HEADS *I* WIN, *TAILS* I WIN

HEADS I WIN, *TAILS* I WIN

Why Smart Investors Fail and How to Tilt the Odds in Your Favor

Spencer Jakab

Portfolio/Penguin

PORTFOLIO / PENGUIN
An imprint of Penguin Random House LLC
375 Hudson Street
New York, New York 10014
penguin.com

ISBN: 978-0-399-56320-1 (hardcover)
ISBN: 978-0-399-56321-8 (e-book)

Printed in the United States of America
10 9 8 7 6 5 4 3 2 1

Set in Mercury Text G1 with Gotham
Designed by Daniel Lagin

CONTENTS

CONTENTS

HEADS **I WIN,** *TAILS* **I WIN**

PREFACE

Hey, good-looking.

Scientific studies have shown that if you survey a large group of people about their relative attractiveness on a scale of 1 to 10, the average answer will be a 7. Speaking as a 7 or maybe even an 8 myself, that's ridiculous. You probably feel the same way.

It's in our human nature to view the world through a distorted prism. In most cases that's basically harmless. When it comes to something such as self-esteem about our appearance, it's arguably even helpful.

Overconfidence is less good for other things. Take driving—an activity at which not only do the vast majority of people surveyed claim to be above average, but even those being treated in emergency rooms for accidents they caused still insist they're better than most.

This book is about money, not something that can leave you or your family members injured or worse. Still, your finances are pretty important—arguably third in terms of priorities after health and happiness. It's also what I've spent nearly a quarter century thinking and writing about every day, most recently for the *Wall Street Journal.*

For all the ink that's spilled about investing, there's a reason the world needed another book on the subject. It's the last area of our lives where even very smart people let hope triumph over experience. We're handicapped not only by the psychological biases that turn the person we see in the mirror into George Clooney or Angelina Jolie, but by an industry with multimillion-dollar marketing budgets and an eye on its own bottom line, not yours.

That bothers me, and it should bother you too. In the United States alone, tens of billions of dollars a year that might be in ordinary savers' brokerage and retirement accounts wind up somewhere else. If you're a typical investor then this year alone that comes to something like 140 times the hardcover price of this book. Over your working years it adds up, with compound interest, to nearly half a million dollars in foregone wealth. What's more, if you're typical you have no idea how much money you could and should be earning or even how much you have earned. It's unbelievable but true, and very much a case of what you don't know *can* hurt you.

Unless you're very handy, you probably don't know how to fix your own car or refrigerator or give a family member a decent haircut. You almost certainly can't fly your own airplane or perform an appendectomy. But most Americans are expected to be part-time fund managers. With gold watches and a steady, livable pension check becoming a rarity, we've been entrusted with our own finances and for the most part failed miserably. The way to measure that is through your returns, and the numbers are so shocking that I'm regularly challenged by people who say they can't be right.

They are, but the skepticism is natural. In fact, the questions come from readers or audience members at speaking engagements who are fairly financially savvy. Having a good idea of what long-run returns have been for stocks and bonds, they find the numbers impossible to reconcile with how little a typical investor makes. The explanation is that we're all players in something called a zero-sum game. That dud investment, high fee, or unfortunate timing that caused you to lose money or earn less than you might have didn't send the foregone dollars to money heaven. They went somewhere else—into the profits of a large financial services company or the pockets of an investor who usually doesn't make those errors.

You've almost certainly heard and read about Warren Buffett, probably the most successful investor of our time. Over the past half century his main investment vehicle, Berkshire Hathaway, grew a dollar by 163 times more than one invested in the stock market. Compared to you, though, it earned about 3,165 times as much.

No, I didn't dig through your trash to read your 401(k) statements. I mean "you" in aggregate. Maybe you're a little bit better or perhaps a bit worse, but that is a huge difference. This book is here to help narrow the gap between you and the market return and perhaps even allow you to do a little better than that. Just whittling away slightly at the difference will add meaningfully to your bottom line.

Maybe that sounds a lot less appealing than saying I can help you double or even quadruple the size of your nest egg, but for the typical investor it's the same thing. The difference really is that big and the power of compound interest that impressive. There's a virtual orchard of low-hanging fruit to pluck and I'll show you where to find it. There are even some juicy treats on the high branches that can help you do a bit better than the market.

The key is to look at investing differently—not just to be told what you should be doing and what you're doing wrong but to understand why. I can't tell you how much stocks will go up in the future or which ones to buy. What I can tell you with a good deal of confidence are your odds of a decent return doing what most people do and how remarkably simple it is to improve them.

Heads I Win, Tails I Win isn't your typical how-to-get-rich book. It isn't a finger-wagging lecture on prudence either. I'm going to shock you—not only to open your eyes to the fact that you're leaving a fortune on the table, but explain how it happens and how unnecessary it all is. If I do my job right you'll be both angry and hopeful by the time you finish.

I'm going to make you two promises here at the outset. The first is that there will be no algebra, Greek letters, or other confusing stuff in these pages. It isn't necessary. Yes, there are quite a few rocket scientists who work in finance these days, but you most definitely don't have to be one to understand and apply profitably what I'm going to say.

My second promise is that this really is my best advice. I already sold you this book (I hope), but unlike a lot of authors in the bookstore's business and finance section, I'm not selling anything else. Over the last quarter century I've worked as a top-rated stock analyst at a major investment bank and more recently as an investing columnist. Whether the market is cruising or crashing, I've seen people's eyes light up time and again when I tell them what I do for a living. I've had to fend off lots of strangers asking for specific advice about what to do with their money and even people offering to pay me when I said no.

It's not that I haven't tried to help people. Why wouldn't I? Their reaction, though, when I tell them that I don't know what stock to buy tomorrow but that there are some principles that could help them be much better investors in the long run is a good indicator of what sort of financial decision makers they are.

For example, the boiler in our house stopped working on a bitterly cold Sunday last winter. My wife called the plumber, who, if he were to come by just a little more often, could be claimed as a dependent on our tax return. He made several trips up and down the basement stairs, his brow looking slightly more furrowed each time. Finally he delivered the bad news about what his repair job would cost. After a short and not too fruitful negotiation about the price, he went out to his truck, came back in with a bunch of pieces of metal and wire, and got to work.

When the time came to fill out the paperwork and settle the bill, he spotted a framed investing column for which I had won an award years earlier propped against the boiler room wall. He looked at it, looked at me, and I knew that what would come next would be nearly as uncomfortable as making out that check. He asked if I had written the article and proceeded to prod me for investment advice. Unlike the usual question about a specific stock—Apple seems to be the crowd favorite—his question was about the market as a whole. Specifically, he wanted to know what would happen to the market *that week*. There had been a bunch of scary headlines that had sent stocks lower the previous Friday, and the Federal Reserve was having a meeting that concluded three days from then.

As I would with friends and strangers alike, I explained to him that I really didn't know if stocks would go up or down that week and that no one else did either. I started to point out that it didn't really matter and how he was better off ignoring those headlines, taking a long-term view, and making sure he wasn't allowing frequent trading or fees to eat up his future returns.

Like so many similar conversations I've had over the years, the words "I don't know" may as well have been uttered in Swahili. The plumber kept pressing for some little morsel of short-term insight. After he described his finances to me in unnecessary detail, I gave up and said that the market probably would be unusually volatile that week—a safe enough statement. He repeated the word "volatile," looked thoughtful, then shook my hand with gusto and thanked me. Then he took $50 off the bill even though, straining against my every cheapskate instinct, I protested that it wasn't necessary and that I don't get paid for investment advice.

I don't know what he did with the one word that got his attention or what he could do with it, but he had already made a silly financial decision. By then the temperature was somewhere in the upper forties in my house and it was getting late on a Sunday afternoon. Without his valuable technical ability and spare parts, neither of which I possessed, my family would be seeing its breath indoors by the next morning. Yet there he was taking $50 off the price of something of considerable, immediate benefit to me for counsel that I had tried to explain to him was worthless.

In fact, there was some useful advice I could have given that plumber, but he was on the clock and not in a frame of mind to listen to it anyway. Sometimes people are a bit more patient, and I've condensed my collected wisdom into a two-minute speech that I dole out to strangers at the gym, to neighbors, or to my seatmate on airplane trips. Sadly, the CliffsNotes version of *Heads I Win, Tails I*

Win isn't detailed or convincing enough to nudge many people from their behavior pattern.

So here's the unabridged advice I've wanted to give all these years. It's not just the product of an entire adult life working in and being fascinated by financial markets but also one fine-tuned after speaking to lots of ordinary savers. It's the sort of message that I think you're most likely to take on board. Even if it only changes your behavior to a small degree, it should be well worth the time devoted to reading this book. However sophisticated you are, I think you'll learn something. I hope that the way the story is told is sufficiently lighthearted to keep the pages turning yet memorable enough to stay with you for years.

It needs to be. Being financially fit is an even bigger challenge than being physically fit. Do you eat red meat, avoid exercise, or push vegetables to the side of your plate because you don't really believe it's bad for you? I doubt it. Sure, that vegan triathlete down the street dropped dead of a heart attack and your grandfather smoked, drank, and ate bacon with abandon and lived to ninety-three, but you know and understand that they defied the odds.

People do those things because they love steak and hate going to the gym and are willing to make that trade-off. Others bite the bullet and do what's healthy. You're significantly improving your odds of a long, healthy life but not guaranteeing it. Yet even the same people who display that degree of self-discipline are on a 100 percent junk food diet of investment behavior without realizing it. In many ways, though, the good advice that boosts your odds of financial success involves less work than what you're doing today—six-pack abs without diet or exercise.

Of course, if it were as easy as it is simple, then middle-class

Americans would be trillions of dollars wealthier. It isn't just that the people selling you financial services have budgets that rival those of the companies flogging Twinkies and Big Macs. The biggest obstacle is that markets behave in a way that confuses and discourages us. Doing the right things and not the wrong ones is a lot harder when we can't see immediate results. Even fewer people would sweat it out at the gym if some of them gained twenty pounds before the benefits began kicking in. That's why this book will spell out as clearly as possible how each strategy affects your chances in the long run.

You've probably heard the saying "Better lucky than smart." The funny thing is, I don't know any professional gamblers with that motto. When you play a hundred thousand hands, you'd better be smart, period. Investing, in the long run, is like gambling, except for the fact that the odds are tilted slightly in favor of making you money rather than sending you to the poorhouse. But, as I said, they aren't all that good for the typical investor. You need them to be a lot better because you don't amass a nest egg through addition—you do it through multiplication. Invest a $10,000 inheritance the day you graduate from college and it'll be worth $35,000 by retirement day at the 3 percent or so annualized return most investors manage. Boost that by two percentage points and it'll be $85,000. Two more points and it'll be $200,000. Two more, which would only get you in the ballpark of long-run market returns, and it's $445,000.

Got your attention yet? Even if most of what I say goes in one ear and out the other and this book nudges your returns just a single percentage point higher, that could translate into a retirement nest egg twice as big. No matter what exotic berry, makeup, or exercise routine they're selling on late-night TV, you probably can't look like a TV star. You can, however, be an investing star or something a lot closer to it. I'm going to explain how to improve your odds and claw your way toward that market return by knowing what to do and what not to do and also why.

Results aren't guaranteed—they never are—but I have a pool of information on which to base my recommendations that would make the people telling you to eat more fruit and exercise green with envy. A huge trove of market history backs up what I have to say, and I'm going to slice and dice it to give you the choicest cuts. The first step is to pay a visit to the shabby place where the vast majority of investors live and don't even realize it: Lake Money-begone.

CHAPTER ONE

LAKE MONEYBEGONE

"If I can tell you where you got your shoes at, can I give you a shoeshine?"

It was near the peak of the technology boom and business had never been better for the investment bank where I was working. Naturally, the director of our research department did what many executives in highly cyclical industries do when their companies are minting money: He decided to spend it like a drunken sailor. The company flew more than a hundred analysts from various countries in Europe and the Middle East by business class all the way to New Orleans for a long weekend full of speeches and "team-building" exercises.

A lot of what happened that weekend is unprintable, and some of it is a little hard to remember. Still, despite acting like drunken sailors ourselves, we learned a few things. One of my inebriated colleagues, for example, discovered that in America, unlike England, police cars and taxis look really similar. We bailed him out the next morning, but weren't around to lend a helping hand to another Brit who took the toothless, elderly African American man up on his offer to identify where he bought his shoes. He certainly wasn't going to guess Marks & Spencer, was he?

"You got your shoes right here on Bourbon Street!"

A good sport and not about to be a pedant about the Queen's English or a dangling preposition, he chuckled and sat down for his shoeshine while the rest of the group kept walking toward the bar. When he was done, the man, not having mentioned the price ahead of time, asked for $25. Whether today or sixteen years ago, that's a lot of money for a bit of spit and polish. But as my colleague began to object, five very large men suddenly materialized and made sure he paid in full.

I love making bets, and I especially love winning them, though I've never relied on linguistic ambiguity, much less the threat of violence, to do so. One way to avoid being the patsy in a wager is to consider how much information the other person has compared to you, and another is to recognize when one of you is being overconfident. Here's a case when those two would cancel each other out. Say I were to bet every person reading this who said they were above average at investing (studies show most of you would claim to be) to benchmark your returns in the same way that people do for their looks or driving ability. The latter two are pretty hard to quantify, but portfolio performance isn't. Many of you wouldn't take me up on it, so it might seem like I'd be setting myself up for a fall by betting against a self-selected group—only the crème de la crème, as it were.

Except I wouldn't be. Studies, among them one by German finance professors Markus Glaser and Martin Weber, show that there's absolutely no connection between how well an investor actually has done and how well they think they have done. None, nada, zip. Or, as the Herren Professors put it in more scientific language (ideally recited in a thick Teutonic accent), "The correlation coefficient between return estimates and realized returns is not distinguishable from zero."[1]

That's pretty amazing. But if I wanted to do better than just break even—much better, in fact—I'd bet you instead on whether or not you keep up with the market return. In Glaser and Weber's study the investors surveyed estimated that on average they had made nearly 15 percent on an annualized basis over the four years in question. Their average performance actually was just 3.7 percent, and only about two out of ten managed to keep pace with the overall market.

Another much longer-term study of U.S. investors is even starker. In April 2015, Dalbar, a firm that evaluates fund managers, released results on how American investors in mutual funds did over the past thirty years compared to the markets that those funds were supposed to track. As I said in the preface, people unfamiliar with these numbers often scoff in disbelief. A handful of other researchers have attempted to calculate this "performance gap" and come up with numbers in the same ballpark. So read them and weep:

The "composite fund investor" earned an annualized 2.5 percent during those 30 years. That is just awful. It's less than inflation during that time. In other words, if a typical saver had a nice nest egg at the end of 30 years it was only because he or she salted away lots of his or her paychecks, not as the result of any real investment gains. And of course this is all before taxes.

Over the same time frame, the main U.S. stock index, the Standard & Poor's 500, earned just over 11 percent a year, and the broadest bond index, the Barclays Aggregate, managed 7.4 percent. Trailing the market in a single year or even for a few years is nothing to panic about, but three decades is an entirely different matter. That great boon to your nest egg, compound interest, works insidiously in reverse too. Fear, greed, naïveté, bad advice, and even the cost of sound advice combine to whittle away the pot of money we should earn after a lifetime of saving relative to what we could have amassed.

Add up the effect of all this behavior and you wind up somewhere I call Lake Moneybegone. Like Garrison Keillor's fictional town of Lake Wobegon where all the children are above average, nearly all investors are below average, and not by a little. But while that sounds bad, a gap expressed in percentage points is just too abstract to resonate with a typical saver.

"You really have to tell them that they should be shocked," says Dalbar's founder, Lou Harvey. "They really need to translate that into 'can you put your kids through college, can you fund your retirement?'"

The sums left on the table really are shocking. To consider a simplified example, let's say your great-uncle leaves you a $100,000 inheritance at age thirty-five but doesn't entirely trust your judgment. He forbids you to touch the principal or change how it's invested until you retire at age sixty-five. Being a frugal and conservative sort, he picks low-cost index funds comprised of 60 percent stocks and 40 percent bonds and they rebalance back to those percentages at the start of each year. Now, let's say your best friend receives a similar gift but is free to invest it as she sees fit, though also without withdrawing any principal. Your friend is a typical investor.

Fast-forward to the day thirty years later when you both qualify for Medicare and your great-uncle's gift would be worth over $1.5 million before taxes—*seven times* the $215,000 your friend has accumulated. That seems like it should be mathematically impossible. How can an average investor be so far below the passive return of the market? Where does all the money she didn't earn wind up?

Like I said before, not money heaven. That foregone income is earned by someone else. While the children in Keillor's fictional town can't really all be above average, there's no reason why the vast majority of investors can't be below it. That's because "average" and "market average" aren't the same thing. Subtract the costs of investing from all the wealth that stocks, bonds, and other investments churn out and you have what investors earned on average, but not what an average investor earned.

The gap of several percentage points between that typical investor's return and what the market as a whole generates each year has to wind up somewhere. Multiply that shortfall by the $23 trillion or so that Americans have stashed in retirement accounts and you begin to understand that the eye-popping compensation on Wall Street isn't conjured out of thin air. They at least owe you a thank-you card.

As financial types put it, investing is a zero-sum game. I compare it to a poker room in a casino where players' money gets redistributed. There's a reason I'm not using the example of a friendly neighborhood game of five-card stud. Unlike your buddy's basement, the casino is a business and takes a "rake," or a small cut, of every pot in order to pay the dealer, its overhead, and of course earn a profit. It's a slow but, over time, not insignificant drag on each player's returns that's analogous to the financial services industry's middleman role.

Calling costs "death by a thousand cuts" is a little too dramatic, but the slow bleed can do a surprising amount of harm. A typical saver spends something like $170,000 in fees by the time they retire and gives up a fifth of their potential return.[2] Can you imagine how people would react if, instead of paying that amount little by little and having to read about it in tiny letters buried in a quarterly statement most of us glance at briefly, we got presented with a bill for $170,000 at age sixty-five? It would make my colleague's shock at the $25 shoeshine pale in comparison. But pay it you do.

For most investors, that isn't even the biggest impediment to keeping up with the market. Much like any poker game by the end of the evening, the chips from investing are redistributed in a very uneven way that winds up costing you more. You, the reader, are like the guy who has to keep checking his little card to see if a straight beats a flush and walks home shaking his head and vowing to get 'em next time. For typical stock fund investors alone, Dalbar calculates that poor timing—zigging when we should zag—costs a typical investor almost two percentage points a year. That's nearly twice what we lose to fees and adds up to hundreds of thousands of dollars over a lifetime of saving. Yeah, really.

You can choose to be upset about that or you can look at it constructively. What sort of world would you rather live in—one in which nearly everyone earned a 3 percent return on their money and the average market return was also 3 percent, or one where most people earned 3 percent but the average return was 7 percent?

Unless you're racked by envy, that's a no-brainer. In the 3 percent return world you'd have to be especially clever and active to earn something like 7 percent, perhaps doing so with the help of an expensive "expert" who would pocket some of that additional return and almost certainly by taking more risk. But in the real world the gap between 7 percent and 3 percent is a result of all the things you thought would get you ahead and backfired instead.

There are few failures in life as significant, surprising, or persistent as that of the average investor who always seems to be running as fast as he can in the wrong direction. The residents of Lake Moneybegone do all sorts of supposedly smart things, take unnecessary and poorly understood risks, pay princely sums to allegedly clever people, and, instead of earning a decent passive return that can build a modest amount of savings during a working life into a respectable nest egg, wind up with a lot less. That's why I say there's a silver lining to the grossly uneven distribution of investment returns. The money you should and could be earning is out there, and a big part of grabbing more of it involves being cheap and lazy. It's really a wonder that I'm not as rich as Rockefeller.

In all seriousness, though, if I do my job properly then I'll have convinced you by the time you finish reading this book that less is more when it comes to investing. Framing investing choices in terms of odds, I'll demonstrate that many of the actions we take in the belief that they'll give us an edge do the precise opposite. And even if we think we can earn a market return or something close to it, we do a poor job of estimating the very wide range of possible outcomes for our nest egg. If you have a realistic idea of what to expect, you can be prepared instead of getting blindsided. Hope is not a strategy.

You'll also see that other things you perceive as risky or even foolhardy can increase your odds of earning a solid, long-run return. Sticking our necks out is hard for many of us at the best of times and especially so during turbulent ones, but doing so allows investors to turn the market's lemons into lemonade.

On the other hand, many risks are unnecessary or even hidden. There are funds, products, and investment practices that tantalize us with the prospect of something for nothing. Please understand that there are no free lunches. Fortunately, though, there are some cheap lunches, and these, oddly, are less popular than inferior strategies that have patrons lining up around the block. A handful of proven techniques and principles have allowed savvy investors to eke out a bit of extra return above what "the market" has produced. Many require a fair bit of patience and sometimes even professional guidance.

Finally, I'll explain why the best kind of expert to follow is almost always the cheapest one. Don't take that to an extreme, though. For some people, either because of their temperament or the fact that investing intimidates them, failing to find wise counsel is penny wise and pound foolish.

Before I start doling out advice, you should get a better idea of what sort of investor you are. That's a two-part question: financial and emotional. Let's tackle the numbers first.

I don't know you, so I can't say for certain that you live in Lake Moneybegone and, if you do, whether it's the rough part of town or the posh side. As Glaser and Weber showed, you probably don't know either. Look back carefully at your own financial history and get at least an approximate idea of how you've been doing and how much you've been paying in fees, commissions, and the like. Leave taxes out of it for now. These calculations aren't rocket science, but they can get complicated.

Just ask the Beardstown Ladies. The mathematically challenged women from a small town in Illinois rose to national fame following their investment club's annualized return of 23 percent during America's late 1990s infatuation with stocks. They doled out both financial advice and cooking tips and the public ate it up. But anyone who read their first bestseller, *The Beardstown Ladies' Common-Sense Investment Guide: How We Beat the Stock Market— and How You Can Too,* should have spotted basic errors in calculating percentage returns. One journalist finally audited their brokerage records and discovered that they actually had lagged the market significantly. There was no word on whether the recipes worked.

Whether or not you find those calculations as daunting as the ladies from Beardstown did, it's important to make certain that you understand one basic mathematical principle, so please indulge me for a couple of paragraphs if this is old hat. Without it, this book, not to mention any fund prospectus or brokerage statement, makes a lot less sense. The average that you learned about in school—adding things together and then counting them up and dividing by that number—is fine for lots of things, but not for investment returns. Instead of that arithmetic average, investment returns are calculated as a geometric average to get what is called a compound annual return. There's a very good reason for that.

Imagine a fund manager who touted his investment results over the past decade to you as a simple average. He would brag about a 35-percent-a-year track record but fail to mention that he lost almost all of the money entrusted to him. By taking huge risks, his fund went up by 50 percent annually until the final year, when things went haywire and his assets sank by 99.9 percent. A dollar invested with him at the outset would be worth four cents after that *negative* 28 percent compound annual return.

A geometric average takes the starting sum compared to the ending one and annualizes the return according to the number of periods. If your savings involve a set amount at the outset with no withdrawals or additions, then that makes it easy to calculate your return. Many brokerage firms have now added online calculators to adjust for the more complicated matter of cash coming in and moving out that tripped up the Beardstown Ladies. I encourage you to find that feature and to be sitting down when you do.

With that little bit of math out of the way, let's turn to your money personality. It may sound like this book is slipping from facts and figures into the touchy-feely world of self-help literature, but bear with me. For starters, I've already violated the first rule of that genre by telling you that you're probably a lousy investor and should be perfectly happy to get back to average rather than strive for greatness. I'm not a highly effective person, I didn't write this book in a four-hour workweek, and I have absolutely no idea who moved my cheese, but I can't stress strongly enough the importance of asking yourself some hard hypothetical questions. It's the oldest piece of self-help advice there is, inscribed on the Temple of Apollo, the location of the mythical Oracle of Delphi: "Know thyself."

Even if I could sit down and read a full transcript of every financial decision you've made in your entire life and point out your successes and shortfalls, I still wouldn't know why. What's more, you might not know why either. There are many psychological foibles that distort our perceptions and sabotage our investing. Great books have been written and a Nobel Prize in Economics has been won on the subject. But while we're all human, we're all individuals too. The renowned mutual fund manager Peter Lynch thought some people just couldn't cut it. In his words, "Everyone has the brain power to make money in stocks. Not everyone has the stomach."

I'm afraid you don't really have a choice. Very few of us can be a highly successful professional investor like Lynch, of course, but almost everyone reading this book has been forced to be an amateur fund manager. If decent returns are what you're after, then risky assets like stocks have to be part of the mix. That terrifies some people and it excites others to the point of distraction, but there are a lot of ways to harness this volatile source of wealth, including, for at least some of you, the help of a competent advisor who can assuage your fears or temper your giddiness at the appropriate junctures.

Behavioral finance expert Meir Statman says our emotions short-circuit steps that we understand should lead to better investing results. "Deeply buried fears can keep us from taking risk—keeping us safe, perhaps, but also robbing us of potential return. A strong tendency to regret past choices can keep us from repeating blunders, but also from repeating sound strategies that simply didn't work out the first time."[3]

In 2013, Statman produced a quiz for readers of the *Wall Street Journal* to judge their psychological makeup for investing. The first question asked what was the maximum probability of a 50 percent reduction in standard of living that someone would accept in exchange for a 50 percent chance that they would gain a 50 percent increase in their standard of living. The quiz had ten choices in increments of five percentage points from 5 percent to 50 percent. Before continuing to the next paragraph, read that question carefully and choose an answer.

The average American's answer is 12.5 percent. If you're right around that level, ask yourself whether it's rational to require a reward four times as great for an equivalent risk. It isn't, and it's probably costing you money.

Statman's second question was whether bad choices bother you. For those who said yes, he pointed out that regret can teach the wrong lesson. Sometimes we do dumb things and learn the hard way, but at other times we played the odds correctly and things just happened to not work out well. A central tenet of this book is that it's better in the long run to be smart than lucky. Luck will run out, but regretting smart choices that turned out badly will only compound your loss by making impossible future gains that could have been had by sticking with them. Some of the techniques that I'll describe in this book for squeezing extra return out of the market can put our portfolios in a hole for months or even years compared to the path of least resistance. Regret is one reason so few people keep on using these strategies and that in turn explains why they still work—a concept called time arbitrage, which I'll also discuss.

His third question was whether you believe that you can beat the market. As I've told you, most people think they can, but few actually do.

It starts out with the widely held assumption that some investors—the guy on CNBC or your brother-in-law who claims to have made a killing in the market—know how to do it year after year. We just have to figure out how to be one of those investors. Maybe you're a doctor, lawyer, engineer, accountant, scholar, businessperson, or just smarter than the average bear. You're a take-charge, well-informed person and you apply it to your finances.

That instinct is like poison when it comes to investing, though. A mental foible called the "illusion of control" convinces us that we can do better than just taking the ups and downs of the market as they come, and instead we make decisions. These may be the purchase or sale of individual stocks or funds or frequent changes in how we allocate our money. For example, we might make a substantial investment in an industry that we heard will be the next big thing, or slash our exposure to stocks after reading that a recent market decline could be the start of a major bear market.

Not much harm in that, though, right? Nope. Research from multiple sources says that the majority of these decisions by individual investors are shown with the benefit of hindsight to have been wrong.[4] The more decisions we make, the wronger we are. A fascinating study by finance professor Terrance Odean divided investors into five groups, from those who trade the most to those who trade the least. The most active ones lagged the least active by an incredible seven percentage points a year.[5]

Are there exceptions? Sure, but you're fooling yourself if you think your odds are good of being one of them. The more passive your approach to investing, the greater the likelihood your results will match the market return—a benchmark most people reading this fail to come anywhere close to meeting. That's the gospel of plenty of smart, successful investors, notably John Bogle, the father of index funds, who says, "Don't just do something, stand there." It can't be repeated enough and is the first, easiest, and most productive step out of Lake Moneybegone.

It might seem counterintuitive that a person who's confident enough to be very active would do worse than another who is largely passive. Surely, that result is skewed by people who think they know something rather than those who do. Investing acumen must have some value—right?

I'm afraid not. Someone knowledgeable specifically about money seems to be at a further disadvantage, according to research done by a firm called Openfolio that was granted anonymous access to a large number of brokerage accounts. In 2014, for example, teachers made double the return of people who worked in financial services. Other studies have shown that fund managers' personal portfolios do no better than those of individual investors.[6]

Please don't equate financial literacy with poor results, though. The culprit is overconfidence and hyperactivity, not knowledge. Investing and the rules around it, particularly taxes and estate planning, are complicated, and you should be an informed consumer of financial services just like anything else.

And if you haven't read much about the actual art of investing, then I certainly don't think a little knowledge is a dangerous thing. Knock yourself out if you want to learn about a subject that I hope fascinates you as much as it does me. Just don't fool yourself into thinking you'll become a stock market genius. The bookshelves in my house sag with dozens of tomes on finance. In addition to that, I read and write about investing and investors all day and used to get paid a lot of money to tell professional money managers what to buy and sell. I even have a collection of bad investment books just for fun, mostly purchased at garage sales or for a penny on Amazon.

Maybe I'm just a bit slow, but all that reading, education, and experience didn't turn me into a world-beating trader. Unfortunately there's a small but active group of investors who think they can defy the odds. Even worse, some pay for the privilege of being "trained" to engage in rapid-fire trading or to be told what and when to buy and sell. Both personal experience and independent research show that these investors are the worst of the worst. Compared to a typical resident of Lake Moneybegone, they live in the skanky trailer park at the edge of town downwind from the slaughterhouse.

The vast majority of you don't have the ego to try turning yourselves into investing masters of the universe and your spare rooms into small hedge funds, thank goodness. Yet many of you seem to believe that financial pundits who appear in the media have achieved that type of mastery over the markets. Either they have won actual accolades or you just assume they must be pretty good to be interviewed on television. Some of these people don't even have funds you can invest in—they just opine on the world in order to get the name of the organization they represent into print or onto the airwaves.

When one of my colleagues at the *Wall Street Journal* takes an expert with a fancy title too seriously, I like to point out that our editor used to call me twenty years ago when he was a young reporter and I was a stock analyst, putting what I had to say in the newspaper verbatim. Today he deletes or rewrites my pearls of wisdom without batting an eyelid.

A vivid memory from my years as an analyst is the time I was bringing a company's management to meet big U.S. investors (I worked in London) and decided to spend the night at my mom's house in Queens instead of the New York Palace Hotel in Manhattan, where they were staying. My bank had hired a limousine to take us around and the driver called to say he could pick me up first, saving me a subway ride.

The neighborhood where I grew up has lots of limo drivers but no limo riders, so my mom's neighbors were slack-jawed as I strolled out to the waiting vehicle in my Savile Row suit and Hermès tie. The value of anything I had to say had risen instantly by about 5,000 percent from the evening before when I had pulled up in a yellow cab from JFK Airport wearing an old T-shirt and jeans. From that day onward I was someone who clearly possessed some sort of highly valuable knowledge about what would go up or down.

The fact that they thought so didn't surprise me, because I once had that misconception myself. The day that I got hired by the bank I felt like I was joining a select fraternity with mastery over money. My first boss, a gruff veteran, sat me down to teach me how to be a research analyst. Looking over one of his reports from the 1980s when he had been a top-rated stock picker, he showed me the basics. But I wanted to know how he knew to slap a "buy," "sell," or "hold" on a stock. Surely he could tell me the secret sauce. He looked at me and laughed: "Spencer, this isn't rocket science."

And it really isn't. What he meant is that once we learned how to calculate all the ratios and make some projections, we knew everything we were going to know. The rest was our best guess. If you regularly turn to a guru for specific advice, then just be aware that his or her odds of making a correct pick in the future are on average equal to or in some cases even worse than a coin flip. I'll get into the ugly details later, but if you can't do without expert guidance, at least hire the cheapest expert.

I say that because another big chunk of the underperformance that lands investors in Lake Moneybegone comes from the expensive experts we hire to actually manage our money. You might have heard that most mutual fund managers don't beat the market in any given year, yet that still doesn't deter you. That's why you spend time reading about their performance or checking services that rate them for you with stars the way a restaurant or movie critic does—so you can put your money on the winners. You may be surprised to hear, then, that these helpful interviews and services actually have been unhelpful, leading investors on average into worse funds for their money.

It's frustrating but true. Even if you go with a true superstar—someone with years of superior performance under their belt—you may be setting yourself up for disappointment. The $23 trillion question is if there really even is such a thing as skill in managing money. Some of the smartest research on this subject concludes that a very small percentage of managers may make their investors a very modest amount of extra money after fees through actual ability. Unfortunately, that skill only becomes evident after many years, so you'd need a time machine to pick those funds.

All funds cost something, but one that almost never has to buy or sell a stock or bond and can be run by a computer is much cheaper than one run by a human—a tenth as much or less in terms of fees. Fractions of a percent may not sound like they're worth your time worrying about, but how about a cool $150,000 or more over a lifetime of saving if you're typical?

Advice on which funds to pick and how to construct a portfolio also costs something. I'll give you some do-it-yourself tips in this book but also lay out the range of services you might want to use, from robots to human beings. The costs vary and they add up, so you should use the level of help you need—no more, no less.

Valuation is yet another unappreciated risk factor. The stock market may seem like a money machine, but the odds of a certain return are greatly affected by how much investors pay at any given time for a dollar of the earnings of the companies that make it up. Wall Street wears rose-colored glasses, regularly casting valuation in the most favorable light possible at times when historically accurate but lesser-known numbers are practically screaming the opposite. I'll show you how to put a much more reliable price tag on the stock market and also how to interpret it.

Finally, we fail to understand that lack of risk can be risky too. A big reason investors end up in Lake Moneybegone is a failure to make calculated bets. I'll demonstrate through stock market simulations that sticking our necks out at the appropriate times can provide a major boost to returns while actually reducing risk. The gap between your return and the market return is largest when financial markets are their most volatile. It's during this small percentage of the time that this book's lessons are most relevant. Don't worry, you won't have to do anything dramatic or complicated to show that profitable level of intestinal fortitude. In fact, you don't have to do anything at all—it happens on autopilot. I'll show you how.

For a variety of reasons this is a tough sell, even after you tell people they can make two, three, or more times as much money over decades with less work. The fact that a modern-day Rip Van

Winkle would beat the pants off of four out of five investors just bothers some people. There are those who are certain they'll be investor five, not one through four, despite the fact that number five was almost always someone who more or less sat on their hands.

Okay, but where's the satisfaction in just keeping up with the market? Well, I'll let you in on a little secret—it's possible to do a bit better. While I can't make any promises, there are some techniques toward the back of this book that have helped some people beat the market by a good margin. I put them at the end for a reason. You need to learn to walk before you can run, and I feel you need to really absorb some of the simpler lessons first.

If all you manage to do is narrow the gap with the market after reading this book, then it will be well worth your time. So keep reading and let me tell you where your returns are at.

CHAPTER TWO

TIMING ISN'T EVERYTHING

A s a newspaper columnist, I may be entitled to my own opinions but not my own facts. A missing decimal place or some other mental slip happens every once in a while, and it's an awful feeling, even when the subject of the error is nice about it. Robert J. Samuelson, the *Washington Post* business columnist, was exceedingly gracious when I used his name in front of a quote by the eminent economist Paul Samuelson, telling me that it's happened before. "Once, the *New York Times* had me winning Paul Samuelson's Nobel Prize. I kept waiting for the $1 million check to arrive, but it never did."

So naturally a reporter like me can be a real pedant when people bring up a quote that "everyone" knows someone made. For example, Willie Sutton never said that he robbed banks because that's where the money is, Ben Franklin's famous dictum about thrift wasn't "A penny saved is a penny earned," and P. T. Barnum didn't say, "There's a sucker born every minute." I have heard a couple of stockbrokers express that last sentiment, though.

A quote one often hears about investing, that Einstein said compound interest is the eighth wonder of the world, is an apocryphal one that I read and hear all the time. Even so, I bet he was pretty impressed. Consider, for example, the famous case of the Dutch settlers who allegedly bought Manhattan from the local tribe for $24. (In fact it was 60 guilders, which would be about $875 in today's equivalent. I told you journalists were sticklers for precision.) Now let's assume that the natives could have invested that sum at an 8 percent rate of interest. By the end of 2015 it would have been worth a whopping $240 trillion, which, despite nosebleed New York real estate prices, gave them the better end of the bargain. In a similar vein, Warren Buffett wrote in a 1963 letter to his partners that Queen Isabella's $30,000 investment in Columbus's voyage would have then been worth $2 trillion at a 4 percent rate of interest. Today that would be $15 trillion.

If you boost the rate of return, then even more astronomical sums are possible over shorter periods. The *Economist* magazine wrote a story in 2000 about Felicity Foresight, a fictional investor born at the turn of the twentieth century who started with one dollar and put her money into the single best-performing asset class in the world each year. A trillionaire by her thirties, she had a fictional fortune of $9,607,190,781,673,150,000 ($9.6 quintillion) at age one hundred.

What if someone had the reverse Midas touch? Choosing the single worst investment each year would get you down to some fraction of a cent pretty quickly, of course, but how about mere bad timing? Money manager Ben Carlson, who writes a smart blog called

A Wealth of Common Sense, went through such a hypothetical exercise.

Beginning in 1970 his fictional investor saved $2,000 a year, doubling that contribution each decade, but he only invested his accumulated principal in the S&P 500 at market peaks. These included late 1972, August 1987, December 1999, and October 2007. His one saving grace is that he never sold. As awful as that sounds, the investor would have $1.1 million to show for it by 2014—quite a respectable nest egg. Calculating those returns is tricky, just as it was for the Beardstown Ladies, since it doesn't involve a lump sum or constant amounts. On an annualized basis it comes to 5.5 percent.

That's far from awful. For example, it's much better than the 3.8 percent rate of return a typical Lake Moneybegone investor earned over three decades invested only in stocks. Think about it for a second—a stock market investor with the worst timing possible over four and a half tumultuous decades still did better. How is it even possible?

The answer is the magic of compound interest. Carlson's investor had lousy timing but never sold, allowing the bulk of his nest egg to keep earning a return. He's no quintillionaire like Felicity Foresight, but he is a millionaire. Just by allowing most of his principal to grow, he took a sum that a middle-class person could quite realistically have saved, made a statistically unlikely succession of errors, and still turned it into a nest egg that a retiree could live on comfortably. I can't think of a stronger argument against outright market timing than that.

A useful way to think about the folly of pulling all of your money out of the stock market to avoid a loss is by considering the contribution to total returns from just a handful of days. Analysts at

Putnam Investments examined the period from 2000 through 2014 and asked what would happen if an investor were to be out of the market completely for the ten best days. A $10,000 investment at the outset would be worth $22,118 if left untouched in an index fund through that period of two bull and two bear markets. But just missing the ten best days—three-tenths of a percent of the period— would see the ending sum cut in half. Missing twenty would see it slashed by two-thirds to $7,297. In other words, around one-half of one percent of the days during that span were responsible for the entire return.

So when were those days? Not at some random point in the middle of a raging bull market. That fact tells you a great deal about why the biggest reason so many people live in Lake Moneybegone is zigging when they should zag. They occurred mostly not when things were great but when they were terrifying. Of the ten best days, seven were in the thick of bear markets, with some of the very best in the weeks after the collapse of Lehman Brothers and the emergency bailout of other major financial institutions. Two were in the first few weeks of the bull market that began in 2009—a time when few people believed and no one knew for sure that the worst stock selloff in seventy years had ended.

I'd like to be a fly on the wall in a retail brokerage on a day that the bottom falls out of the market. The people picking up the phones—those who put their clients' well-being first, at least— would be playing the role of psychiatrist as much as order taker. It's hard to say how any individual reacted to market crises, but because mutual funds publish information weekly and monthly on how many dollars investors contributed or redeemed, the swings of the pendulum between fear and greed are there in black and white.

Dalbar calculated the individual months when investors did

the most damage to their long-run returns based on those flows. Top of the list is October 2008 when the Dow had its largest single-day drop after investors learned that Congress didn't pass the bailout bill. They came to their senses and pushed it through days later. The stock market was still down by nearly 17 percent for the month, but Dalbar calculates that individual mutual fund investors probably lost over 24 percent—the sort of deficit that would normally take a couple of years' worth of errors to rack up.

The third-worst month came following the crash of October 1987 and the fifth-worst in August 1998 when Russia defaulted on its debts and hedge fund Long Term Capital Management threatened to blow up the world financial system. The second-worst month for investor timing, on the other hand, was a good one overall: March 2000. Stocks rose by nearly 10 percent, but investors lagged that by six percentage points, probably for two reasons. It was a very volatile month that saw technology stocks peak, but also an era during which many investors had abandoned so-called old-economy stocks that still made up a big chunk of the benchmark S&P 500 stock index. It was a bad time to own Cisco or Pets.com but a pretty decent one to own, say, Pfizer or Ford.

There's a reason that five of the seven worst months were bad ones for the market rather than good ones. Losing money hurts in two ways—financially and psychologically. The pain of a loss has been shown to be far worse than an equivalent monetary gain, a concept called prospect theory that won its cocreator, psychologist Daniel Kahneman, the Nobel Prize in Economics.

Those brilliant experiments measured the loss or gain of an equivalent dollar amount. A far less brilliant insight, but one more relevant to what I'm about to discuss, can be gleaned from some arithmetic that you probably learned in fifth grade or thereabouts: that it takes an increasingly large percentage gain to make yourself whole the bigger your initial loss. It's why Warren Buffett, probably the greatest investor of all time, quipped about his two rules of investing. Rule number one is "Don't lose money," while rule number two is not to forget rule number one.

Back when I was a stock analyst and had clients I had to fawn over, a fund manager actually explained this exercise in multiplication and division to me over dinner as the heart of his fund's investment strategy after the 1997 Asian crisis had reduced the value of some stocks in the region by half.

"You see, Spencer, we did some calculations, and getting back to their precrisis value would mean we stand to make 100 percent in these stocks."

I nodded and smiled politely as a little piece of my soul died. This wasn't the sort of investing brilliance for which his clients should have been paying him 2 percent of assets and 20 percent of profits. But then he had his reasons and made a bundle, a great example of being lucky rather than smart. The 90 percent or so loss his fund suffered on Russian stocks several months later, on the other hand, was pretty unlucky. Win some, lose some.

If you take away only one lesson from *Heads I Win, Tails I Win*, then, it's that being smart is way more important than being lucky. Investing is a repeatable exercise and there's no avoiding losing money or, almost as painful for some people, letting a hot stock tip go by that makes someone else a fortune. The people who wind up with the biggest pot of money at the end, though, are almost always the ones who didn't worry about that and played the odds correctly.

It isn't only losses that wrongfoot investors. Gains—especially a long streak of gains—can be awfully intoxicating. If you follow my advice you may feel frustrated during such times because it will involve selling stocks and buying bonds regularly to get back to a target allocation. Markets are a little like a rubber band, though—the more stretched they get, the likelier they are to snap back in the other direction.

To illustrate this, let's play a game devised by fund manager John Hussman. His weekly musings about finance—perhaps not surprisingly, since he made the transition from academia to money management—are sophisticated and well written to boot. One of the best commentaries he's published on his fund's Web site dates from February 2007 when his skepticism about the stock market was about to be proven right in spectacular fashion. Dispensing with complicated formulae (which I promised I wouldn't subject you to anyway), he made his point with a child's game he dubbed "Baron Rothschild."

That was a real person, by the way, a British member of the famous banking family who profited handsomely through contrarian investing during the Napoleonic Wars. A memorable quote of his, which is the basis for Hussman's game, was "I made my fortune by selling too early."

The rules go like this: A dealer lays down a card and then another and another. Each one represents an annual investment return of 15 percent, 20 percent, 25 percent, or 30 percent. You multiply a dollar by those returns one after another. For example, drawing 25 percent followed by 20 percent would equal $1.50.

But there's one card somewhere in the deck that equals negative 20 percent, the unofficial threshold of a bear market, at which point the game ends and everyone adds up their winnings. The catch is that a player can say "Baron Rothschild" at any point and receive 10 percentage points less than the amount on the next up-turned card. For example, 25 percent would be counted as only 15 percent. But if the next one that comes up is the 20 percent loss then it becomes a 5 percent gain instead. Saying "Baron Rothschild" is like buying insurance by putting a big chunk of your money into super-safe but low-return bonds.

Hussman points out that saying "Baron Rothschild" after just a few cards have been laid down (yearly returns ranging from good to great) usually beats pushing your luck. In each case below, a player was three turns or years early in becoming defensive:

15%, 15%, 15%, 5% beats 25%, 25%, 25%, –20%
Or:
20%, 10%, 5%, 5% beats 30%, 20%, 15%, –20%
Or:
5%, 5%, 5%, 5% ties 15%, 15%, 15%, –20%

Caution paid off because losing a fifth of your money gets progressively more expensive from a larger base. Also, since this is a card game, the longer you go without the bad card turning up, the higher the chance that it's in the remaining stack—a property shared by the real stock market.

That comment deserves some explanation. All sorts of mental mistakes stem from streaks. Something random such as the "hot hand" of a basketball player or a roulette wheel that has come up on black five times in a row will convince some people that a similar outcome is more likely than probability would dictate the next time. We do the same thing with the stock market, but actually the opposite is true. The catch is, nobody can tell you exactly when today's great returns will come at the cost of tomorrow's mediocre ones. But they will.

Our brains trick us into the exact wrong conclusion. Surveys of investors show that an uninterrupted streak of gains will cause respondents to extrapolate the last few years of returns even when that's unrealistic. For example, in the summer of 2000 an annual poll done by the Securities Industry Association showed that the average investor surveyed expected a 33 percent annual gain on his or her stock investments going forward.[1] The S&P 500 had returned 37.2 percent, 22.7 percent, 33.1 percent, 28.3 percent, and 20.9 percent, in that order, in the preceding five years, while the technology-heavy Nasdaq Composite had done far better. The next three years had returns of –9 percent, –11.9 percent, and –22 percent. By the end of that streak of three losses, the average expectation had slumped to 10 percent. And remember, this was supposed to be a long-run expectation.

The shocking figures about investor ineptitude in Dalbar's study start to make more sense when you grasp how unrealistic it is to expect a 33 percent long-run return. Just consider that an eighteen-year-old could, instead of going to see a movie one night, save that $10 and stick it into a stock index fund. Between that day and retirement he could never save a single additional penny as a working adult and still have over $8 million at age sixty-five.

The stock market is random in the short run, but it actually tilts the odds slightly in the opposite direction of what our biases lead us to believe. What I mean to say is that many good years in a row could be followed by a few more good ones, but they do heighten the risk of the opposite. A stock fund, after all, is just ownership of all the future profits of the businesses it represents. Those profits don't grow by 33 percent a year or anything close to that much, so a red-hot stock market is either playing catch-up or getting way ahead of itself. In 2007, Hussman correctly guessed the latter and saved his clients a lot of money.

Unfortunately for his investors, he also stayed cautious for far too long and kept his fund braced for another plunge. From the time of his bold call in February 2007 through October 2015 a dollar in his main fund would be worth just 68 cents, while one invested in stocks, even after the huge bear market, was worth $1.67.

Don't misinterpret the lesson of Baron Rothschild. It isn't to be hypercautious at all times or to ever dump everything. If the market clearly is frothy, though—a time such as late 1999 or early 2007—then you should adjust your expectations and your investments accordingly. I'll show you later how a regularly rebalanced portfolio does that on autopilot.

If Hussman could have declared victory at the depth of the bear market, he would have "won." But the real-life game of investing and growing your assets doesn't work that way. In fact, the aftermath of a bear market not only is a time when you should stay invested but one when you should make sure that your allocation to stocks is up to your full, age-appropriate comfort level. Since nobody will ring a bell at the bottom of the market, just as they don't at the top, you may increase your stock holdings when prices continue to fall. As I'll discuss in more detail later, it's better to be fairly early than slightly late in boosting stock market exposure, because the returns early in a new bull market tend to be excellent.

Still think you can sniff out danger and come out smelling like a rose? I can see why it's tempting to try dodging a bear market. Sitting out just a couple of awful days in history could do wonders for a portfolio's growth. Analysts at Invesco illustrated that by examining an even longer period than their counterparts at Putnam. From 1928 through 2014 they calculated that the cumulative return of the S&P 500 and its predecessor index would have grown $10,000 into $1.166 million. An investor who missed the ten worst days during that span—they include the 1929 crash, 1987's Black Monday, and some panicky days around the Lehman Brothers bankruptcy in 2008—would have been left with $3.65 million at the end of 2014, or over three times as much money.

See what I mean by tempting? I did point out, though, that very good days tend to come around the same weeks or months that very bad ones do, so your timing would have to be practically perfect. We're talking about less than one-tenth of one percent of all trading days during that span.

Sure, the payoff from missing a major selloff would be huge. The very smartest people on Wall Street would give up a major bodily appendage to identify even one of those episodes, though, and there's no evidence any of them has managed to do it with any consistency. Their statistical models aren't even very good at predicting how bad those bad days will be once they arrive—potentially a fatal miscalculation for those using borrowed money to enhance returns.

For example, the October 1987 stock market crash was what risk managers call a 21 standard deviation event. That's a statistical definition and I won't bore you with the math. In a nutshell, about 68 percent of daily moves by definition should fall within one standard deviation from the mean (average) daily return, while 95 percent should fall within two (notice I use the word "should" and not "will").

But 21 standard deviations aren't merely a tenth as likely as two standard deviations—oh, no. The odds of the drop in prices seen on October 19, 1987, were so long that I would fill this page with numbers if I wrote them out. To put it in stark terms, it shouldn't have happened in the entire history not only of this universe but of many others.

Then there are days like October 21, 2008. The S&P 500 rose by over 9 percent, a 10 standard deviation event that "should" have happened once every 355,120,000,000,000,000 years. Maybe you thought you saw 2008 coming and maybe you're really being honest with yourself. Fine, but you didn't anticipate October 1987, because that month's crash was like a bolt from the blue. There was one strategist, Elaine Garzarelli, who actually predicted it through some nifty analysis, parlaying it into a career as the best-paid strategist on Wall Street. And if you believe her, I have a broken clock to sell you that can tell the time correctly twice a day with stunning accuracy. (There'll be much more on Garzarelli and similar prophets later.) How about September 11, 2001? The only people who knew about it, besides the hijackers, were in a cave in Afghanistan.

Wall Street professionals armed with massive computing power just aren't very good at identifying these periods of extreme volatility, and while you may not do worse, you probably can't do much better either. If you've been paying attention, for example, then you should be asking why at least three events that shouldn't have happened even once since the Big Bang have occurred in the past three decades alone. It's because even the most sophisticated traders make poor predictions. When people with pointy heads and absolute conviction in models that claim to do so are united with billions of dollars of borrowed money, trouble often ensues. See Long Term Capital Management, Bear Stearns, and Lehman Brothers.

You won't blow up the global financial system, but you could blow a big hole in your nest egg by dipping in and out of the market. If you have done so successfully in the past (I plead guilty to a few naïve attempts), then it involved at least some luck. Sitting out for any length of time will be costly because missing bad days usually means missing some really good ones too. That means a foregone gain. Consider the fact that sitting out that entire eighty-six-year period that the Invesco analysts measured and merely earning interest on idle cash would grow a nest egg to just $193,000. That's just a sixth of what someone investing passively in stocks throughout would have earned.

The two points that all these figures are meant to illustrate are critical for keeping you out of Lake Moneybegone. One is that you've got to be in it to win it. Unless you're unbelievably lucky, prolonged periods on the sidelines will cost you. The other is that financial markets can make a fool out of the smartest person you know. In fact, they made a fool out of the smartest person almost anyone has known.

No less a genius than Isaac Newton took a bath in a speculative mania. He even sold for a nice gain but jumped back in near the peak. It was called the South Sea Bubble, and at one point it was worth about five times all the money in Europe. And you thought Pets.com was loony!

"I can calculate the motions of the heavenly bodies, but not the madness of people," said Newton at the time.

One definition of madness is doing the same thing over and over and expecting a different result. Burned by a previous round of poor timing, for example, we find it hard to let go and allow the ebb and flow of the market to take over.

I've already mentioned a concept in behavioral finance called the illusion of control. Successful people are bold and active, not resigned and passive. When it comes to investing, though, it gives us the impression that activity—buying and selling—is fruitful when it actually is a waste of time or even acts as a drag on our returns. Lottery organizers hit on this behavior early on when they replaced random numbers with lotto cards that people could fill in themselves. They were able to sell a lot more tickets and offer poorer odds because people felt they had some influence over the outcome.

Naturally it's tempting to think you can find a pattern in the market that no one has noticed before. It would be not only gratifying, but also hugely profitable. I admit that I enjoy flipping through each year's new edition of *The Stock Trader's Almanac*—a long-running tally of every calendar pattern out there that breaks down returns for every single day of the year and every major and minor holiday. "Sell Rosh Hashanah and buy Yom Kippur," anyone?

The best-known patterns include the Presidential Cycle, in which the third year of a president's term is about two and a half times as profitable as the dismal first year. Traders trying that one missed out on the start of a bull market in 2009 and a fantastic year in 2013. Then there's "sell in May and go away," the granddaddy of them all. In the sixty-four years through 2014, $10,000 invested in the Dow Jones Industrials only from November through April grew to $816,984, while the same amount invested only from October through May actually shrank slightly.

That sure sounds good, but nobody can say why it works or if it will in the future. I would caution against adopting any such timing strategy. If you search hard enough you can find all sorts of odd coincidences. Once I wrote a column about some researchers who devoted serious computing power to find the single indicator that best predicted the direction of the stock market. Drum roll, please . . . the price of butter in Bangladesh. As ridiculous as it was, I got an e-mail from a reader who didn't get the joke and asked where he could look up the price of butter in Bangladesh.

I would say that there's only a fine line between market timing and astrology, except that sometimes even that distinction vanishes. Another phenomenon that I wrote about many years ago stems from a 2002 paper by graduate students at the University of Michigan: "Are Investors Moonstruck? Lunar Phases and Stock Returns." It found that returns were a dramatic 5.4 percent lower on an annualized basis between the fifteen days around a full moon compared with those around a new moon for the years they examined. I got e-mails about that one too, of course.[2]

The rule of thumb I apply to all of the above is akin to Murphy's law—they all work until you personally try them. Trust me on this one. There are hedge funds out there with teams of mathematicians on staff using supercomputers to slice and dice any and every anomaly that exists. They'll find one before you do and that will be the end of it.

Investors who lose confidence in their own ability to time the market, or those who never harbored such delusions in the first place, aren't out of the woods either. There are literally hundreds of services out there that purport to have successful models to get us in and out at the right time. Occasionally they become so influential that they can, at least briefly, create a self-fulfilling prophecy.

For example, the late Joseph Granville, who died at age ninety in 2013, once had the ability to move markets through his pronouncements. In 1981 he sent an alert to his subscribers to "sell everything." The market plunged by 2.4 percent on then-record volume. The reputable *Journal of Portfolio Management* even claimed in 1982 that Granville's "algorithm" had some predictive value. That was before he missed the greatest bull market of all time that was to begin that year. In 2005, *Hulbert Financial Digest,* which tracks newsletters, reported that Granville's recommendations actually lost money over the preceding twenty-five years. Luckily in one case, and arguably both, two of Granville's predictions failed to pan out—a massive earthquake in Los Angeles in April 1981 and his winning the Nobel Prize in Economics.[3]

I could go on and on, but the final nail I'd like to hammer into market timing's coffin comes courtesy of investment blogger Barry Ritholtz. Having read about Ben Carlson's terrible market timer, a reader of his calculated what returns a perfectly good market timer would have earned. The results obviously are better, but, once again, they aren't at all what you'd expect. He only bought stocks when the index was trading at a fifty-two-week low and at least 17 percent lower than his most recent purchase. When it came to U.S. stocks, the perfect timer slightly lagged an investor who put money into the stock market on a schedule without attempting to time it.[4]

It might not have Einstein's official seal of approval, but that's a testament to the awesome power of compound interest. What's more, I'll demonstrate in the next chapter that even a technique Einstein did know a thing or two about—time travel—wouldn't necessarily help you beat the market.

CHAPTER THREE

TURNING LEMONS INTO LEMONADE

K eep Calm and Carry On" may have been a dandy slogan during the Blitz, but it doesn't sell newspapers. You shouldn't be surprised to hear, then, that publications like the *Wall Street Journal* and channels such as CNBC see their best Web traffic and viewership on the very worst days for financial markets. You don't even have to put on your glasses to read how bad it was because the font size on the headline is roughly proportional to the number of points the Dow Jones Industrials dropped the day earlier. And if the news makes it to the front page of your local, generalist paper, then you just know there's been a bloodbath on Wall Street.

There's a well-worn formula for what sorts of images accompany a story about a major market swoon: a floor trader cradling his head in his hands or perhaps an anxious throng outside a stock exchange in some Asian city, along with a jagged and ominous-looking line on a chart pointing sharply down and to the right. (The shell-shocked trader meme may soon be as anachronistic as a ticker tape as physical trading floors where actual human beings work give way to vastly more efficient computers.)

It's interesting that bad news about stocks is featured far more prominently than good news, even when the percentage change is the same and the only difference is a plus or a minus sign. And a string of several minuses in a row is way more newsworthy than the inverse. Sure, there are stories in the paper every day about finance, but you'll never see "market humming along" given prime real estate, except perhaps when some major milestone such as a big round number for the Dow or Nasdaq Composite indices is breached. The more prominent the scary headlines about the market, though, the smarter it is to commit some more money to stocks.

Don't take my word for it. A group of analysts at Bespoke Investment Group quantified the prominence of financial stories and came to the same conclusion. They focused on a single, influential news source, *The Drudge Report,* which aggregates items from all over the Internet and enjoys thirty million page views per day. A story that makes the main *Drudge* headline is the epitome of big news.

The analysts looked back at headlines from 2003 through 2012 over rolling fifty-day periods that ran during the hours when most financial news is consumed, between 9 a.m. and 4 p.m. eastern time, and developed something called the "Drudge Headline Indicator." The measure hit its all-time peak on February 27, 2009, just a handful of trading sessions before stocks hit their bear market low. Once the new bull market was well under way a couple of months later, the indicator hit zero, suggesting that the stock market had turned ice cold as a general news story. Then it reached another peak in August 2011 as the Eurozone crisis flared and the credit rating of the United States was downgraded by Standard & Poor's, setting off tremendous market volatility. It also marked a fresh swoon for stock prices. Both peaks in the Drudge Headline Indicator were great times to buy stocks, not sell them.

Despite the surge in newspaper readership on tumultuous days, it's not as if reporters are rooting for bad news. Boom times are better for our odds of remaining employed, not to mention our own 401(k) balances. But crises are exciting and provide plenty of interesting material. The atmosphere at work on such days is totally different now that I'm a journalist compared to my earlier career at an investment bank. Back then, with the majority of our pay in the form of bonuses based on the firm's profitability, not to mention a lot more money at stake, period, there was a palpable tension in the office. As we fielded anxious calls from clients, potential cars, vacation homes, and early retirements were going "poof" in our minds.

In a newsroom, by contrast, there was electricity in the air the day in September 2008 when Lehman Brothers hit the wall and panic broke out in the markets. We felt we not only were living history but writing its first draft. In common with most journalists, my thoughts were more along the lines of "What does this all mean?" than "What does this mean for me?" It was weeks after the heat of the crisis that I heard anyone mulling the impact of the meltdown on his or her personal finances. That's probably a good thing, and maybe it even makes financial hacks slightly better-than-average investors. Knee-jerk reactions to dramatic news can get expensive.

But what if you thought you knew when all hell was about to break loose? Take an economic recession—something so unpleasant and costly that companies and the government spend tens of millions of dollars annually trying to predict it, without much success. If you could see one coming before everyone else, it seems like it wouldn't be worth just millions but billions. That idea is so wrongheaded that we have to turn to fiction to find the right way to overturn it.

I saw *Back to the Future II* when I was in college and I ended up thinking an awful lot about it. I happened to like it nearly as much as the original, but there was one little detail that bugged me. For the purposes of this book, I finally satisfied my curiosity and found the answer to be surprising. I think you will too.

In case you haven't seen it, or just to refresh your memory, part two of the *Back to the Future* trilogy starts out with Marty and Doc flying thirty years into the future to the year 2015 to prevent Marty's son from committing a crime and going to prison. (Marty went thirty years back to 1955 in the first movie.) As you would expect from Hollywood, all sorts of laughably improbable things were supposed to be going on, including the advent of flying cars, self-tying shoes, and the Cubs finally winning the World Series. Marty does wind up keeping his progeny on the straight and narrow, but that's where the fun only begins. While walking around the future Hill Valley, Marty buys an antique sports almanac covering the years 1950 through 2000.

It turns out to be a very bad idea. Doc convinces him that he risks wreaking havoc by using it to enrich himself and jeopardizing the space-time continuum. Before he can get rid of the book, though, his now-elderly nemesis, Biff, sees Doc's DeLorean time machine parked on the street and, unbeknownst to Doc and Marty, borrows it to make a quick round trip to 1955. Meeting his teenage self, he hands him the almanac. After Doc and Marty accomplish their mission, they return to 1985 to find a dystopian world dominated by a fabulously wealthy and corrupt Biff.

So here's the detail I felt could be improved: I questioned the relative usefulness of a sports almanac. The amount you can bet on any given event is limited, and too much success will earn you a visit from a guy named Dominic with no neck. On the other hand, a single page of stock quotations from a newspaper (which still existed in the real live 2015, if barely) or a history book telling you when key events such as wars or recessions took place would seem to be far more valuable.

As you can tell, I would be an awful screenwriter. But was I right? It sure seems like there's more money to be made in stocks than gambling. Old Biff wouldn't even have to give young Biff anything in writing. Just whispering the names Polaroid, Xerox, Apple, and Microsoft into teenage Biff's ear along with the relevant decade to ride them to gains of several thousand percent apiece would have turned a small sum of money into billions. But let's say he did the next best thing and gave him an economic history book. In it would be the dates of every recession for the next thirty years.

Contrary to popular belief, a recession isn't merely two consecutive quarters of negative economic growth. A group of experts at the National Bureau of Economic Research decides on the precise period during which economic activity was at its worst. Since 1929, this committee has dated the beginning and end of a recession based on plenty of hindsight. For that reason, recessions aren't declared until long after they've begun and sometimes when they're nearly over. Likewise, the ensuing upturn usually is well under way by the time the NBER gives the all-clear. The downturn coinciding with the financial crisis ended in June 2009 but wasn't declared over until September of the following year. The recession that preceded the roaring 1980s expansion ended in November 1982, but the economists at the NBER didn't stick an official fork in it until July 1983.

It might seem a bit like those analysts who unhelpfully down-grade a company from "buy" to "sell" the day its stock has plunged because the CEO got arrested. Cut the NBER some slack, though. They're there to get it right, not to provide investors with an early warning system. Biff, on the other hand, would have done just that by knowing the precise starting date of a recession well in advance. Not only would the official arbiters of economic cycles not have be-gun to fire up their slide rules yet, but virtually all private-sector economists would be complacent at that stage too. They only tend to form a consensus that an economic slump is under way months after the fact.

Economic contractions come in different flavors, none of them appetizing. During the thirty years Biff could act on his list of reces-sions, there were six of them lasting between six and sixteen months. The economy was in a recession about a fifth of the time. All recessions saw the economy shrink and unemployment rise, and one, from 1973 to 1975, worsened by the Arab oil embargo, was the sharpest since the Great Depression until the even nastier one from 2008 to 2009. Needless to say, deep downturns are bad for business and lousy for consumer sentiment, making a perfectly awful combi-nation for stock prices.

Armed with this information, Biff would begin to invest in the stock market but make sure to sell everything and put his money in cash on the day before a recession began. His surprised stockbroker would urge him to remain in the market, perhaps suggesting a hot new initial public offering, but Biff would just reply that he "had a gut feeling" and leave it at that. Fast-forward (or is it backward?) to the day Marty and Doc return to 1985 and everything should be pretty much the way they left it, save for a very frustrated Biff. You see, there's a cost to interrupting the stock market's steady stream of gains. If you choose to sit it out then you had better be pretty sure something awful is about to happen.

Awful things did happen, but they manifested themselves at slightly different times for investors than the dates circled on Biff's cheat sheet. It turns out that stocks are a lot better than economists or strategists at "knowing" that a recession is about to hit and usually start falling earlier. Naturally there are some false alarms as well. Take the October 1987 crash, the stock market's worst ever single-day decline in percentage terms, which led to widespread but unfounded speculation that it would mark the start of a recession or something even worse. After all, the less severe Black Tuesday in 1929 is popularly seen as the cause of the Great Depression, even though the story is actually far more complicated. Such head fakes led economist Paul Samuelson to quip that "Wall Street indexes predicted nine of the last five recessions."

Be that as it may, the stock market seems almost clairvoyant sometimes—sort of like a fortune-teller with some smudges on her crystal ball. I'll admit that up until this point in the book, I haven't encouraged you to pay its gyrations much heed. But if you were in the prediction business rather than the business of preserving and growing your nest egg, you would be better off taking more notice of stock prices than professional seers do.

A few months before the official start date of a recession, at the time the market has started to falter, few or no mainstream economists are sounding warnings. The same goes for the latter stages of a recession, except in reverse: Stocks begin a new bull market before the economy has turned the corner. When stocks form what we ultimately will recognize as their trough, the recession usually will be more than halfway over. At that point, though, few economists will be willing to stick their necks out to say they see the light at the end of the tunnel.

Which brings us back to poor Biff. He sold his car, cashed in his savings bonds, and managed to scrape together $10,000 in 1955—quite a large sum for a teenager at that time. Over the thirty years he had possession of the beginning and ending dates of the economic expansions and contractions, between the end of 1955 and 1985, he dutifully switched his portfolio to cash only during recessions and remained fully invested in the S&P 500 at other times. We'll be generous to Biff and ignore capital gains taxes and transaction costs. By the end of 1985, he would have accumulated a portfolio worth nearly $122,000.

That's not too shabby—an 8.7 percent compound annualized return, which is far better than what most investors earn. But, shockingly, it's less than the over $149,000, or 9.4 percent, that he would have netted by just staying invested in the S&P 500 throughout the entire thirty years, in good and bad economic times alike. So I stand corrected: Biff would have been better off with the sports almanac.

To be fair, choosing this specific thirty years involves a tiny bit of cherry-picking on my part. The more severe and long a recession, the sharper the downturn in stocks has tended to be. The worst-ever slump in American equities came between September 1929 and July 1932, with a drop of almost 90 percent in the Dow Jones Industrial Average. As nasty as economic downturns have been in recent decades, the early 1930s were on an entirely different scale. The rate of unemployment rose from just over 4 percent in 1928 to nearly 25 percent at its worst. Industrial output plunged by close to half and prices of most goods fell. Several thousand banks failed and, since deposit insurance didn't exist, many people lost their life savings even if it wasn't in the stock market. The second-worst stock market slump in anyone's lifetime came recently, between October 2007 and March 2009, when the housing bubble collapsed and the S&P 500 fell by over half. Still, we're talking about different orders of magnitude.

Just consider what losing 90 percent of your savings means. It amounts to seeing your portfolio shed half of its value followed by another third and then half of its value again, capped off by losing an additional third of what's left. It is utterly devastating.

If someone in 1929, say Biff's father, had been able to avoid the brunt of that calamity by staying out of the market during the initial, very sharp phase of the Great Depression, even though stock prices began to rebound strongly more than three hundred days before the contraction of the U.S. economy officially ended, it would still leave him better off. So some recessions—once-in-a-century calamities—are bad enough for stocks that they would warrant interrupting the market's steady compounding. I hope that we don't see a similar episode in our lifetimes, and though I wish I could tell you the warning signals, I can't.

I have heard several "sky is falling" predictions of a new Depression during my career, including some from renowned forecasters, that made them look like Chicken Little. On the other hand, Irving Fisher, the most respected economist of his era, said on the eve of the actual Great Depression that stock prices had reached a "permanently high plateau." Predicting a hundred-year financial flood is simply beyond the ability of most forecasters, so reacting to such warnings will probably cost you, even if it happens to be someone who nailed a similar prediction in the past. I'll explain why in chapter 7, "Seers and Seer Suckers." By the time it becomes obvious to the experts that a garden-variety contraction has turned into an economic catastrophe, it'll be too late to sell anyway.

As for the majority of downturns, the time to sell is never. Instead, you should leave the decision making to a formula outside of your control that adds to your flattened stock portfolio. That's because the most interesting and hopeful statistic about downturns, particularly sharp ones, is how strong the rebound can be. After the Great Crash of 1929–32, at the market's normal rate of appreciation, about 9.5 percent a year compounded including reinvested dividends, it would have taken a quarter century, or until 1957, to recover from the loss. But that isn't what happened. It took just around eighteen years, from a trough in June 1932 through the middle of 1950, to get back to the high hit in September 1929. And, oh, by the way, those eighteen years included World War II, the bloodiest, costliest conflict in human history, and also three additional bear markets.

Much more recently, the S&P 500 shed over half of its value between its peak in October 2007 and its trough in early March 2009 during the global financial crisis. At a normal pace of appreciation, that should have taken over seven years to recoup, but instead it took just three years and two weeks.

In every case, the time to recover from a devastating bear market was far shorter than what one might have assumed by plugging in the normal rate of gain. That makes perfect sense, though, because not only are stocks not in a bull market and therefore not rising 100 percent of the time, but they have to compensate for the declines when they're moving higher, making hay while the sun shines, as it were.

Imagine going on a road trip with your family and realizing when you've already been on the interstate for half an hour that you left your wallet on the kitchen counter. After wasting an hour getting back to where you were plus stopping for your kids to use the bathroom, you reach your destination six hours after you first set off and calculate that your average speed was 50 miles per hour. Then you check MapQuest, which informs you that it should have taken you only 4 hours and 40 minutes to travel those 300 miles. In theory it should have at 65 miles an hour, but computer programs don't adjust for children's bladders and parents' absentmindedness.

By contrast, the MapQuest of the stock market, its advertised long-term gains, accounts for all of its detours, big and small. The corollary of that fact is that the market really has to put the pedal to the metal when it's on the superhighway known as a bull market. What's more, even those fairly rapid gains aren't spread evenly. As some furious people might after being forced to go home and retrieve their wallet, it starts driving at a seemingly reckless speed to make up for lost time when it first gets back on the highway heading in the right direction.

That's the silver lining to bear markets. Just as with the old saying "The bigger they are, the harder they fall," the inverse is true for downturns. The worse the fall, the more impressive the rebound. The gains from the new bull market accrue disproportionately during its early stages. Unfortunately, they also occur during the times when individual investors are most likely to have reduced their exposure to equities. Attempting to time the market is, as I've already said, a big reason why most investors live in Lake Moneybegone. Their behavior during these turning points, when bear markets turn to bulls, is when the most severe damage is done. It isn't your losses but your foregone gains that hurt the most.

What's that—you weren't one of those nervous nellies who sold into the teeth of the 2007–2009 bear market? Good for you, but did you buy more stock with proceeds from the safer part of your portfolio? If you didn't, then your exposure to stocks was less than optimal.

This book's basic goal is to get you as close to your fair share of the market return as possible. That involves, first and foremost, making peace with the market's volatility. Even better than that is seeing those gyrations as an opportunity to turn lemons into lemonade.

Of all the hard habits to break, the way you think about bear markets may be the toughest. Yes, they are scary and devastating. They also happen to be fantastic opportunities to enhance returns. There is serious upside in maintaining your stock exposure after a downturn has taken a bite out of the number at the bottom of your brokerage statement rather than waiting for the all-clear. In fact, as Biff learned the hard way, some of the best gains are to be had before a recession has ended.

How good? How about 68 percent annualized, or about seven times what passive investors earn in the long run. Of the eight bear market recessions highlighted in the chart below, the lowest annualized return earned between the day stocks bottomed and the official end of the recession was 28 percent, or two and a half times the long-run market return. The best was 124 percent at the start of the great 1982–2000 secular bull market. Those returns were earned during just 1,311 days over an eighty-year period. Those also happen to be the times when a retail investor is most likely to be leery of the market—not only when both a recession and major bear market are well under way but before the decline in economic activity has reversed, much less been spotted by economists.

ANNUALIZED RETURN BETWEEN START OF BULL MARKET AND END OF RECESSION

Bull market start	Return
Jun-32	50.40%
Jun-49	58.05%
Oct-57	28.16%
May-70	56.91%
Oct-74	77.07%
Aug-82	123.78%
Oct-90	56.10%
Mar-09	94.50%
Long-term return	*9.60%*

Source: Author calculations; S&P Dow Jones Indices

One reason that economists are so slow to declare the beginnings or ends of recessions is that economic growth is calculated by government statisticians with a significant lag and often revised sharply higher or lower to boot. For example, the third and final report on how quickly the economy grew in the fourth quarter of 2014 from the Bureau of Economic Analysis was published on March 27, 2015, or nearly a full quarter later. Waiting for economists to measure the economy accurately is like watching grass grow and even less profitable.

It sure seems like timelier statistics would be more helpful. They do exist, but it really doesn't matter, because there's no magic bullet in the form of economic data to provide a trading signal. The unemployment rate is as fresh as it gets. The Labor Department reports this number on the first Friday of the following month, making it the most watched government release of all on Wall Street. A good or bad jobs report can jolt not only the U.S. stock and bond markets but those all over the world, creating or erasing hundreds of billions of dollars in value as prices rise or fall.

As an investing columnist, I spend more time slicing and dicing the minutiae of the monthly jobs report than anything else. In addition to writing my column, I usually make an on-camera appearance to interpret the numbers at 8:30 a.m., when the release hits the wires. A big deal is made out of positive or negative surprises. Oddly enough, though, knowing the unemployment rate ahead of time wouldn't be particularly useful to investors aside from anticipating the market's immediate, knee-jerk move.

Take the period from the peak of the technology boom in early 2000 through the middle of 2003. Unemployment hit a low of just 3.8 percent in April 2000—about as good as it has been in recent decades. It deteriorated from that point, and eleven months later a formal recession would begin. Then came the 9/11 terrorist attacks and the wars in Afghanistan and Iraq. Joblessness kept rising until June 2003. In the three months leading up to that peak, the unemployment rate would go from 5.9 percent to 6.3 percent—a substantial deterioration. Yet those were three fantastic months for equity markets. Stocks would post a return of nearly 15 percent—equivalent to a stellar 60 percent gain on an annualized basis.

The same pattern, to a greater or lesser extent, held true for each peak in the unemployment rate since the Great Depression, some fourteen episodes in all. Not only did stocks always rise in the three-month period that saw the jobless rate continue to grow, but they usually rallied handsomely. In fact, if you were to be a sort of anti-Biff, only holding stocks during those seemingly inauspicious three-month periods, you would make seven times your money.

Strung end-to-end, that's a period of just three and a half years spanning almost nine decades. There is no single bull market that even comes close to matching those sorts of gains. The worst of times for the economy truly were the best of times.

ANNUALIZED S&P 500 GAIN THREE MONTHS BEFORE UNEMPLOYMENT PEAKED

Peak date	Return
31-May-33	291.3%
30-Jun-38	151.7%
28-Feb-47	26.3%
31-Oct-49	33.6%
30-Sep-54	49.2%
31-Jul-58	40.7%
31-May-61	25.1%
31-Aug-71	2.8%
30-May-75	53.3%
31-Jul-80	64.7%
31-Dec-82	74.1%
30-Jun-92	11.8%
30-Jun-03	59.8%
31-Oct-09	16.1%
Long-term return	9.60%

Source: Author calculations; Labor Department; S&P Dow Jones Indices

As much as it pains me to say this given the fact that my newspaper column is about the flow of private and government numbers that affect investments, the day-to-day news itself all really amounts to noise. A good earnings report or economic statistic will send an individual stock or the market as a whole rising during the trading session after it's released, to be sure, but the value of making investment decisions as a knee-jerk reaction to that number is less than zero. Stocks not only react but frequently overreact to good and especially to bad news. The fact that certain investors believe this to be true, at least some of whom know what they're doing, is lost in the media's flair for the dramatic in covering the news. Just think about the typical headline after a nasty piece of economic or corporate news has jolted the market: "Wave of Selling Hits Stocks"

Oh, really? Why not a "wave of buying," then? All those sell orders don't make stock certificates disintegrate. Each share that was sold was also bought by someone else, so clearly those people thought the lower price, despite the news, was an opportunity to buy.

As I noted at the beginning of this chapter, such headlines not only sell papers but also make it into the parts of the paper that someone not particularly interested in business news is most likely to see. Unlike Biff, we don't have even a faulty indicator of which ones are false alarms and when even bigger selloffs in the stock market actually may be around the corner. But when we see scary headlines about losses that have already occurred, we react the same way one of our primeval ancestors would have (or should have) when faced with danger. We run.

Take the period from January 2007 through February 2015. Over that time, some months saw inflows into and some outflows from equity mutual funds according to data maintained by the Investment Company Institute. When I sorted those flows based on the performance of the S&P 500 that month and the month earlier, a clear pattern emerged. The ten periods with the worst trailing two-month stock market performance saw a gigantic outflow of a cumulative $220 billion. The ten best two-month periods coincided with an inflow of a cumulative $60 billion.

It's classic evidence of retail investors zigging when they should zag. Looking at mutual fund sales and purchases another way makes this even clearer. During the first ten months of 2007, which were also the final ten months of that bull market—when prices were both highest and the market closest to a sharp reversal—a net $84 billion was invested into equity mutual funds. That's a large number and reflects many people who were late to the party, preferring to see evidence of a multiyear trend in prices before committing more of their savings to stocks. We know with the benefit of hindsight that it was a mistake. For many people it probably was two mistakes combined. Unlike Ben Carlson's hypothetical example of an investor with perfectly bad timing that I presented earlier in this book, those most likely to buy near the top didn't remain invested in those funds forever. People skittish enough to wait for five years of gains for affirmation are also most likely to have had a change of heart, selling near the ensuing bottom. Those people enjoyed less of the 2002–2007 bull market, and because they were demonstrably flighty, the very same people were more likely to be among the big sellers and to lock in losses in the ensuing downturn. That also means they probably missed the best part of the recovery. They were buying first-class tickets to Lake Moneybegone.

As bear markets are to bull markets, periods of mutual fund outflows are shorter and thus more concentrated than those experiencing inflows. The ten-month period between June 2008 and March 2009, the heart of that downturn, saw a whopping $250 billion leave equity mutual funds. You may recall that March 2009 was the market's nadir and the start of another raging bull market. Someone who waited until just the end of April to get back into stocks—and the record shows that many people waited far longer—missed out on gains of 30 percent.

If you can ignore the scary headlines or remain oblivious to them then you'll avoid this wealth-destroying error, but how exactly do you do that? Later in this book I'll discuss the pros and cons of having a professional act as a buffer between you and your investments—a cost that may be well worth it for the most jittery investors. But the simplest remedy for sleeping well at night, and a prudent step on its own, is to have a mix of lower-risk assets like bonds alongside stocks.

That's pretty standard, but many investors in charge of their own portfolios are either overly cautious or adopt a "set it and forget it" approach, exposing themselves to nasty swings. In other words, either low-return assets like bonds make up way too much of their portfolio or they choose a certain mix of riskier assets like stocks but never adjust it. In the latter case that share of risky assets will grow over time to make up a possibly excessive slice of the whole pie.

The volatility of a portfolio is measured using something called standard deviation (a higher standard deviation means a choppier portfolio). Take two hypothetical portfolios both invested 60 percent in stocks and 40 percent in bonds—a pretty typical mix—in 1926. Over the next eighty-four years an unchanged portfolio would have 98 percent of its assets in stocks, a minimum stock weighting of 36 percent at the worst point, and a standard deviation of 14.4 percent according to calculations by Vanguard Group. Its annualized return would be 9.1 percent, but an investor may just as well have eked out a bit more by putting everything in stocks.

A portfolio rebalanced each year, on the other hand, would be far less volatile. The farthest that stocks would fall would be to 52 percent of the total, and the standard deviation would be only 12.1

percent. Naturally some return would be sacrificed for peace of mind, but it still would have been a very respectable 8.5 percent annualized.

There's a reason that the portfolio rebalanced each year still did pretty well. While I've urged you to avoid outright market timing, automatic rebalancing is a way to buy low and sell high on autopilot. It's a form of timing requiring no human judgment or the possibility of cognitive errors.

Take a portfolio that started a year with 60 percent in stocks and 40 percent in bonds. Stocks suffer a bear market, dropping by 20 percent, by the time of the investor's next scheduled rebalancing, while the bond portfolio appreciates by 3 percent. The simple act of getting back to a 60/40 split means going against the flow and buying 11 percent more stocks, raising that cash by reducing bond holdings. In other words, buying low and selling high. The same works in reverse. Say stocks rose by 25 percent and bonds lost 1 percent the previous year. Getting back to a target weighting means selling 8 percent of your stock holdings and increasing your bond holdings by 16 percent.

Those sales and purchases almost certainly won't be made at the bottom or top, but they don't have to be. Faithful rebalancing is in and of itself a successful contrarian strategy. The more volatile the market is, the bigger the bargains available and the more likely that other, less disciplined investors will hand them to you on a silver platter by zigging when they should zag. While it will reduce your portfolio's volatility, it still will be psychologically demanding at times, because you often have to go against the flow. It may involve selling relatively safe bonds and buying stocks at a scary juncture for the economy. Doing so in January 2009 would have seen stocks continue to plumb new depths for sixty-eight more days.

Rebalancing regularly is nearly as frustrating during good times. Take a period such as 1995 through 1999 when stocks turned in gains of 28.2 percent compounded, their best five-year stretch in history. Each year's rebalancing would see a 60/40 investor reduce his or her potential gain the following year. In the long run, though, rebalancing and staying invested benefited an investor far more than it hurt.

As maddening as stocks can be from year to year, their long-run edge over "safe" investments is compelling. It's so compelling that debating the merits of what sort of information would be most valuable to receive from a time traveler from the future is a bit silly. A surefire way to make a tidy bundle over pretty much any thirty-year period would have been to fly back in time with a bunch of money and force our younger selves to put it in the stock market with no option to sell when headlines got frightening.

A big reason for the extra return investors get from stocks is that we're not forced to tie our money down. The fear of losing money in the interim is what robs some people of return and improves it for others. As I'll show in the next chapter, most investors take too little risk, particularly at the appropriate stages of their lives, leaving lots of money on the table.

CHAPTER FOUR

WHO WANTS TO BE A BILLIONAIRE?

Yeah, I know—that's not the actual show's name. Adding extra zeroes to the prize might boost ratings, but if anyone ever won, it would put the TV network out of business. In fact, there's never been a payout in any game of chance that reached ten figures. That's more due to a lack of imagination than a lack of cash, though.

Allow me to explain. I was commuting to work one day recently and pondering how to best explain the paradox of the stock market's superior returns in this chapter. My daily trip to and from the *Wall Street Journal* in midtown Manhattan is the least fun part of my day since it involves taking a crowded bus between suburban New Jersey and the Port Authority Bus Terminal, the biggest in the world but certainly not the cleanest or best-organized. On this particular day I had to work my way around a line of people snaking out the door of a shop that sells nothing but lottery tickets. It didn't take long to find out why: After several weeks without a winner, the Powerball jackpot had grown to $564 million—the third-largest ever.

As you can probably guess from reading this far, a 1-in-175,223,516 financial bet holds little appeal for me, even if I only have $2 on the line. But I got to thinking what the people who won would do. I don't mean the fact that the typical lottery winner blows through his or her winnings within seven years, runs a higher-than-average risk of bankruptcy, and often winds up regretting ever having played. I mean the decision they make the day that they're presented with that humongous check.

I looked up past lottery results when I reached the office. The recipient of the largest ever Powerball jackpot, eighty-four-year-old Gloria MacKenzie of Zephyrhills, Florida, made the same choice that 98 percent of those in her position do: She took the winnings in a lump sum of, in her case, $371 million (not the $590 million in the headlines). The other option would have been to receive that larger dollar value over thirty years in payments that start low and rise by 4 percent annually.

Obviously the desire for immediate gratification plays a role in most people's choice to take the money and run. The winners of the $564 million jackpot (it was split three ways) probably were a bit underwhelmed when told the annuity would pay them *only* $2 million in the first year after taxes. That's hardly private-island money, after all. But accepting an annuity also exposes a winner to the ravages of inflation and could make the prize worth potentially far less in real terms.

I'll admit that I used to think of lottery players, and especially winners, as pretty naïve. Okay, so I still do. But while some of them may not spend the proceeds very wisely, and few ponder how much a gallon of milk will cost in the year 2046, I have to concede that they generally make the correct choice by taking "less" money up front.

Let's imagine, though, that they also offered winners a third option with a much bigger prize. Naturally, there would be a catch. Just like the annuity, once you decided to defer your payout you wouldn't be able to change your mind and get at the principal, so the lottery organizers would leave you with some financial risk. In this case, though, it would be of an entirely different nature. Instead of promising you a specific dollar amount, they would say you "probably" stood to make more overall but that you would get less money to start as a yearly payment. Your annual checks would "probably" rise over time and total $316 million over the thirty years—not much less than the safest option of an up-front cash payment. But here's the big bonus: At the end of thirty years, you "should" expect to receive a check for "at least" $932 million. Add up the periodic payments plus the lump sum at the end and the winner would have received $1.25 billion, with a "b," in total over thirty years. And while they wouldn't be able to guarantee that amount, the lottery organizers inform you in a letter couched with all sorts of caveats in legal boilerplate that you're likely to earn much more. A typical outcome would be to receive $4 billion in total over the thirty-year period.

Gloria MacKenzie, eat your heart out!

As you've probably guessed, the only way the lottery organizers could offer this third option would be if they invested the lump sum in the stock market. That's the reason for the uncertainty. I calculated the odds using thirty-year rolling returns for U.S. stocks from 1870 onward. The worst compound return over any thirty-year period was 4.9 percent starting in 1873, while the very best began in 1969 and was 13.6 percent. The average return was 9.3 percent. The

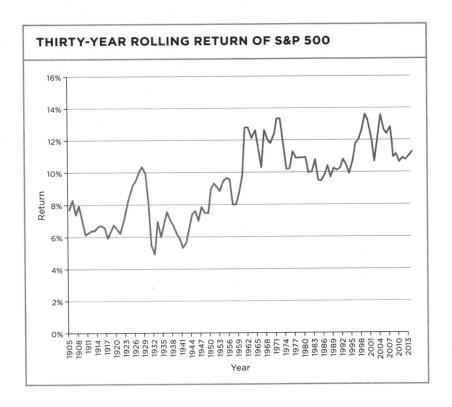

THIRTY-YEAR ROLLING RETURN OF S&P 500

annual lottery payments are the current dividend yield of the S&P 500, and they tend to grow in line with earnings.

Think about that for a minute. By accepting the third option, what historically would have been the worst outcome would leave a winner with over twice the annuity and three times the up-front cash amount. The typical outcome would leave a winner with *seven times* the guaranteed annuity. Aside from the fact that the regular payments would be a bit lower at the outset, choosing option number three seems like a no-brainer—reward with barely any risk.

Not only would a sum in the billions attract a lot of players, but I bet many more would go for the big, uncertain number than the up-front option. That's certainly what I'd recommend. But according to two authors who arrived on the scene when America's love affair with the stock market was at its apex, you're a fool not to choose all stocks all the time. Kevin Hassett and James Glassman, authors of the bestseller *Dow 36,000: The New Strategy for Profiting from the Coming Rise in the Stock Market,* argued in October 1999 that a "perfectly reasonable price" for the market was at least four times as high as the record level it had just reached. Hassett, an economist who would go on to serve as one of John McCain's chief advisors, and Glassman, a financial journalist, basically said that we had been totally wrong about stock prices over the last few centuries. Irrationally exuberant investors briefly cheered their conclusion.

Yes, stocks make a lot more money than other investments in the long run. But as your mother probably told you, there's no such thing as a free lunch—you have to stomach a lot more volatility to get that reward. Financial types call this reward the "equity risk premium," and between 1928 and 2014 it was 4.6 percentage points a year as measured by the gap between the average annual return of the main U.S. stock index and the ten-year Treasury note. Hassett and Glassman neglected the word "risk" in that definition and were saying, in a nutshell, that the difference was there to be grabbed because all the conventional wisdom linked to fear of volatility was wrong. "If you own stocks or mutual funds, this book will remove the fear. If you are worried about missing the market's big move upward, you will discover that it is not too late," they wrote in the introduction.[1]

Other books appeared around the same time that remind me of the scene in *There's Something About Mary* in which Ben Stiller picks up a homicidal hitchhiker touting his business idea that's going to blow "8-Minute Abs" out "of the water." His idea: "7-Minute Abs."

"Think about it. You walk into a video store, you see '8-Minute

Abs' sitting there, there's '7-Minute Abs' right beside it. Which one are you gonna pick, man?"

Despite aiming higher, *Dow 40,000* and *Dow 100,000* sold less well, which is why my editor talked me out of titling this book *Dow 36 Trillion!* In all seriousness, though, the argument that Hassett and Glassman were making was more sophisticated, not to mention far more audacious, than just declaring that the bull market had a lot further to run. What they were saying was that stocks already deserved to be worth much more and that, like a lottery player boneheaded enough to choose the safe fixed annuity in my hypothetical example above, you were leaving money on the table.

"The stock market is a money machine: Put dollars in at one end, get those dollars and more back at the other end. The history of these remarkable returns is vivid and undeniable," they wrote in an article in the *Atlantic* introducing the book.

Coming when it did, the book played to investors' confirmation bias. That's a fallacy in behavioral finance and other fields that leads people to seek out information that underpins what they already believe or want to believe. Faith in the stock market was so high that President Bill Clinton, in his 1999 State of the Union address, broached the idea of investing part of the Social Security Trust Fund in stocks for the first time. It has always been in the special federal IOUs and remains so to this day. There were a few skeptics, though.

"The public can see for itself that the sky's the limit on Wall Street. A best-selling book purporting to prove, mathematically, that the party has just begun may outsell even the latest eat-all-the-fat-you-want-and-still-lose-weight self-help guide," wrote the snarky and insightful financial journalist James Grant at the time *Dow 36,000* was published.[2]

As Grant pointed out, with the help of well-known value investor Seth Klarman, price-to-earnings ratios of 100 would lead to impossible distortions. Entrepreneurs would rush to start businesses in order to cash in on the valuations on the stock market. We hear about similar or even higher figures being slapped on hot new companies launching initial public offerings, but the multiple Hassett and Glassman suggested as "perfectly reasonable" would also apply to those that could only hope to grow in line with the economy.

Their conclusion would, of course, apply to privately held companies as well. A business doesn't magically become four times as valuable when it's given a stock ticker, after all—at least not outside of Silicon Valley. For example, in a "Dow 36,000 World" I could take $50,000 in savings and borrow another $50,000 from the bank to open a convenience store. In the first year I might make $300,000 in sales and conservatively expect to eke out $5,000 in profit. Even if I could fetch just fifty times those earnings, around $250,000, I would be a fool not to sell the store, repay the loan, and take my $150,000 gain, a 300 percent one-year return. Then the guy who bought the store from me could work twelve-hour days selling Slurpees, Marlboros, and, of course, lottery tickets, and, if he was lucky, keep making a 2 percent annual return on his investment while I sat on the beach. Potential buyers would get wise to the game pretty quickly.

"New eras are cut short by the financial behavior they reward and condition," wrote Grant.

It's easy to laugh at *Dow 36,000* as a sign of bubble-era excess. I have a first-edition hardcover copy on my bookshelf, along with other mementos, to remind me not to get carried away during the next mania. But Hassett and Glassman actually were correct about stocks' returns and risk in the long run. The problem occurred when they extrapolated that conclusion to a naïve one about valuation.

I already told you that if a friend of mine won the lottery and stocks were one of the choices, I would advise them to go for it. That's because I'm confident, just like the *Dow 36,000* authors were, that the long-run outlook for stocks is vastly superior to bonds. And if I were an advisor to the people who run the lottery, I'd tell them to charge four times as much for a ticket since that would be a "perfectly reasonable price" for a prize that read "Expected Payout of $1.25 billion" followed by an asterisk and some fine print.

That was the gist of Hassett and Glassman's argument—that people should pay four times as much for a ticket to long-run equity returns. Aside from the distortions it would create that I just described, people don't for two other reasons. One is that we're not inclined, much less forced, to choose between tying down our money for decades or to having it sit in readily spendable cash. There are countless choices and permutations in between. The other is that there will be a huge amount of choppiness over the years if we do commit it to equities, and losses sting more than profits please.

As I briefly mentioned a couple of chapters back, there's a scientific basis for that assertion. The two psychologists who laid the foundations of behavioral finance, Daniel Kahneman and Amos Tversky, showed in the 1970s that we feel the pain of a loss more acutely than the pleasure of a gain and that this affects our financial decision making. The bias exists even among savvy subjects.

Kahneman, who went on to win a Nobel Prize in Economics for those insights, offered his students a coin flip in which they can lose $10 or win a higher amount. In terms of expected outcome, it seems like people would take that bet as long as the prize is even a little bit more than $10. In practice, though, they demand at least $20 on average before agreeing to play. In other words, lots of ostensibly free money is left on the table. Rejecting an offer of, say, $15 for a potentially winning flip means that an extra $2.50—the average of a winning and losing flip—was considered insufficient by many subjects for the risk of possibly losing. The amount of free money has to be at least $5 to get people to accept the risk, on average.

The same phenomenon plays out in the stock market every day. Superior long-run returns—the equity risk premium that Hassett and Glassman thought should be zero—are a necessary inducement to play in the market, and it still isn't enough for some people.

Remember Felicity Foresight? Not surprisingly, the best investment in much of the century that she racked up nearly $10 quintillion was stocks—sixty-nine years out of one hundred, to be precise. But there were sixteen years when U.S. bills or bonds or British gilts—investments for widows and orphans—were the best performers. That wasn't because they rose dramatically. It's because they were the least bad thing to own, appreciating a little bit, usually when stocks and commodities lost value. The worst year for U.S. stocks in the past century was a loss of nearly 44 percent, and there were several other years when losses exceeded 20 percent. Those times, and many others too, were trying ones for stock investors.

Therein lies the rub of investing in stocks. In order to unlock their extra return, you have to be willing to accept big losses in the interim. Reacting to those ups and downs by selling or buying at the wrong times is a big reason why investors wind up living in Lake Moneybegone.

The good news for you, the investor, then, is that Glassman and Hassett were absolutely wrong about how to value stocks. If they had been right, it would have been magnificent for people who had lots of money in the market the day the scales fell from everyone's eyes and stock prices quadrupled. But anyone trying to save money after that would be stuck with a measly 2 percent return—even less than the residents of Lake Moneybegone make after lots of costly errors. A lump sum of $10,000 at age twenty-five would grow to a mere $24,000 by retirement day.

You're lucky because that bumpy but superior long-run equity return is still out there. And while I'm not going to go all Dow 36,000 on you, my recommendation is to rethink the riskiness of stocks. Though it isn't one of the reasons Dalbar quantified for the awful returns of the typical investor, the fact is that most people look at the choppiness of the stock market in a very odd and counterproductive way. I'm going to explain why lack of risk in your portfolio at certain stages of your life is actually risky.

To do that, we'll look at an example of what can go wrong for a typical saver with a typical mix of assets. While there may be decades between the day that first dollar is put away and the one when that money first needs to be drawn upon for retirement income, what happens to the market in the last few years of asset accumulation takes on outsized importance.

Let's take the example of a hypothetical saver making a salary of $40,000 at age twenty-five and able to stash 7.5 percent of it in a tax-free account. That percentage remains constant while the saver's salary, and thus his retirement contribution, rises by 2.5 percent each year that he works. He puts 60 percent into stocks and 40 percent into bonds, rebalancing that amount at the beginning of every year. Unlike the typical investor in Lake Moneybegone, let's give our saver the benefit of the doubt and assume he holds his emotions in check and is perfectly robotic. He also invests in the cheapest index funds available. (Yes, I realize index funds weren't always around.)

It turns out that even after a period as long as forty years, it matters when an investor starts saving. What's more, periods that seem auspicious may not be quite so promising. Others that seem lousy at first turn out to be pretty good.

Take the forty-year period that began in 1935. The first couple of years would have strengthened the investor's resolve in staying the course with this stock market thing. The S&P 500's total returns in 1935 and 1936 were excellent, nearly doubling in just two years the value of a dollar put into stocks. After starting out like gangbusters, the market's compound average return over the entire forty-year period came to a respectable 9.7 percent.

Unfortunately, our retirement saver had relatively little money invested in the market in those early years. Also unfortunately, the end of the forty-year stretch was a doozy for stocks and just so-so for bonds as well. The market fell sharply in 1973 and 1974, by which time our saver had a large nest egg at risk. The result? An ending balance of a little over $850,000.

Now let's compare that to a different forty-year period that began with the sorts of bumps likely to discourage a novice stock investor. Starting in 1960, the market would fall in four out of the following ten years. But he didn't have that much money to lose early on and was rewarded if he stuck with it, because the average stock market returns including dividends would be 12.1 percent over the entire forty years. More to the point, he would end his investing odyssey with a bang, benefiting from the late 1990s bull market. His retirement nest egg would be a whopping $2.75 million, or over three times as much despite a shaky start and more bad years overall.

We're constantly reminded about stocks' superior long-run returns and the importance of allowing our money to compound as long as possible. It's true that getting an early start is critical, but an issue that's often overlooked, which I just highlighted, is that the sums don't really become meaningful for several years. Through a cruel twist of history, people planning on retiring in years like 1975, 2002, or 2009 received a drubbing if they didn't reduce their stock exposure. Even those who were some years away from retirement grew more pessimistic about having enough money to live on. A Gallup survey of nonretired Americans showed that in 1996 just 14 percent expected to work beyond the normal retirement age of sixty-five. By 2002, after the tech bubble had burst, that jumped to 21 percent. By 2012, after yet another stock market crash, the proportion had risen to 39 percent. A big reason was shattered nest eggs. But then the years leading up to those market reversals were good times for stocks when "everyone" knew that they were a great vehicle for saving. People who hadn't saved enough or who wanted to buy a slightly bigger retirement home had a hard time resisting the allure of what in hindsight was a dangerously frothy market.

Based on the examples of the two investors I just gave, then, you might expect me to recommend a more cautious approach. What I'm going to suggest, though, is the opposite. Embracing risk at the appropriate time actually can reduce it in the long run. By doing so, it's possible to kill two birds with one stone—reducing sharp swings that can send a portfolio's value plunging at the exact wrong time while enhancing overall returns. It's the investing equivalent of Lite beer—tastes great, less filling.

Let's revisit the example of our twenty-five-year-old. So far we have looked at two actual historical periods—a mediocre one and a great one. This time let's also look at two scenarios, but ones that never existed. I'll use actual stock and bond returns, taking data from eighty-seven years of investment history and then shuffling them into thousands upon thousands of different combinations through what's called a Monte Carlo simulation. Named for the principality with the famous casino, Monte Carlo simulations have nothing to do with gambling. Instead they involve running many simulated outcomes to determine probable ones. Each time there will be forty randomly selected stock and forty randomly selected Treasury note returns.

The first scenario uses the same asset allocation as the original example, a 60/40 split between stocks and bonds rebalanced annually. The second scenario employs what at first might seem like a riskier strategy. Instead of 60 percent we'll start with an aggressive 85 percent stock allocation at age twenty-five and reduce it by a percentage point each year. By age sixty-four the allocation to stocks would reach 46 percent, while bonds would be 54 percent.

The effect of this is twofold: You're likely to earn more because the average allocation to stocks is modestly higher throughout and their long-run return is markedly superior to bonds. But at the same time, you're much less likely to suffer a devastating loss in your final years of accumulating assets. That's because you have less invested in stocks by then.

A good way of comparing the two scenarios is to see how often certain values fall within certain ranges. In the case of the 60/40 split, when I ran the simulation a hundred times, the majority of ending values at age sixty-five fell between $600,000 and $1.8 million. The range for a saver who starts with 85 percent and slowly dials back stock exposure is clearly better, falling mostly between $1 million and $2.2 million. What's more, not only were the odds of coming up short lower, but the median nest egg was a third higher at $1.66 million. Starting out with more risk and finishing with less, even if you save the same amount, both reduces your total risk and enhances your payoff.

It's no surprise, then, that prudent advisors used to tell their clients that a good rule of thumb for stock market exposure was to subtract their age from one hundred and put that amount into stocks. If you were twenty-five it would be 75 percent, and if you were fifty-five it would be 45 percent, and so forth. Since then the industry has become a lot more sophisticated and, unless you're willing to take an unemotional look at your portfolio and get back to your age-appropriate setting yourself on a regular basis, choosing a cheap fund that does it automatically is often the best bet.

Such funds go by different names, including "target date" or "life cycle" (not to be confused with "lifestyle funds"). The basic idea is to do more or less what I did in the second example by establishing a "glide path" of asset allocation that rebalances and gets less risky as retirement nears. For example, one offered by mutual fund giant Vanguard Group supposedly appropriate for me, a forty-six-year-old, is the Vanguard Target Retirement 2035 Fund. Nearly 50 percent of assets are in U.S. stocks and a bit less than a third in international ones. A fund offered by the same company for someone who might retire around 2060 has 54 percent and 36 percent in those two categories, respectively.

I can't recommend one product over another, but will point out that all target date funds are most definitely not equal. One factor is frequency of rebalancing (more is better). Investors in some target date funds with a 2010 retirement date that hadn't rebalanced stock holdings recently lost 23 percent of their value in 2008 according to Morningstar.[3] That's a fairly painful experience two years before retirement.

Even more important is costs. A study by FutureAdvisor compared target date funds based on fees and expenses and found that it was an accurate predictor of total return. I learned this the hard way myself. The *Wall Street Journal*'s 401(k) plan is run by Fidelity Investments, and in addition to various actively managed funds that I avoid like the plague (I'll explain why in chapter 8, "Where Are the Customers' Yachts?"), there are some low-fee index funds they offer that are run by a computer. When a big chunk of my savings was automatically put into the Fidelity Freedom 2035 fund, I assumed that it just held a mix of index funds similar to the Vanguard fund I used as an example.

I contribute the most I can but have a policy of only checking my 401(k) rarely. With my investments automated and a target date fund that was supposed to handle rebalancing, that seemed prudent. As I wrote this chapter I decided to take a peek and spotted my fund's expense ratio. It's 0.75 percent, which I had never noticed. That seemed awfully high, and I realized it was run by an actual human being who put on a suit and tie and went to an office building every weekday and tried to pick stocks and bonds for me based on my age.

Sure enough, I compared my Fidelity 2035 fund to one targeting the same date by Vanguard, which uses index funds only, rebalancing them each year. Vanguard's expense ratio is 0.18 percent. Over the last ten years, as a result of costs but also investing decisions, $10,000 invested in the Fidelity fund would have grown to $16,876, while it would have grown to $18,145 in the Vanguard fund. That's a pretty big difference—possibly enough to justify using Fidelity's lower-cost stock and bond index funds alone and rebalancing them myself manually once a year.

Or I could have a service tell me what to do. I tried one out called MyPlanIQ. Their free service asked me for my risk profile (moderate) but not any other information and suggested a portfolio of five index funds available in my company's plan that it would tell me by e-mail to rebalance quarterly. I "backtested" the results and found that the returns over ten years would have been 26 percent better than the higher-cost Fidelity 2035 fund. An enhanced version of the service that claims to have a more optimized formula costs $200 a year.

Human financial advisors are more expensive and may or may not assist you with a 401(k) plan since it's not under their control. On the other hand, they can provide tailored advice that a Web site can't since everyone is unique. You may have different life goals beyond retirement or specific issues such as a disability, a special needs child, or a large sum of money in taxable accounts. What every person reading this does have in common, though, is being human. Fear and greed are hardwired into your brain to varying degrees. If personal intervention is what it takes not to sell at the point of maximum pessimism, then it may be worth the money.

For most people reading this, though, a low-cost target date fund may be the best bet. According to a recent snapshot of 401(k)s by the Employee Benefit Research Institute, people in their forties like me had less than 16 percent of assets in target date funds. More alarmingly, 7 percent of their money was in company stock—an unnecessary risk since your chances of remaining employed shouldn't be tied to an investment you hope to live on. Enron employees learned this the hard way. Some 3.3 percent of forty- to forty-nine-year-old Americans' assets were in money market funds earning zero, and 26 percent of 401(k) participants took loans from their accounts—an awful, wealth-destroying idea except in case of emergency.

Many people have substantial savings outside their workplace savings in taxable or other tax-deferred accounts. You can simply stick that money into a target date fund too, of course, but there are some other techniques—possibly requiring some professional help—that are even better at harnessing market risk to your benefit. One is tax-loss harvesting—taking advantage of inevitable, occasional losses to minimize Uncle Sam's take.

Another technique, called mean variance optimization, pinpoints, in theory at least, the optimal mix of return and reward. While one might think that the two are just opposite sides of the same coin, a clever man named Harry Markowitz, one of the fathers of modern financial theory, showed that that wasn't true. Mixing and matching assets that aren't closely correlated will trim the choppiness of a portfolio over time. What this means is that while the individual components may be choppy too, they don't mimic one another's movements too closely. Finance geeks call this "moving out on the efficient frontier"—a visual way of thinking about the curved rather than straight line that represents the risk/reward trade-off on a chart. It all sounds complicated, and the benefit may not be immediately obvious, but it usually does work over time.

The more an investor can diversify, the better, as long as it doesn't cost too much. Institutions such as endowments with long time horizons are uniquely positioned to do this. In addition to stocks and bonds, they may own commodities, farmland, timber, or private equity stakes in unlisted companies. Some of those are unavailable to ordinary savers or prohibitively expensive.

David Swensen, the fund manager who has led Yale University's endowment to phenomenal returns, in his book *Unconventional Success: A Fundamental Approach to Personal Investment* proposed a model portfolio that could get some of that extra risk-adjusted return through funds that are both accessible and affordable for individuals. In the portfolio's recent incarnation in May 2015, only 30 percent is in a U.S. stock index fund, with a fifth in international stocks and half in income-producing securities. The mix has changed over the years, but performance has been excellent. With lower risk than a typical split between just U.S. stocks and Treasury bonds, Swensen's portfolio returned 8.3 percent annually—over a percentage point more. It even beat a risky portfolio 100 percent invested in the S&P 500 by a smidgen.

One can't argue with success, but I don't think going out and buying Swensen's book and trying to recreate his portfolio yourself is the wisest course of action for many people reading this. First, one size doesn't fit all. Second, this can get complicated and you may be tempted to tweak your holdings.

A decade ago you would have turned to a human advisor to help you with this and hope that he or she knew what they were doing. You might still want a human being in charge of your money for emotional reasons, but today there's no technical part of investing that a person can do that a computer algorithm can't do more cheaply and efficiently.

For example, a firm called SigFig can construct a portfolio for you out of the lowest-cost mutual funds. Between tax efficiency, automatic rebalancing, and costs, they claim they can beat typical investor returns by a whopping four percentage points a year. Most of their money under management is actually held with three large brokerages. Clients give them access and pay 0.25 percent of assets annually as a fee.

Another company called Asset Builder maintains several free model portfolios with differing amounts of risk, from "capital preservation" and "stable" at one end to "growth" and "aggressive growth" at the other. For a fee they'll offer frequent updates much like

MyPlanIQ. One of the portfolios listed under aggressive growth looks like this:

U.S. small-capitalization stocks	20%
U.S. large-capitalization stocks	10%
Real estate investment trusts	11%
International stocks	13%
Fixed income (bonds)	30%
Emerging-market stocks	16%

The standard deviation of this portfolio over the last five years (as of March 2015) was higher than stocks alone, though not by too much. But one dollar invested in the portfolio in 2000 would have grown to $3.17, compared to $2.01 in the S&P 500 Total Return Index. That's a big payoff for a small increase in risk.

And then there are full-fledged "robo-advisors"—companies with names like Betterment and Wealthfront—where you deposit your savings and open an account. Wealthfront boasts a marquee name among its staff, with Princeton University professor Burton Malkiel acting as chief investment officer. Betterment's advisors are also impressive. Both will, like SigFig, apply modern portfolio theory, tax-loss harvesting, and other techniques to your portfolio. Wealthfront claims that doing so should add about a half percentage point a year to a saver's long-run performance. That would mean a 20 percent boost to a retirement nest egg after forty years before costs. More recently, discount brokerage firms such as Charles Schwab have launched similar services.

A more appropriate choice for some of you would be an actual human being on the other end of the phone. The typical cost of a fee-only advisor—one whose interests should be aligned with yours in growing your nest egg—is 1 percent of assets annually. Whoever does it for you, and as attractive as an optimized portfolio sounds, there's often a catch when you think you're getting something for nothing. At times of severe market stress such as the 2008 financial crisis such attempts at diversification were dubbed "de-worse-ification" as market panic became an equal-opportunity destroyer of assets. People and institutions under the impression that they were insulated from wild market gyrations suffered with everyone else and often sold near the bottom, whether out of necessity or panic.

Stocks aren't quite the magical money machine that the *Dow 36,000* authors make them out to be. Sometimes they shower investors with riches, and at other times the market can be capricious. While there's no way to predict exactly what it will do, I'll demonstrate in the next chapter that investors aren't exactly flying blind.

CHAPTER FIVE

ACTUALLY, TIMING *IS* EVERYTHING

They say that, on Wall Street, denial is just a river in Egypt. But then who am I to talk? A couple of chapters ago I railed against the folly of market timing, and, based on this one's title, I seem to have made a complete U-turn. There have been investment authors who have foretold a coming boom and then warned of an impending bust, but at least they had the decency to wait until their next book.

The sort of timing I'm about to discuss, though, is entirely consistent with this one's overall message. It can help you know what to expect from stocks and bonds and perhaps squeeze out a slightly higher return from your savings. As for my snarky take on Wall Street, I stand by my words.

Here's a vignette from my days as a stock analyst that sums up the investment industry's odd way of thinking. It concerns the rise, fall, and renewed rise of a pharmaceutical company that I "covered." I visited its headquarters and toured its plants dozens of times and spent many hours poring over its financial statements and product lineup. I came away impressed. This was twenty years ago, so I can't remember the exact numbers any longer, but my target price based on all this research was something like $90, and its market price had been around $60 when I first wrote a report. With that 50 percent potential gain, naturally I had a "buy" recommendation on it.

But then there was an emerging-markets crisis and any stock with that label, including this one, fell sharply. Now, the origin of this particular swoon was Mexico, and the countries where this company did business were at least six thousand miles away from Mexico, so this baby was being thrown out with the bathwater. Some of their currencies weakened in sympathy with the "tequila crisis," so I trimmed my valuation a bit to $85. The stock's price, though, fell to something like $40. In other words, despite the fact that I cut the target a little, the implied gain for anyone who bought the stock had gone from 50 percent to well over 100 percent.

Having been an analyst for only a year at that point, I didn't see anything wrong with what I was doing. I had learned that the only proper way to value companies was to make a forecast of their future profits and "discount" them back to the present. They didn't seem to have changed much, so neither did my target. But I soon got a call from a fund manager who was one of our largest clients. He and I got along well, but he sounded peeved, pointing out that my target price on this and some other stocks was unrealistic and made me look silly. Who in the world sets a target price at double the market price? It just wasn't done.

I felt like a wet-behind-the-ears amateur but explained that I had my model and that I was comfortable with it. Things eventually sorted themselves out on their own as the company's stock began to rise steadily. Less than three years later it had gone past my original target, and though I also had raised it along the way as the company's business boomed, it was getting hard to find a reason to maintain my "buy" recommendation. But clients were by then so in love with its stock that I felt like I had to find any excuse to accentuate the positive.

Then I went on a trip to Russia to do some research. That country was about to suffer a crisis that would make Mexico's stumble three years earlier look like a fiesta. My pharmaceutical company made most of its profit there. It also had extended lots of trade credit to its local wholesalers, who, if they faced a shortage of dollars to pay it back, would leave it high and dry.

As soon as I got back to my office I cut my target price to reflect that risk and downgraded my recommendation on the stock. Not just the company's management but many clients were livid. In less than five months, though, its price had dropped much more than I had anticipated—by some 80 percent. In the weeks after the crash I called many of the same clients and talked about the companies I covered and especially this one. The drop was an overreaction, I said, and they should try to pick it up while it was unreasonably cheap. I found very few takers. These were people who had just lost their investors a lot of money on paper, and the idea of buying more of one of the worst-hit stocks was going over like a lead balloon. The irony of the fact that the same people had reacted angrily for suggesting it was overpriced just months earlier wouldn't have been very diplomatic of me to point out. In any case, it made back most of the loss, a gain of several hundred percent, in the next few years.

The moral of my story isn't that I'm brilliant (I get plenty of things wrong) but that Wall Street has a warped view of what is and isn't attractive. The default setting is to assume what's recently been heading in a particular direction will keep on doing so. That's particularly true about the highfliers also most likely to be in a retail investor's portfolio. At the moment that means companies like Tesla, Apple, Facebook, or Chipotle, but the list may have changed by the time you read this. What stays the same is the practice of accentuating the positive in order to keep up with a market darling's momentum, justified or not. An analyst covering a stock fitting that description, if they know what's good for them, will find a reason to keep upping his or her target price.

And if they really want to go for the big time they'll come up every once in a while with an aspirational, pie-in-the-sky price target. Remember Henry Blodget? Before getting banned from the securities industry, the Internet analyst went from obscurity to fame and fortune by raising his target price from $150 to $400 on Amazon.com in December 1998. The online retailer's stock rose by nearly a fifth that day and hit his target in less than a month. He was promptly hired by a much bigger firm, Merrill Lynch, at a reported $4 million a year in salary and bonus. His predecessor, who said Amazon was overvalued, got fired.

Now, *that* was good timing, but it isn't at all the sort that I want to discuss in this chapter. The same career pressure that applies to recommendations on individual stocks affects the whole market, you see. The Dow Jones Industrials or S&P 500 won't soar so much so quickly that they require such frenetic updating of targets, but they will go up a lot over the years. Since World War II there have been seven major bull markets in the United States that saw an average gain of around 250 percent and as much as 500 percent.

Much like one of its individual companies, the market will appreciate more quickly than the combined earnings of its constituents. As with my pharmaceutical company, that doesn't bother people. On the contrary, it excites them. That's why they say stocks are the only market where people run away when there's a sale and line up at the door when prices have just doubled or tripled.

Almost every investor has heard of the price-to-earnings, or P/E, ratio, but very few appreciate what an important role it plays in their returns. Just as a stock has a price and earnings per share and the ratio of those two numbers, its P/E, denotes how cheap or expensive it is, the entire stock market does too. The Standard & Poor's 500 index and its predecessors have fetched an average P/E multiple of 15.5 times the earnings that those companies produced over the preceding twelve months going back to the late nineteenth century. That has moved in a broad range from as low as 5 times to north of 40 times.

One other piece of information, "growth," completes the picture. Despite being half of the formula for knowing exactly what price stocks will fetch at a given point in the future, it hogs almost all of investors' attention. Turn on financial television or read a strategist's comments in a newspaper article and you'll see lots of references to how quickly sales or earnings or the economy are or aren't likely to expand. This makes for pretty shallow analysis, though—even if analysts were any good at predicting it.

As I'll demonstrate in painful detail in a later chapter, and as I can tell you from personal experience as a former analyst and later head of a research department, growth forecasts are to be taken with a gigantic grain of salt. As odd as it sounds, very high analyst expectations for earnings growth are a bad sign for stocks, according to Ned Davis Research. Times when they predict historically high growth usually precede stock market tumbles and vice versa.[1]

Sometimes growth forecasts are way, way off. When stocks hit their bull market peak in October 2007, for example, strategists looked at what thousands of analysts were predicting for the companies in the S&P 500. Those "bottom up" forecasts called for record earnings of $103 a share according to figures compiled by Brown Brothers Harriman. When all was said and done, they actually earned $57. Ouch.

One reason why analysts were so sanguine in 2007 about where stocks were headed is that the market had been rallying at that point for five years but fetched almost the same P/E ratio based on forecast earnings for the following year as it had when they had started their run. That was possible because corporate profit margins had expanded from very low to very high.

But in 2008 they fell sharply. To rub salt in the wound, investors were willing to pay even less for a dollar of those lower earnings a year and a half later than they were a dollar of the higher ones at the outset. In other words, the P/E ratio fell even as the "E" plunged. The result was that stock prices, the "P," were worth well under half of what those strategists thought they would be. A collapse like the global financial crisis doesn't happen very often, but even more modest changes in valuation or profit margins can have a surprisingly big effect on your returns.

Let's suppose, for example, that you have complete faith in forecasters and, despite what that spoilsport Spencer Jakab says, you're finally vindicated. The projections you hear from strategists and economists for what will happen to the economy and profits of U.S. companies for the next ten years turn out to be exactly correct. Would that also make you confident in what direction the market is going, though? Well, it shouldn't. It's almost completely meaningless without knowing what the P/E ratio will be. I'll give you two hypothetical examples to show why.

In the first scenario, analysts and economists think that companies will be able to grow their earnings by a very respectable 7 percent a year over the next decade. That's enough for earnings to nearly double. Valuations aren't in the stratosphere, but they're sort of high at nineteen times last year's earnings. At the end of the ten-year period, though, investors only are willing to pay a slightly below average multiple of twelve times for each dollar of earnings.

In the second scenario, analysts and economists are fairly pessimistic about earnings growth. They see them growing by just 4 percent annually over a decade. Because of compound interest, a dollar of earnings would grow by just half as much as in my previous example. But in this case stocks are trading right at their average earnings multiple at both the beginning and the end of the decade. Even though earnings grow by just half as much, the value of stocks rises by double what it did in the previous example.

Convinced yet that valuation matters? Twice the price gain from half the profit growth is pretty compelling. Surely that's a stylized example meant to prove a point, though? Nope.

For example, between June 1949 and June 1959 the earnings of companies in the S&P 500 rose by 44 percent. That's not spectacular or even good, but the stock market rose threefold over the same time—a fantastic gain. It did that because the price people were willing to pay for stocks was very low at the outset at less than 6.5 times earnings and fairly high at the end at over 19 times.

The inverse held true in December 1964. In the next decade, earnings for the S&P 500 were destined to grow by 80 percent, or much faster than in the first example. With only that piece of information provided by a time traveler, a stockbroker might have urged everyone he met to buy stocks with abandon. That would have been a big mistake, though, as the S&P 500 actually fell by a fifth over the ensuing decade. That was because the P/E ratio was a fairly high 19.4 times at the outset and fell to an unusually low 7.7 times by the end in December 1974.

Timing really is everything. But the good news is that what you really need is a history book, not Doc Brown's flux capacitor, and those exist. Just ignore the P/E ratio you hear quoted by pundits on TV. Unlike the examples I gave above, the most commonly cited P/E ratio is based on a forecast of the following year's earnings. As I said earlier, that measure gave false comfort by showing that in October 2007, at the end of a bull market, stocks were just as cheap as when it had begun five years earlier. We only knew with the benefit of hindsight that the forecast "E" was completely wrong.

There's a much more stable and reliable P/E ratio you should use instead. Though he wasn't the first person to tweak the measure in some way, Yale University professor Robert Shiller has done so much excellent work on valuing assets that his version of a modified P/E ratio is the most famous. It's also free to see on his public Web site. The "Shiller P/E," also known as a cyclically adjusted P/E, or CAPE, mostly gets rid of the problems of corporate margins bouncing up and down that I mentioned earlier and also adjusts for inflation. It does that by taking the current price of the S&P 500 index and dividing it by the real (inflation-adjusted) average earnings of the last ten years. That usually covers at least an entire business cycle. The CAPE has averaged 16.6 times since 1881 and extreme highs or lows have marked major turning points for the stock market.

For example, the CAPE got to an all-time low of 4.2 times in December 1920. Stocks would rise by almost 370 percent in the Roaring Twenties rally that followed, and the measure hit a then all-time high of 32.6 in September 1929. That was followed by the Great Crash and Depression, and in less than three years the CAPE had plunged to a very low 5.6. The highest reading of all time came shortly before the technology bubble burst when the CAPE hit 44 times. It dropped to a little over 13 times at the March 2009 bear market low. Stocks fell by 41 percent over that nearly nine-and-a-quarter-year span.

You won't be surprised to hear, then, that the CAPE can be a remarkably good predictor of what sort of short- and medium-run returns to expect from the stock market. I took every available measure for more than fifteen hundred months of U.S. stock market history and sliced it into tenths, or deciles, from low to high. The lower it was, the higher the subsequent one- and ten-year returns. For example, the one-year return for the cheapest decile averaged over 22 percent. That went down to 17 percent for the next cheapest, 15 percent for the following one, and so forth, all the way down to

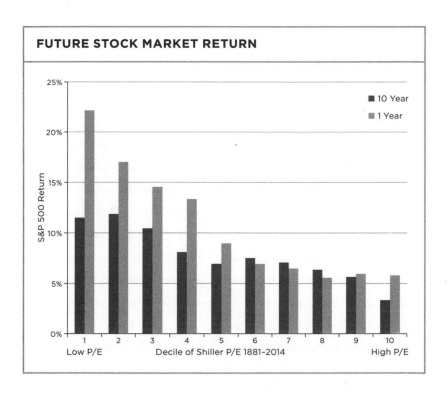

FUTURE STOCK MARKET RETURN

below 6 percent for the most expensive one. The same pattern repeats over ten-year periods. Returns were 11.5 percent a year for the
cheapest decile and just 3.3 percent for the most expensive one.

If the regular old P/E sounded like a virtual crystal ball to you,
then Robert Shiller must seem like Nostradamus. But curb your
enthusiasm. The CAPE would be a disastrous short-term timing
tool because what I just described is what happens on average. Valuations can stay low or high for years. For example, there was an
occasion when the market fell by 18 percent in the following year
after one of the cheapest readings. At the other extreme, the most
expensive tenth of readings should be lousy for stocks and mostly
was. Even so, there was a time when stocks rose by almost 48 percent in the following year. A cheap market can get cheaper and an
expensive one more expensive for quite a while.

While you should never, ever use the CAPE or any other measure as a short-term trading tool, it still can be very useful. Back in
chapter 2, "Timing Isn't Everything," I laid out the very wide range
of outcomes that the stock market presents. I emphasized that the
future was unknowable.

It still is, but you just saw that the market's valuation can tell
you a lot about your odds. In theory you could even use the CAPE in
a way that would give the buy-and-hold crowd conniptions. Just for
fun I did that in a column a few years ago, and I received more
e-mails than for almost anything I had written on any subject. Its
title was "Yes, Virginia, You Can Time the Stock Market!" With
the caveat that there are better and easier ways to squeeze out
extra return from stocks (I'll discuss them later in the book). I've
reproduced the calculations below.

I already sliced market history into deciles from cheap to expensive. Within a portfolio that rebalances annually, my model

overweighted stocks when they're historically cheap and underweighted them when they're expensive. Across a long period that would mean no change to average stock exposure, since there would be about the same number of overweight and underweight years.

So here goes. Two portfolios from 1881 through 2014 had a 60 percent weighting in stocks and a 40 percent weighting in bonds, but one was tweaked according to the CAPE and the other just rebalanced annually without regard to valuation. The years were split into five categories: very cheap, cheap, normal, expensive, and very expensive.

When the CAPE is in the middle four deciles, the weightings were identical between the two portfolios. But when stocks were cheap or expensive, their weighting is multiplied by 1.3 or 0.7, respectively. The cheapest and most expensive tenth gets multiplied by 1.5 or 0.5, respectively. For example, in the third most expensive CAPE decile a 60 percent stock allocation would become 42 percent (0.7 times 60 percent), while bonds would make up the remaining 58 percent.

Here's what happened. Even though the average equity weighting through the entire period was 60 percent for both a CAPE-weighted and unweighted portfolio, the compound annual return was 8.3 percent for the adjusted one and 7.6 percent for the unadjusted one. Over that extremely long period of 134 years, a dollar in the adjusted portfolio grew by 2.4 times as much as the other one.

Buying at the bottom of the market or selling at the top is pretty much the holy grail of investing. Sadly, unless you're armed with Doc Brown's flux capacitor, it's not possible. What my experiment did was buy a bit more *near* the bottom or pull back a little *near* the top, on average.

There's no "Yes, Virginia" fund out there and I think people would lose patience with it before it showed results. Tweaking a portfolio in the way I've just described would have to be done on your own and would only show results in the long run. It's also an awful lot of work to eke out a bit of extra return from the market. Just like my column, then, this was meant as an illustration that valuation matters, not a template that many readers would lack the intestinal fortitude to adopt faithfully.

But while there isn't a "Yes, Virginia Fund," there are thousands of actual investment funds that reap billions of dollars in fees with the claim that they can help us do better than the market. Some even deliver the goods. I'm about to explain why you should take not only the claims but even the results with a large grain of salt.

CHAPTER SIX

THE CELEBRITY CEPHALOPOD

W hat did an octopus and a middle-aged man from Baltimore have in common? Both got famous as a result of luck.

The celebrity cephalopod was the late Paul, formerly of the aquarium in Oberhausen, Germany, who for a while had a perfect record of picking the victor of international soccer matches. People from all over the world would tune in to hear Paul's verdict before key contests, sometimes lending more weight to it than the opinions of the paunchy former stars who serve as on-air analysts. At the height of his fame, businessmen from Spain arranged to pay a 30,000-euro "transfer fee" for Paul that was rejected.

The human in question was Bill Miller, who became one of the most quoted and followed fund managers around. His unprecedented fifteen-year streak of beating the performance of the Standard & Poor's 500 stock index was seen as extraordinary, frequently being compared to slugger Joe DiMaggio's feat of hitting safely in fifty-six consecutive games in 1941—considered a virtually unbreakable record. Miller's favorable opinion on a company or sector was the sort of thing stock market columnists like me would treat as pure gold, given their likely market impact.

His record certainly ushered in a gilded age for Legg Mason, the Baltimore-based money management firm where he worked. At Miller's peak his fund alone was earning $130 million in fees annually from retail investors. There also were spillover effects for the rest of the firm for having "the greatest investor of our time," as *Fortune* magazine dubbed him, on staff. Miller became the chairman and marketer in chief for Legg Mason. In just the last ten years of the streak, Legg Mason's stock delivered a total return of 5,500 percent.

But that was fool's gold according to a prominent school of thought. Efficient market theory holds that all information is reflected in stock prices, so there's no such thing as a talented stock picker. While some funds will do better than others due to sheer randomness, investors waste their money and enrich a bunch of empty suits at their own expense by hitching their wagon to star managers like Miller. The following analogy, or variations on it, is used to explain the existence of great performances:

Imagine that every person in America is asked to flip a coin. Those who get heads—about half—are asked to flip again, and this is repeated twenty times, by which time the odds of having kept the streak going, at less than one in a million, are truly infinitesimal. But that still would leave around 310 people who might be hailed as coin-flipping geniuses. They would become minor celebrities, and acquaintances would ask them their secret. "Is it all in the wrist?"

Um, no. On the other hand, mere thousands of fund managers,

not millions, ply their trade. That makes Miller's accomplishment look exceptional. If you were simply to take a group of, say, three thousand mutual fund managers and repeat the coin-flipping exercise, the likelihood of there being a Bill Miller are small, though not infinitesimal, because the chances of flipping heads fifteen times in a row are 0.003 percent times the number of managers.

Ah, but more than one party pooper pointed out that, since mutual funds had been around for forty-five years by the time Miller's streak ended, the probability was actually higher. There were, after all, thirty different fifteen-year periods when a streak could have occurred. The surprising thing is that there weren't two or perhaps more people who achieved the feat. A sober look at the odds seems to point to the conclusion that some money managers, through sheer luck alone, will look brilliant.

Others begged to disagree. A year after I switched careers from investment banking to journalism, one of my former colleagues, Michael Mauboussin, who was also an adjunct professor at Columbia Business School, wrote a report in which he extolled Miller's talent. At the twelve-year mark of the streak, Mauboussin calculated that Miller's odds of beating the market for so long almost certainly weren't a fluke because they were way less probable than a coin flip. Since most managers fail to do so—in some years only 8 percent achieved the feat—Miller's record was a 1-in-477,000 accomplishment.

This was music to the industry's ears. After all, a world in which financial pros are good or bad, not lucky or unlucky, was what brokers, fund managers, and everyone else in between wanted to hear. By the time the streak was over, Mauboussin had left my old firm and joined Legg Mason as a strategist. By then he pegged the odds of Miller's streak at 1 in 2.3 million.[1] It seemed like a record for the ages. Miller wasn't only DiMaggio but also Orel Hershiser, Cal Ripken Jr., and Ty Cobb rolled into one.

Or was he? I read the calculations with more than the usual amount of interest because my new job as an investing columnist gave me the chance to meet with Miller during the height of his fame—what would have been year sixteen. He was closely shadowed by public relations professionals so that his pearls of wisdom could be doled out to those journalists likely to portray him and his firm in the most favorable light. I barged my way into his presence at a conference and found him to be soft-spoken and approachable.

What was most striking to me, though, was that he was no plain vanilla moneyman with his nose buried in company filings all day. Miller drew on many ideas outside of finance to influence his investing and, because he was so famous, the management at Legg Mason humored him. These ranged from having his team study ant colonies to assigning them all to read *The Landscape of History*.[2] Some of his ideas crossed the line from offbeat to outright silly.

For example, at the time he was avoiding energy stocks but was up to his eyeballs in home builders and companies extending risky mortgages. The reason he didn't invest in oil and gas was the "abiogenic" theory of hydrocarbons. It holds that, contrary to overwhelming scientific evidence, those fuel sources come not from once-living fossils that will eventually run out but from deep inside the earth. If that were true then the rarity of reserves, oil companies' key asset, would be exaggerated since more would just make its way up from below. That theory had proved convenient during most of Miller's streak, with energy companies in the doldrums, but had begun to hamper his performance by the time we met.

Meanwhile, despite rumblings that there was an unsustainable housing bubble under way—in hindsight, it was just peaking when we had our first conversation—his past experience told him those fears were overblown. He had bet big on banks after the savings and loan crisis and eventually profited handsomely. And he had made a massive wager on tottering mortgage guarantor Freddie Mac in the 1980s with great success. What his firm failed to highlight was that he also had gambled and lost on Enron and WorldCom, two of the biggest bankruptcies in history, narrowly escaping with his famous streak intact. At the time we spoke he was also making what seemed like a foolhardy wager on Eastman Kodak, a onetime blue-chip company getting clobbered by the shift to digital photography.

So, back to the question of luck versus skill. The real answer is more complicated than professors assuming that financial markets are just like games of chance using dollars instead of dice, and also not as black and white as Mauboussin's calculations would have us believe. Understanding the truth is of more than academic interest. It may make you a better investor.

The best take I heard on the Bill Miller phenomenon was from Miller himself. More modest than his firm's marketing department and far less prone to hyperbole than sycophantic journalists, he explained his success to a colleague of mine in 2005 at the start of what would be his epic run's final year:

> As for the so-called streak, that's an accident of the calendar. If the year ended on different months it wouldn't be there and at some point those mathematics will hit us. We've been lucky. Well, maybe it's not 100 percent luck. Maybe 95 percent luck.[3]

I'd say that's just about right. A thoughtful stab at the question of the mutual fund manager luck-versus-skill debate was written up in the *Harvard Business Review* by complex systems scientist Samuel Arbesman and expanded upon in his book *The Half-Life of Facts*. For the study he teamed up with none other than Mauboussin's teenage son Andrew. A few years earlier Arbesman had mined a far richer seam of data, baseball statistics, to ask just how exceptional DiMaggio's fifty-six-game streak was. He and a colleague reran baseball history ten thousand times and determined that there would be a player with a fifty-game streak or better about half the time. They also calculated that the players likely to achieve those streaks were great ones such as Ty Cobb and Rogers Hornsby.

To that second conclusion, my scientific response is, "No duh." I mean, it's within the realm of possibility that Ramiro Mendoza, the otherwise forgettable Mexican shortstop who gained baseball immortality for "the Mendoza Line"—a batting average below .200—could hit safely for fifty-six games in a row if you repeated baseball history enough times, just as a chimpanzee could randomly peck away at a typewriter ten trillion times and eventually produce the complete works of Shakespeare. Obviously, though, a great player has a better chance of being like another great one.

Arbesman and the younger Mauboussin applied a similar analysis to mutual funds over five decades. To do this they used something called a null model that gave each fund a typical chance of beating the market and ran the scenario ten thousand times. What they found was that, though there were streaks, they weren't as common as in reality. Therefore, some skill exists in fund management.

I agree but, before you run out and place your life savings with the fund manager who has the best performance or longest streak at the moment, please keep reading. I've already mentioned that

Miller had some kooky views and that his track record allowed him to get away with large, unorthodox bets. That practice could in and of itself make it more likely that a performance will be good.

You don't have to be a master statistician to see why. My oldest son, who entered a national stock-picking contest when he was still a high school freshman, figured it out on his own. Since it lasted just two months and involved play money rather than actual dollars, he grasped right away that having the craziest portfolio was the key to winning. He asked me what the most volatile things on the stock exchange were that he could possibly buy. I gave him a list that was the financial equivalent of nitroglycerin.

It worked . . . for a while. He quickly amassed the highest rank in his school and was close to snagging the lead in the entire state. Then Russia invaded Crimea and he nearly dropped to last place in a few days. Instead of being discouraged, he knew he was on to something and repeated the exact same strategy in his high school stock market investment club's biannual trading contests. He has won every single time by a wide margin.

Now, the apple may not fall far from the tree, but I wouldn't advocate giving my son your savings to manage. What he's doing is making sure that he's an outlier. He just has happened to be the right kind of outlier since that first contest. The incredible swings in his fortunes were made possible by having a portfolio that was like Bill Miller on steroids.

And remember, unlike my son, who was trying to beat other reckless teenagers with play money, Bill Miller only had to beat the market. Since a mere 44 percent of managers can do that in a typical year, sticking too close to that herd means you'll usually lag the market too. An iconoclast like Miller, who was given a relatively free rein, had a better chance of being at one extreme or the other and hence moderately higher odds of beating the market. Most fund managers aren't stars and can't risk their careers by eschewing entire sectors like oil and gas or making huge bets on possibly failing companies. In other words, the null set looks pretty pedestrian.

Could that still mean Bill Miller was special? There just isn't enough information to tell. Anyone claiming Joe DiMaggio was just lucky would be viewed as a crank, and with good reason. Aside from that fifty-six-game streak (which was followed by another sixteen-game one, by the way), he was an excellent hitter for many years, batting .325 over close to seven thousand plate appearances. Proclaiming greatness in sports and in fund management are two very different things, though.

Two of my three sons play baseball quite well. Putting it mildly, I never did. On our visits to the batting center near our house I'll usually pop into the cage for the last round just for a bit of exercise. While they will have taken around 120 swings apiece and will have mostly good and some off days, my 15 swings usually aren't too impressive. Every once in a while, though, I'll smash a handful of balls into the far corner of the net and turn around, chest puffed out, only to see both my sons laughing and imitating my lame batting stance. I'm under no illusion about signing up for a minor-league contract or even the local over-forty league.

Unlike a sweaty, nearsighted, middle-aged dad in a batting cage, a fund manager's ability is harder to judge. Sure, you can see what's in his or her portfolio, but when they swing for the fences, there's a fine line between ineptitude and brilliance.

"Hey, that guy just bought 20 percent of a failing company. What is he thinking? Whoa, it miraculously survived and he made 200 percent on the stock. What a genius!"

Such home runs notwithstanding, an individual fund manager

has too few "at bats" to reach a firm conclusion about skill. Just looking at Bill Miller's fifteen-year streak won't get us much closer to an answer. There are plenty of other stars in the fund manager firmament for which the same holds true.

Take Jim Gipson, who was voted "Domestic Equity Manager of the Year" by fund rating company Morningstar in 2000—a year when he pretty much hit the cover off of the ball, beating the index his fund was benchmarked against by over 45 percentage points. That excess return is known by finance geeks as "alpha." Another term, "beta," denotes just the market return. I said I'd avoid Greek letters at the start of this book, so I'll stop after one more telling statistic, called "standard deviation of alpha." That means, in a nutshell, how much a fund's returns bounce around relative to its benchmark.

Remember when I said that Miller's concentrated and unorthodox bets increased the odds that he would either beat or lag the market in a given year? Over many years his fund had a standard deviation of alpha of 9.8 percent, which is huge. But the Clipper Fund managed by Gipson made him look like steady Eddie with a standard deviation of 12.3 percent. The fund also lagged the market in seven out of ten years both before and after the one when he won the award. Analysts at Institutional Fund Advisors looked at those numbers (Gipson left the fund in 2005 and a manager with a similar style was chosen as his replacement) and calculated how many years of performance would prove that the fund's award was a reflection of skill, not luck. It was 4,574 years. It's safe to say, then, that we'll be waiting a while to see if the Clipper Fund's success was a fluke.

There's another reason why it's so hard to tell if someone has skill at managing money. Unlike dads flailing away in batting cages, their technique is invisible. In other words, while investors get frequent snapshots of what stocks are held in a mutual fund's portfolio, they may not have much insight as to why those particular ones were chosen.

Imagine, for example, if two fund managers, Bob and Sally, put together enviable records over many years and attracted large amounts of money. The two of them are profiled by a widely read financial magazine and asked about the secrets of their success. Sally cites her hours spent poring over financial statements, tells the interviewer what she looks for in a company, and so forth. Then Bob reveals his technique. He says he closes his eyes, puts his finger down on the stock listings once a month, and buys whatever he points to. He spends the rest of the time playing *Tetris* in his office. Once this information leaked out, people either would assume he was joking or believe him and yank their money out at the first opportunity, perhaps putting it into Sally's fund instead.

While no fund manager in his right mind would do that, or at least admit to it, some very smart people will tell you that it's entirely plausible. "A blindfolded monkey throwing darts at a newspaper's financial pages could select a portfolio that would do just as well as one carefully selected by experts," wrote Burton Malkiel, the Princeton University professor and author of the bestseller *A Random Walk Down Wall Street*. It turns out, based on actual studies, that he was wrong. The monkey just might do better.

Robert Arnott, who runs asset management firm Research Affiliates, did a study in which one hundred random portfolios of thirty stocks each were created from the thousand largest U.S. companies, and ninety-six beat the index. And since the majority of managers lag the market, that means they trounced human fund managers.

The secret to Arnott's success may lie in part in the way his monkey portfolios were constructed, though. They bought an equal amount of each stock and then bought a new bunch of stocks each year. An index such as the S&P 500, the one tracked by most stock fund managers, owns them in proportion to their market value. Apple, for example, is the index heavyweight at the moment and is represented as heavily as more than one hundred companies at the bottom of the rankings. That seems like it shouldn't matter, but it does, because an index owns more of what just went up in price and less of what just went down. Most fund managers mimic this pattern too. The stock market is the only place where millions of people rush to buy what just got pricier, and even when it's done through a low-cost index fund, it affects performance.

Arnott's study also illustrates a point that goes beyond the luck versus skill debate, though. Basing a portfolio on something other than company size is a good alternative, even if stocks are picked randomly. As I'll explain later in the book, this fascinating effect can be used to enhance your own investment returns.

What about actual monkeys and actual fund managers? The evidence is more mixed. The *Wall Street Journal* began a series in 1988 in which it pitted investment analysts against what were supposed to be dart-throwing primates, but the liability insurance for bringing animals into the office proved too expensive. Instead, they used the next best thing: dart-throwing journalists. On the hundredth iteration of the contest a few years later it looked like the pros had proved their worth, with sixty-one wins to thirty-nine for the ink-stained wretches. But a follow-up study by Professor Bing Liang showed that once dividends were counted and distortions from publicity about the pros' picks immediately after they appeared in the newspaper were weeded out, the results were dead even.[4] The difference, of course, is that professional fund managers don't work for peanuts. (Journalists, however, come pretty close.)

I was in a graduate microeconomics lecture at Columbia University right around the time the series was running, and our instructor split us into two groups to demonstrate efficient market theory using a similar experiment: random stock pickers versus those who selected them based on personal research. I remember both that the random portfolio won and that my own pick, arrived upon with my eyes closed from a newspaper stock listing, did well. But at the time I was an avid reader of investor hagiographies such as Jack Schwager's *Market Wizards* and John Train's *Money Masters of Our Time.* As I pored over those interviews with gurus and their very smart-sounding techniques, it seemed like the professors in their ivory towers who said that stock picking was futile really needed to get out more.

I didn't become convinced that markets were mostly efficient until I started spending twelve hours a day with highly compensated fund managers a few years later. Most of my clients were pretty bright, but a handful weren't, and one achieved a sort of fame among my fellow analysts for being astoundingly thick. Everything had to be explained very slowly and carefully and usually more than once to this young man, yet he kept his job through good and bad times at the large and prestigious asset management firm where he worked. We theorized that maybe he had compromising photos of the chairman or was his nephew or something until he moved on to an even bigger position as a fund manager at another reputable firm.

Of course the answer wasn't nepotism or naughty pics—it was far simpler. He was a perfectly pleasant, good-looking guy, and spoke in complete sentences. More to the point, he also did fine as a portfolio manager. If a monkey can do it, then he, with an IQ well above simian level, could too.

Bill Miller, by the way, is no fool. Even if he were, people pouring money into his fund were convinced, largely on the strength of gaudy results and flattering press coverage, that he was a genius who could make them rich. The more money he managed, though—his fund's assets had risen from $800 million when the streak began to over $20 billion at its peak as his fame spread—the bigger, more counterintuitive bets he had to make.

Miller's penchant for concentrated, unorthodox wagers that had helped him beat the index finally came back to bite him. Oil prices doubled between 2006 and mid-2008, peaking at over $140 a barrel. Home builders and shares of many of his concentrated holdings in banks, meanwhile, did abysmally during the financial crisis even as he kept adding to his fund's positions on the way down. Kodak filed for Chapter 11 bankruptcy protection a few years later. Another major holding, subprime mortgage lender Countrywide Financial, had to be bought at a fire sale price by Bank of America. Miller had kept on buying the stock as it fell, compounding his losses. Not only did his streak end, but his fund was among the worst-performing over a ten-year period by the time all was said and done.

It wasn't just Mom and Pop who got sucked in by "the streak." Even sophisticated investors who probably had a good chuckle at Paul the Octopus's exploits thought Bill Miller was no fluke and felt disappointed when his magic ran out.

"Why didn't I just throw my money out of the window and light it on fire?" lamented a well-known venture capitalist and substantial investor in Mr. Miller's fund to a colleague of mine. The strategy "worked for a long time, but it's broken," he said.[5]

Of all people, someone who manages money for a living should have understood that the reversal would be especially sharp and nasty when it came. Miller had admitted that his success was mostly luck, but people who read glowing articles about the wonder investor from Baltimore and put their savings into his fund probably chalked it up to false modesty. It's comforting to believe that you've entrusted your savings to "the greatest investor of our time."

Miller's "crucible," as I dubbed it in a column at the time, also served to highlight a mathematical fact that the vast majority of investors fail to appreciate. A larger chunk of personal savings was incinerated in the decline than one might guess based on the sorts of data investing firms publish. While few were riding Miller's streak in the early years, many piled in just as the wheels were ready to fall off. The fund's assets, as I said, had surged to over $20 billion. By the end of the following year, his assets under management would sink to $4.3 billion through a combination of dismal performance and redemptions by disillusioned clients. By the spring of 2011, shortly before he resigned as manager, that had shriveled to just $2.8 billion. Much of the money invested in his fund enjoyed an all too brief taste of his good performance and then locked in losses during the very worst years.

Failing to take that into account, Miller's defenders pointed out that his overall record was decent, citing compound average returns better than most managers. Even following his disastrous last few years, after all, his fund had beaten the S&P 500 by a couple of percentage points a year on an annualized basis if you held it from day one. That wasn't really accurate, though, because the assets he managed at the time of his fall from grace far exceeded those when he was building up his track record. On a dollar-weighted basis, then, he lagged the market by about seven percentage points annually, hardly earning any money at all in eighteen years—other than fees for his firm, of course. Though not as extreme, the same dollar-weighted calculations mean that the vast majority of funds earn less than they advertise.

The phenomenon applies not only to shooting stars that flame out but even to managers who have been more successful overall than Miller. Just consider the best-performing stock mutual fund of the previous decade, the CGM Focus Fund run by Ken Heebner. Its investors lost about 11 percent annually over that stretch.

That isn't a typo. As far as the record books go, the fund was a winner. Its 18.2 percent compound annual return was around three percentage points better than the next closest fund in the same category and much better than the stock market overall. That's fantastic. But since Heebner's portfolio was fairly concentrated—even more than Miller's—his fund also was extremely volatile. In 2007, for example, it had a stellar 80 percent return. On the back of that excellent performance it attracted some $2.6 billion in fresh cash in 2008, a year when many competitors saw clients flee in droves. Unfortunately, the fund's performance swung sharply in the opposite direction that year, plunging by 48 percent. The following year saw $750 million go out the door.[6]

You certainly can't blame Heebner for his awful dollar-weighted return. The damage was done by investors reacting to good performance by piling money into a hot fund. Then they did the inverse. And while the effect isn't as extreme as with Heebner's fund—an annual difference of nearly 30 percentage points between paper returns and actual ones—it exists across the whole industry and is one of the main reasons investors live in Lake Moneybegone: zigging when they should zag.

Just as it's dangerous to time highs and lows in stocks, attempting it with funds also is filled with pitfalls. A paper coauthored by Jason Hsu of the UCLA Anderson School of Management and colleagues, "Timing Poorly: A Guide to Generating Poor Returns While Investing in Successful Strategies," measured the effect across the whole universe of stock mutual funds from 1991 to 2013 and showed some interesting results. The actual or dollar-weighted return on all funds during that period was 6.9 percent annually, while the buy-and-hold return—the one reported in those glossy mutual fund brochures—was 8.8 percent. Over that twenty-three-year period that nearly two percentage point drag would have seen a typical investor turn $10,000 into just $46,000 even as the published returns suggested that he or she could have made $70,000, or one and a half times as much. The $24,000 difference went straight into Lake Moneybegone.

Given Miller's fall from grace and the billions of lost investor dollars, he sure doesn't sound just 95 percent lucky. I told you near the beginning of this chapter that I'm not a believer in complete market efficiency. The reason isn't only Arbesman's finding that there must be some small degree of skill among fund managers. Just the fact that heads or tails came up a little more frequently than they should is interesting but not too helpful. After all, there are thousands of managers and you can only identify potentially skilled ones with years of hindsight. But what if managers who flipped the coins with their left hands showed up disproportionately as winners of the contest again and again? Then efficient market theorists would have to pay attention.

It turns out that the equivalent of left-handed managers exist, and Miller was a mild devotee of this left-handed school of thought. Just like the great returns of the monkey portfolios put together by Arnott and his team, the preponderance of these investors at the top ranks tells you something very interesting and potentially very profitable. A disproportionate share of successful managers are so-called value investors. In fact, the man who probably does deserve the moniker "the greatest investor of our time" and arguably even "all time," Warren Buffett, is a dyed-in-the-wool value maven. Over the long run, simply sticking with funds that use such strategies, even when there is no human manager behind them, can enhance your odds meaningfully. I'll discuss this in more detail later in the book.

When it comes to the entire mass of managers, though—left-handed, right-handed, or ambidextrous—is there any collective skill? You'll hear conflicting takes on that question in part because they're measuring the results in two different ways. To cite just one example of studies that say active management may be worth it, a recent one by researchers at Japanese investment bank Nomura showed that the stocks favored by active funds did slightly better and those shunned did slightly worse than the market.[7]

But what matters is your bottom line, not some measure that shows some modicum of stock-picking ability. A longer study by two of the most distinguished finance professors around, Nobel laureate Eugene Fama and Kenneth French, found that fund managers eked out alpha, or extra return, of 0.1 percent a year. Unfortunately, their net result after accounting for the expense of running a fund was negative 0.8 percent a year.

We didn't need these brilliant men to do thousands of calculations to tell us that, because common sense would dictate the same conclusion. Fund managers, you see, own so many stocks that they come close as a group to *being* the stock market. In order to do better as a group, the small sliver of stocks owned by others would have to do really badly. However inept individual investors may be, we're not *that* terrible. So that slight edge that professionals earn is nice, but it's swamped by fees and expenses.

While that part should come as no great revelation, Fama and French went on in the same study to measure fund manager skill in a very interesting way. They took the top tier of funds by long-run performance and then "cloned" them into funds that did the same through sheer luck. Comparing the two groups, they found that there is indeed a small sliver of fund managers—around 3 percent of the total—who can be said with some confidence to possess skill sufficient to justify what they charge.

Hold the confetti, though. By their calculations, these managers possess just enough ability to cover their costs plus perhaps a bit extra. Now it's time to look in the mirror and ask how skilled *you* are at picking a fund manager. Remember, their ability only evidenced itself years after the fact. Hindsight will only make you money if you have a time machine to go along with it, so you would have to see something in a manager's style or written statements that made him or her one of those 3 percent of stars. I doubt you can.

Even if you pay little attention to the name of the man or woman managing your fund and instead are more of an asset allocator, picking a category of fund you think will do well, those numbers also need to be viewed with a jaundiced eye. Their actual results may in fact be worse than what asset managers claim. Industry statistics slice and dice the performance of every single fund and also every category in mind-numbing detail, but there's one important piece of information they leave out: the funds that are no longer with us.

This matters a lot more than you might think, because there's a distinct pattern of fund openings and closures that mirrors overall market performance. In horrible 2009, for example, 870 funds were liquidated or merged into others—about one and three-quarter times as many as the number of new funds. In 2006, a great year for the stock market, only 437 funds vanished, or 56 percent *fewer* than the number opened. How did those closed funds do? Fund management firms and their industry body, which produces a huge statistical yearbook, had no clue.

Mark Hebner, founder of a firm championing passive investing called Index Fund Advisors, paid $1,000 to the one group that keeps track of such things, the University of Chicago's Center for Research in Security Prices, to find out over five decades, from 1962 through 2012, that there were thirty-nine thousand mutual funds in existence at any time, but a third, or thirteen thousand, no longer existed by the end. Over that period Hebner calculated that $100 invested in all existing mutual funds would have grown into about $2,100, but based on the industry's performance data for existing funds, it would have grown to $2,500.[8]

Were you an investor in the FrontierMicroCap Fund? How about American Heritage Growth or Helios Select International Bond A? I certainly hope not, because those now-defunct funds lost 99.5 percent, 98 percent, and 92 percent over their lives, respectively. But their existence has been scrubbed from industry statistics. I doubt somehow that many world-beating funds were shut down. In fact, Hebner's return statistics show conclusively that it was poorly performing ones that got the chop.

When you're looking at existing funds, please realize that history is written by the winners and can be misleading. People thinking of buying a certain type of fund will look up how its peers have done over the years. For example, a colleague of mine wrote about a fund category called "market-neutral" that appeared on the scene around 1997 after rule changes allowed mutual funds to sell stocks short (bet that they would fall with borrowed shares). She noted that there were just six of them at the beginning of that year and sixty-two more introduced over the next decade. But that category struggled during the financial crisis and in 2012 just thirty-two remained. Those were the only ones that could be counted when tallying the performance of long-short funds.[9]

Looking at those funds then existing, the group turned in a great performance in 2003 of 19.2 percent. Okay, maybe "great" is being a bit generous, since the overall stock market did an even better 28.4 percent including dividends. But the published return and the actual return of all the funds in the category that were in business in 2003 were very different. The average market-neutral fund actually made just 8.5 percent, or nearly 20 percentage points less than the market overall. Like dead men, dead funds don't talk.

You know who does talk, though? Pundits. When Bill Miller, Jim Gipson, or any of their thousands of fund management brethren are wheeled before the cameras to opine on how financial markets will do, there's at least a body of work to consider. Television hosts rarely put them on the spot for how their funds are doing, of course, but you're free to get on the Internet and look up their one-, three-, five-, and ten-year performances calculated out to two decimal places and decide whether or not to believe what they say.

Few people do this, and I don't see much point in it anyway, but at least there's a form of accountability. On the other hand, many of the people on the same shows can't be evaluated in the same way and they seem to be the most confident in their assertions. These are the professional talking heads who go by such titles as "strategist," "analyst," "chief investment officer," and many others.

The saying goes, and perhaps you agree, that talk is cheap. As I'm about to show, though, it can be pretty expensive.

CHAPTER SEVEN

SEERS AND SEER SUCKERS

I am the greatest investor who has ever lived.

If you don't believe me, just ask my coworkers or check my 401(k) statement. On March 9, 2009, I stood up in the newsroom of the *Financial Times,* where I was then a columnist, and called the exact bottom of the bear market, moving my account from 100 percent cash to 100 percent stocks. I had cut all equity exposure in August 2007, less than two months before the market peaked.

Now, if I failed to mention that I got cold feet about six weeks later and temporarily went back to cash, missing a good deal of the bull market's rise, or if I didn't show you my merely so-so long-run investment returns, I wouldn't exactly be lying. What I would be doing is cherry-picking the facts in the way that all too many pundits do.

Investors should be under no illusion that financial prognostication is a business, whether or not they pay for it directly. All told, the amount of money Americans spend on forecasting has been estimated to be as high as $300 billion annually,[1] much of it for choosing investments, so the people selling it naturally put a lot of effort into promoting their products. In the same way that Procter & Gamble wants you to believe that you'll get whiter whites with its detergents, Coca-Cola insists that it's the real thing, and McDonald's doesn't leave your lovin' it to chance, market seers need to shout their prowess from the rooftops while downplaying their foibles.

As a stock market columnist, I get more than my fair share of exposure to this industry. I used to be in the fortune-telling business myself and made a nice living out of it. Like you, I receive lots of recommendations, largely unsolicited, on what to do with my own savings.

After spending years thinking about the value of advice, the smartest take I've read on punditry comes from an academic paper, "The Seer-Sucker Theory: The Value of Experts in Forecasting," published more than thirty-five years ago in the *Technology Review* by J. Scott Armstrong. It's available for free online and is very short and readable for its genre, with no Greek letters or algebra. I'll save you the effort of googling it by giving you the money quote:

"No matter how much evidence exists that seers do not exist, suckers will pay for the existence of seers."

That probably sounds a bit harsh. Who are you going to believe, this Armstrong guy you've never heard of or your own eyes and ears? Most people reading this follow the financial media closely enough, perhaps including my own columns, to point to some shrewd calls by analysts, money managers, journalists, or some hybrid of those such as Jim Cramer. But the fact that there are some great predictions doesn't mean that the people who made them have special ability or that they can continue to make them consistently enough to matter.

First off, it's important to be clear what sort of predictions Armstrong is and isn't talking about. The people who are interviewed in the media about economic or financial matters are right about a lot of things and make sense more often than not. Will the Federal Reserve raise rates next month? Can Apple's newest iPhone sell more units than the last version? Will falling gasoline prices spur consumers to spend more on clothing and eating out? Given the fact that analyzing such things is his or her job, a smart observer can usually be correct about them or at least will come off sounding smart. By the time you hear these nuggets, though, they already have become conventional wisdom and financial markets have braced for it accordingly.

You almost certainly have expertise in some area to do the same. Picking the winner of a sporting event might be one example—particularly if a stronger team is playing a weaker one. But even if you told me that you haven't missed an episode of *SportsCenter* in years, I wouldn't cash in my life savings and pay you for your expertise to try to make a killing in the Las Vegas sports book. The odds already reflect the information and opinions of thousands of bettors, not to mention the vigorish that makes the words "professional gambler" an oxymoron for all but a few.

Likewise, saying something smart about a company or interest rates rarely translates into knowing which stock or bond to buy or avoid. Being able to do so consistently would make an expert a seer by Armstrong's definition.

Purported seers need followers. Anyone can make predictions, but having people pay attention to them is another matter. Scientific evidence shows that such influence is more a function of self-confidence than accuracy. In my experience, most forecasters are themselves convinced that they have the ability to pick winning investments with regularity despite their own mixed track record and that of the profession on average. What I mean to say is that rather than being populated with con men, the prediction business is mostly filled with people conning themselves. They relish their hits and find excuses for their misses. It's certainly a pleasant thing to believe about yourself, and I speak from experience.

While I didn't really think I was an investing genius for accidentally ticking the bottom of the great bear market in my 401(k) account, praise from others can be intoxicating. For example, a couple of years ago my wife and I were having dinner with a neighbor of ours who runs a small investment fund. A regular reader of my column, he complimented me on being "right" what he estimated to be about 70 percent of the time and also noted that I had recommended at the sidelines of our sons' basketball practice a year before the stock that wound up being the best performer in the entire S&P 500 that year. I feigned modesty, don't think my stock picks are all that accurate, and only vaguely recalled the recommendation I had given him. Nevertheless, I felt a warm glow.

My wife's reaction when we were alone was telling, though not exactly the ego-stoking praise I expected. If I had dispensed all this fantastic advice free of charge, then why hadn't I acted profitably on it myself? Knowing our finances, she could see that our retirement portfolio was growing steadily but that it wasn't exactly the work of an investing guru.

That's the question you need to ask about any purveyor of advice. Why would someone tell me which stocks to buy or sell, whether for free or in exchange for compensation worth less than my potential profit? He wouldn't—he would keep it to himself. Perhaps some do. Remember the old saying: "Those who say don't know, and those who know don't say."

Believing the contrary is only human nature. We want to think that the world isn't quite so random and that some expert can make sense of it. I certainly do. Shortly before sitting down to write this chapter, I was contacted repeatedly by a particularly persistent public relations professional who wanted me to speak with his client, Charles Nenner. I get such calls all the time, and the number that turn into interviews is very low. I accepted this one because Nenner literally sent chills up my spine the first time we spoke, years earlier.

Back then he trotted out some uncannily accurate predictions that made him out to be a financial Nostradamus. As I look over my notes, they included almost the exact top in the Dow Jones Industrials in 2007, the 2008 peak, 2009 trough, and subsequent recovery almost to the dollar in crude oil prices, plus a handful of other bull's-eyes. Some, but not all, of the claims were backed up by media appearances bookmarked on his Web site. But then I looked back at what he predicted would happen *after* we spoke. It was almost the polar opposite of what did happen. Searching the subsequent media appearances on his Web site, though, I couldn't find any reference to those inaccurate calls.

Paid for his services by investors "managing hundreds of billions of dollars," according to him, Nenner claims to have a proprietary algorithm based on something called a neural network that is calling not only for a stock market crash but possibly a nuclear war, though the date is a little vague. Given the long lead time in the book publishing industry, if you're reading this it was probably a false alarm. And if you're reading this by candlelight in a fallout shelter then please pass on my posthumous apologies to Mr. Nenner.

As far as I can tell, there are three ways to become a financially successful seer. An obvious one is to derive your authority from the name of the firm on your business card. "Strategist" on its own won't impress anyone, but "Global Equity Strategist, Goldman Sachs" lends to your predictions the imprimatur of a firm that has had huge success in financial markets, whatever your own track record. And even if it's rotten enough to cost you your job eventually, you still can dine out for years by sticking "former" in front of that appellation.

If you lack such an insta-pedigree, a slower but still proven way to hit the big time is to make lots and lots of unremarkable predictions and then emphasize those you got right. Yet another is to swing for the fences and make outrageous forecasts that grab attention right away. That method may at the very least gain you notoriety and, if you're ever right, a rich vein of marketing gold that can be mined for years. Like the path to the dark side in *Star Wars,* there are also shortcuts. If you have any desire to give up what you happen to do for a living and be a paid guru, at least briefly, then here's a foolproof way of doing it.

First you have to find a large number of people, preferably all strangers to you and one another, to contact in some way: phone, e-mail, or through an old-fashioned letter. Say you start with two thousand and inform exactly half of them that your proprietary system tells you with absolute certainty that the market will rise next Tuesday. You tell the other half that the market will fall. It's important to sound confident and scientific. The next week you contact only the thousand people who received the correct advice and repeat the exercise. After five weeks there will be seventy-five people left who, if they've been paying attention, should be convinced that you can see the future. The next step is to sell them each a subscription to your service for hundreds of dollars—a bargain given how much money they'll make.

That's an actual scam, by the way. I'm not at all suggesting that Nenner and other gurus I'm about to discuss are doing anything similarly illegal or even dishonest. What I am saying is that they achieve the appearance of prescience by selectively emphasizing which calls they've made. If you make a lot of predictions for long enough, then you're bound to be right, and if you ascribe your successes to a methodology too complex for ordinary people to reproduce, then you have a decent shot at turning them into paying customers.

Possibly the most famous financial prognostication ever was made on September 5, 1929, by Roger Babson, a well-known research provider who foresaw a "crash" in stock prices. Stocks promptly fell, and the drop became known as the "Babson Break." Although they recovered in the following days, the stock market really would crash the following month. The Dow Jones Industrial Average only regained its early September highs a quarter century later.

Babson, a genius as a publisher, was the first modern stock market pundit, attracting subscribers through easy-to-understand graphics that supposedly were constructed by an arcane formula known only to him. He said his "Babsoncharts" were based on Newtonian physics and its effects on the economy. People remember Babson's famous call, and his legacy lives on because he parlayed his fortune into endowing Babson College in Massachusetts.

What many forget is that Babson was extremely bearish as early as 1926 when stocks still had tremendous gains ahead of them, and he repeated his prediction of a crash many times. Then in 1931—far too early—he called for a recovery, ensuring steep losses for any who followed him. Since he likely gained many new subscribers on the strength of his famous 1929 pronouncement, those people not only didn't have the benefit of avoiding the crash but compounded their losses if they listened to him in 1931. Bizarrely, he went on to run for president on the Prohibition ticket years after the unpopular amendment had been repealed and later funded research to discover an antigravity device.

Speaking of defying gravity, a modern-day Babson still gets the occasional plug in the press and supports himself selling newsletters. Robert Prechter earned his claim to fame in the late 1970s, predicting a top for gold prices, which had been red-hot throughout the decade, almost to the exact month. More significantly, he also said a roaring equity bull market would begin in 1982, missing the date by only a few months. He claims to have made these predictions using an arcane technique called the Elliott Wave Theory developed by accountant and amateur social theorist Ralph Nelson Elliott in the 1920s.

Subscribers to Prechter's paid newsletter swelled to twenty thousand, with an annual subscription price of over $200, in the mid-1980s. Then he made a very optimistic and tantalizingly specific call on stocks, predicting that the Dow Jones Industrials would hit 3,686 in 1987 or 1988. Many people, most of whom probably read about that target in the newspaper due to Prechter's sudden fame rather than as paid subscribers, fixated on the number reached so scientifically by this investing guru. Whether intentional on Prechter's part or not, the use of that Dow target rather than a round number like, say, 3,650 or 3,700 that was less than a percent off is significant. As Charles Seife explains in his fascinating book *Proofiness: How You're Being Fooled by the Numbers,* precise-sounding figures trick us into believing that there is a more scientific and therefore valid method for reaching them.

Unfortunately for Prechter, not to mention his clients, the market never got close and the Dow suffered its worst-ever single-day crash in October 1987. Some sources point out that he did warn subscribers of a 50/50 chance of a 10 percent decline several days earlier, but he advised his institutional clients to hang on. The Dow dropped to just above 1,700.[2]

Things got worse from there for Prechter. In 1993 he predicted a devastating crash and depression around the time the Dow really did break through 3,600. He said it could fall to 400. Even at that time he still had forty-five hundred subscribers, or over $1 million in annual income, for some very costly advice. In 2002, just as stocks were bottoming from a horrific slump, he published *Conquer the Crash: You Can Survive and Prosper in a Deflationary Depression.* He became briefly bullish with extraordinarily poor timing in 2008. Then, for good measure, he re-upped his pessimistic call by publishing a second edition of *Conquer the Crash* in, wait for it . . . 2009. The most recent version on Amazon is a paperback update: *2014: Last Chance to Conquer the Crash.* Again, if you're huddling for warmth and only reading this before burning pages of my book for kindling in a modern-day Hooverville circa 2017, then I owe Mr. Prechter an apology.

If 1987 was Prechter's Waterloo, then it was for Elaine Garzarelli too, except she was Wellington, not Napoleon. A Wall Street strategist at Shearson Lehman, she appeared on CNN in midOctober of that year and predicted "an imminent collapse in the stock market."[3] The Dow would go on to have its largest-ever percentage drop days later, and *BusinessWeek* magazine dubbed it the "call of the century."

Garzarelli went on to become the best-paid strategist on Wall Street and made millions through newsletter subscriptions after she hung out her own shingle. To hear her tell it, Garzarelli's record from well before her famous 1987 coup through today has been eerily accurate. A chart on her public Web site shows a stock market chart spanning decades with "buy" and "sell" arrows at every single market peak and trough. It practically makes her look psychic.

But William A. Sherden, an expert on experts, says otherwise. He tracked down several of her verifiable predictions between 1987 and 1996 and found only 38 percent to be accurate. More damningly, a mutual fund that Garzarelli ran somehow lagged the market for five out of six years that it was in business, barely edging out the S&P 500 in the winning one. Since Sherden's results were published I found at least one whopper of a bad call, though no reference to it can be found on Garzarelli's Web site. She claims there that she advised clients to get out of stocks in 2008. But in *BusinessWeek*'s annual investment outlook for 2008, a year when stocks would suffer horrific losses, Garzarelli didn't just recommend a 100 percent allocation to stocks but named the specific ones that wound up doing the worst.

"Garzarelli is advising investors to buy some of the most beaten-down stocks, including those of giant financial institutions such as Lehman Brothers, Bear Stearns, and Merrill Lynch. What would cause her to turn bearish? Not much. 'Our indicators are extremely bullish.'"[4]

Oops. I could go on for a long time naming dozens of false

financial prophets, but I don't want to beat a dead horse. And since all of the evidence I've mustered against the value of market seers is anecdotal, it's a matter of my stories against theirs. This book seeks to provide you with hard, quantifiable evidence. It's coming. First, though, here's a quote from Sherden that, while not mathematically precise, gives an elegant explanation of why there are so many one-hit wonders in the realm of market punditry:

> Given that there are thousands of stock market predictors, pure chance guarantees that at least one of them will make what seems to be remarkably accurate calls and attain guru status. Being a market guru, however, is a short-lived honor, because the likelihood of a repeat performance is remote. The odds of making a truly spectacular prediction in any year is one in a thousand, the odds of a repeat performance is one in a million, and the odds of getting it right three times in a row is one in a billion. The eventual fall of the market guru is inevitable.[5]

From what I can tell, though, it's a long, slow, and highly lucrative fall. You may not have availed yourself of the services of the category of seer I've discussed so far in this chapter, or even heard of them. The line between market sages who swing for the fences and those who focus on singles and doubles is a blurred one. The latter group have a higher batting average, to be sure, but not high enough.

If you're at least an occasional follower of financial advice, many and probably most of the names I'm about to discuss are familiar to you. There seems to be no connection between fame and accuracy. Armstrong claims that there may even be a slightly inverse relationship for the most famous experts. There are pundits who made astoundingly ill-timed calls, such as a bank analyst who enthusiastically recommended buying Lehman Brothers shares days before it went bust, who seem to be more in demand on financial television than before.

Naturally the best and worst predictions are what stick in an observer's memory and may present a skewed picture. Luckily, a smart research outfit called CXO Advisory Group regularly gets questions from subscribers asking them to evaluate the prowess of one or another well-known investing expert. They painstakingly comb through every publicly verifiable announcement and come up with a "guru grade."

I take their individual rankings with a pinch of salt because the sample sizes can be small. What they do with thousands of grades, though—6,582 in all between 2005 and 2012 from sixty-eight people or organizations—is significant and probably the most thorough evaluation of popular market analysts around. Their conclusion: You may as well flip a coin. In fact, the average across all forecasts is slightly worse than that, with just 47.4 percent of them being correct. They think one reason it's lower than 50 percent is that some of the gurus in the study, such as Robert Prechter (accuracy of 20.8 percent), who make extreme forecasts also tend to make more frequent ones.

Gracing the list are familiar names such as Jim Cramer (46.8 percent), Doug Kass (49.2 percent), Abby Joseph Cohen (35.1 percent), and Marc Faber, a.k.a. "Dr. Doom" (44.6 percent). I'm pleased to see a couple of names up high on the list that you may not know but probably should. One is John Buckingham (58.8 percent), a friend who both runs AFAM Capital and writes the top-rated investment newsletter of recent decades, the *Prudent Speculator.* Also there is David Dreman (64.4 percent), an investor and author of one of my favorite financial books, *Contrarian Investment Strategies: The Psychological Edge.*

But wait, didn't I say that there is no such thing as a market seer? Yes, but as I'll explain later, their success is most likely about their process. Certain investment strategies have had fairly remarkable results over long periods. Prominent among them is value investing, to which both of these gentlemen adhere. While no guarantee of success, it's akin to playing a game of chance with loaded dice, which is all you can really ask for as an investor.

Despite the contribution of those value mavens, the overall showing of seers is just about what you would expect—some

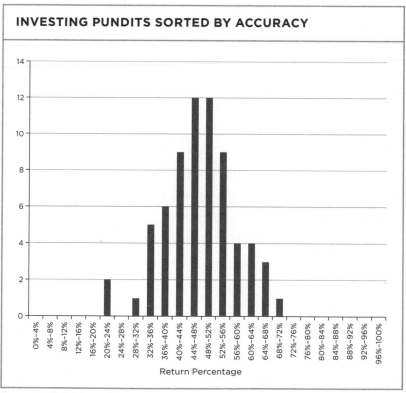

INVESTING PUNDITS SORTED BY ACCURACY

Return Percentage

Source: CXO Advisory Group

winners, some losers, but no one who can manage to be consistently correct (or even consistently incorrect), and lots of people right around the middle. That's best described using a type of chart called a histogram that shows the number of values falling in a certain range right around the middle. Just like annual rainfall or children's height, most observations bunch up around the average, while outliers are rare. Likewise, some pundits will seem prescient (or hopeless) because some must be in a large sample, but that says nothing about the ability of prognosticators generally. The shape of the curve, on the other hand, says it all.

It pains me somewhat to pan the advice business, because I'm a part of it (sort of) and was very much a part of it back when I worked for an investment bank. But that also puts me in a stronger position to explain how to digest the flow of advice and analysis that you receive. Let's get started by taking a trip down memory lane.

Many years from now (I hope), when my teary-eyed sons are reminiscing about me and going through the junk in my basement, they're going to find some strange stuff. That isn't because I'm into deviant behavior. Tucked away in a cardboard box are the so-called tombstones from all the deals I worked on during my years as an analyst—miniature term sheets embedded in blocks of transparent Lucite meant to serve as bragging rights displayed prominently in the offices of investment bankers to show how much money they've made for the firm. Also scattered among them are the prizes that I or any sensible analyst would display most prominently: *Institutional Investor* covers.

Getting voted to an "all-star" team in the magazine's yearly poll is the equivalent of the professional investment world's Good Housekeeping Seal of Approval. It means that fund managers from all over voted you as one of the top three analysts covering a particular country or sector.

Like countries with their medal counts during the Olympics, investment banks would add up first-, second-, and third-place finishers—the equivalent of gold, silver, and bronze—and then rank themselves accordingly. If you happened to be a director of research and your team slipped in the table, then your bonus or even your job might be in jeopardy. If your team was number one, as ours was for a year, you were untouchable. Showing all the modesty and decorum of a six-year-old, our boss had gigantic posters reading "#1" put in the windows of all the analysts whose offices faced across the street toward Morgan Stanley when we overtook them to claim first place.

Of my eight years as an analyst, I spent five as an all-star and three of those as the number one–rated analyst—the equivalent of winning an Oscar in the geeky world of research.

"Mr. Jakab was wearing navy Brooks Brothers with a crisp white shirt and Hermès tie last night as he accepted his prize. He said he wanted to thank . . ."

Okay, it's not all that glamorous, but it was a very big deal for me at the time. Each number one's picture would be made into a caricature sporting a jersey (soccer in the case of the European all-star team) and put alongside the other winning analysts on the cover of the magazine in February. By late December I would be anxiously rehearsing my shpiel for "the call" I hoped to receive from one of the magazine's writers. She would ask a few questions, including a couple about stock picks I had made during the year. I would try to act nonchalant but had memorized out to two decimal places what percent so-and-so stock had risen after I bravely bucked the trend and slapped a "buy" rating on it, along with an example of another one I had shunned that had fallen or at least lagged the market.

The day the magazine came out there would be a few paragraphs with the details that made me sound like an investing genius, along with flattering quotes from some of the anonymous fund managers who had bothered to vote. Of course, not just me but every single "first team" all-star came off looking brilliant.

Were we really, though? I'd like to think so, if only for my own self-esteem, but I had nagging doubts even then. Now that I sit on the other side of the phone, not to mention in a lower tax bracket, I view my former profession in a harsher light. Not too harsh, mind you. Good analysts play an important role by interpreting the reams of complicated information coming out of companies and turning it into something sensible, or at least more sensible. They often keep management honest and, despite negative publicity garnered by a few bad eggs during the dot-com boom in particular, are generally honest people themselves.

What analysts most certainly are not is good stock pickers. That's strange because, in the general public's mind, that's their only job. I found this out the hard way by trusting the opinions of a few of my older, wiser colleagues early in my career when they seemed particularly convincing. I actually had a colleague, an economist and later a stock strategist, who seemed to prove an exception to that rule, except he was eerily prescient about all sorts of things in reverse. Almost every single piece of investment advice that I heard come out of his mouth turned out to be dead wrong. If someone had set up a fund that just did the opposite of what he said it would have been like printing money.

After I had left the business, and after he faced an eventual reckoning and was asked to leave, I attended his wedding. He was in the process of setting up a hedge fund with a couple of friends who didn't seem much luckier than him. While I was waiting in the reception line, a couple of his dad's well-heeled friends, by then lubricated with champagne, asked what I thought about investing in the fund.

Now here was a dilemma. Anything short of a glowing endorsement would be akin to throwing my former colleague under the bus as he was trying to raise money to get his venture off the ground. I have a personal rule about never giving explicit investment advice to strangers, yet here I was being asked if this Wrong Way Corrigan would make them some money. I hesitated awkwardly for a second before heaping praise on his intellect and work ethic, both more or less true, without explicitly saying anything about his fund's prospects. It was a sin of omission, but I told myself that, after all, I didn't know he would struggle.

Of course he did. After the fund folded, he "blew up" a proprietary trading desk at a European bank. The last I heard he was employed again at another U.S. bank. I'm happy for him and figure that, as long as he's giving advice to people who themselves are paid to manage money, they have only themselves to blame for acting on it.

But what about the advice of analysts in general? The hard evidence seems to jibe with my personal experience. Exhibit A in my assertion that it's a bad idea to follow their picks is the distribution of their stock recommendations. One might think that they would be split between buys and sells, with wishy-washy holds to balance them out, since only half of stocks can outperform by definition. Right?

Not even close. In a recent tally of analyst rankings for stocks in the S&P 500, more than twelve thousand in all, only 6.2 percent were rated "sell," while just over half were rated "buy"—a ratio of nearly ten to one. The ratio of buy to sell recommendations is even starker for stocks with the greatest momentum and hence those with the most retail investor activity. In March 2015, for example, Facebook had thirty-eight buy recommendations and a single sell, Amazon.com had twenty-one buys and one sell, and Apple had thirty-four buys compared to two sells.

Believe it or not, the current distribution of buys and sells is actually more balanced than it was before then–New York attorney general Eliot Spitzer's legal crusade against research analysts. Zacks Investment Research looked at recommendations for stocks in the S&P 500 in late 2000 and found that of eight thousand recommendations, only twenty-nine were sells.[6]

The modern investment bank equity research department really began in the 1960s, and the first *Institutional Investor* all-star team was selected in 1972. Back then the recommendations were more balanced, but the stigma of a sell recommendation and its potential to damage the prospects of winning corporate finance work grew over time. It's akin to the phenomenon of grade inflation at Ivy League universities. Just as there are no more "gentleman's Cs," a hold recommendation is now like a sell from an earlier era. An actual sell, meanwhile, is like a red flag in front of an open manhole screaming, "Stay away!" Except, as I'll show, it's often placed there after plenty of people have fallen into it already.

Meanwhile, buy recommendations issued by firms that stand to win or have won banking business might be even less valid of a reason to buy a stock than they might be otherwise. A 1999 research paper by Roni Michaely and Kent Womack calculated that the twelve-month excess return of stocks recommended by an analyst working for the underwriter of a stock offering was negative

7.5 percent, whereas it was positive 7.4 percent for similar recommendations by analysts not working for an underwriter.[7] Another conclusion one might reach from that data, but probably an incorrect one, is that independent analysts really do have skill, because their picks generated "excess return." But understand that this was for initial public offerings during the technology bubble—a time when almost every issue was technology-related and when that sector did far better than the broad market. In a more sedate period, as I'm about to show, buy recommendations aren't worth much.

If memory serves me right, my personal ratio of buys to sells was more balanced. That, though, was probably because I worked in emerging markets where the bulk of my compensation came from client commissions rather than investment banking fees. The lopsided distribution of analyst ratings in developed markets like the United States is fully explained by the lopsided nature of revenue at big banks these days. Analysts have the common sense not to bite the hands that feed them.

Since one shouldn't take analyst recommendations literally, are they at least directionally right? I tried to answer that question by looking at not the absolute rating put on stocks but the change, negative or positive, in buy or sell recommendations. Analysts at Bespoke Investment Group periodically rank all stocks in the S&P 500 on each, so I looked at the twenty companies with the biggest increases in buys and sells at the beginning of 2014.

The results confirmed my suspicions. Analysts are, as a group at least, like the farmer who bolts the barn door after the horse has run into the meadow. If you read financial Web sites or watch television you'll have noticed the occasional "thanks for nothing" headline about a rating change after some awful news has sent a stock plunging:

ANALYST BEN WRONG OF BANK OF AMERICA
DOWNGRADES CONSOLIDATED WIDGETS INC. TO SELL
AFTER WIDGETS WERE LINKED TO SEVERAL
HORRIFIC ACCIDENTS

Most recommendation changes aren't so egregiously unhelpful, but my tally of the top twenty's performance a year before and after showed a clear pattern. Of the stocks that had seen the largest rise in buy recommendations, most had been on a roll, but there was a whopping 31 percentage point drop in their total gain the year after the change compared to a year before. In other words, you *should have* bought them before the flurry of buy recommendations. On the other hand, the stocks that had the biggest increase in sell recommendations had done poorly as a group over the past year, often issuing profit warnings, facing legal problems, and the like. Despite 2014 being a weaker year for stocks overall, they did better as a group than they had in 2013.

Giving my former profession the benefit of the doubt, I left open the possibility that this didn't mean the recommendations themselves were bad. Some buy and sell ratings are less enthusiastic than others, after all. So I looked at a list of stocks in the S&P 500 that at least 80 percent of analysts rated as a buy. Of those thirty-four stocks, though, only fourteen, or 41 percent, would go on to beat the market over the next year. Some did very well, but others declined, so an equal-weighted portfolio of those stocks would have lagged the market.

Since you've bought my book, perhaps you're curious to know whether as an analyst I knew what I was doing and was any good at picking stocks. To be perfectly honest, I'm not sure. Like most analysts (or investors or drivers), I might have said and believed at the time that I was above average.

I know I was good at getting voted onto all-star teams, writing reports, wining and dining customers, and helping to win corporate finance business, but no one kept track of how my picks and pans did. The few examples I would have at hand for the yearly call from *Institutional Investor* made me look great but were cherry-picked ahead of time. I wasn't even allowed to buy a stock that I covered.

The fact that I didn't "eat my own cooking" as an analyst (I assume the same rules still apply in the industry) would seem like a possible explanation for why the profession can't stock-pick its way out of a paper bag. If analysts had some money on the line, maybe it would concentrate their minds, or at least weed out choices made due to ulterior motives.

Sadly, I don't see any evidence of that when I compare the "sell side" and the "buy side." The latter refers to fund managers who, in contrast to investment bank analysts like me vying for their business, are paid to pull the trigger on stock purchases and sales. Their performance is measured in dollars and cents against a benchmark, and some, though not all, invest a bit of their own money in their funds.

As a group, though, mutual fund managers aren't able to beat a passive index most of the time. Still, if one were to ask a professional investor for his very best idea, he might possess an advantage over a sell-side analyst at a bank like I was. That's because while there are thousands of companies, my choices were restricted to the handful I knew a lot about, all of them in the same industry. I couldn't very well have recommended a stock covered by another analyst or one in my field on which I hadn't expressed a formal opinion. If I'm the widget analyst and every single widget maker stinks, I can't pick a single good stock, just a less bad one. A fund manager, by contrast, can cherry-pick the best ideas of every analyst or brokerage firm or come up with his own.

It turns out, though, that fund managers' batting averages aren't any better than those of analysts when thrown this fat pitch. To cite just one example, *Fortune* magazine in December 2013 selected twenty highly regarded fund managers to each give their best stock pick for the following year. Not only did fewer than half of them beat the S&P 500, but the average stock pick lagged the broad market by nearly 12 percentage points.

Fund managers may manage your money, but they aren't the ones who shape the market's expectations. That's the job of the sell-side analysts like I used to be. Whenever a company reports earnings there's an instant assessment of whether it was good or bad. The estimates of all analysts, while not known to the public individually, are compiled by services such as Bloomberg, Thomson Reuters, and FactSet into a "consensus" forecast for earnings per share to which the actual number is compared.

But here's a curious fact about those forecasts. Almost every quarter about 70 percent of companies "beat" consensus, constituting a positive surprise. About 10 percent to 15 percent are considered in line with expectations, and 15 percent to 20 percent "miss." So, to be clear, analysts as a group routinely guess too low on earnings three or four times as often as they guess too high. If that happened every once in a while, it would be the sign of a strong economy and booming corporate profits, but the "surprise ratio" violates the definition of a surprise by persisting.

It shouldn't come as a surprise to you, then, that the odds of a company's stock rising following its quarterly results is the same or even slightly lower than it is on any other day. If that weren't the case, then having an investment strategy of buying any stock on earnings day would be a surefire moneymaker. Investors could plunk their money down on some blue chip at 3:59 p.m., a minute before trading ends on the major exchanges, and sell at 9:31 a.m., a minute after their shares begin trading on the morning they released earnings.

The reason this doesn't work is that investors have caught on to this game—and I use the word "game" intentionally. To cite one example, sportswear company Under Armour Inc., at the time of this writing, has beaten the analyst consensus compiled by FactSet by between one and three cents for the last twenty-four quarters, or six years in a row. The odds of that happening if the outcome were random would be 0.00001 percent. (Actually it would be even less since the chance of meeting expectations, a nonsurprise, wasn't counted.) On the session following its earnings release, though, it fell thirteen times and rose eleven times, for a median loss of 0.6 percent during that stretch.

Anyone who closely follows the stock market's price-to-earnings ratio—it's published in the *Wall Street Journal* and elsewhere—may be scratching their head right now. The so-called forward P/E, which is based on the expected profits of every company in the index in the following twelve months, is usually pleasingly low, which is to say that the assumed profit growth of the market is high. That's based on thousands of individual forecasts from analysts covering each company. Oddly, not only is the valuation rarely as "cheap" when the dust settles and those earnings are reported but, as I've just said, analysts set the bar too low for most companies.

It seems mathematically impossible—either analysts are too optimistic or too pessimistic. The way they accomplish both is that they shift those numbers over time. Take the fourth quarter of 2014. Two years before that earnings season wrapped up, the sum of those thousands of forecasts for the companies in the S&P 500 index implied that earnings would grow by 16.5 percent compared to a year earlier. That's a very good number and made the P/E ratio for 2014 look attractive.

The closer the actual date of earnings got and the more information that became available, though, the lower analysts' actual forecasts got. A year and a half before the date, the growth forecast was just 13.2 percent, a year before it was 10.5 percent, and six months before it was 9.9 percent. Then it really started to fall sharply, reaching an anemic 2.9 percent just before companies began to report their actual earnings.

But guess what? The actual earnings growth turned out to be 5.1 percent—better than expected. That allowed the quarter to be cast in a good light and most companies to "beat" consensus despite growth being just a third as high as the forecast back in 2013. On Wall Street you really can have your cake and eat it too, and it's nothing new. A McKinsey study looking back at twenty-five years of similar data showed that while actual earnings grew at 6 percent a year on average, analyst forecasts a year before were nearly twice as high.

Spare a thought for poor analysts, though, or investing columnists for that matter. Not only do we spend hours slaving in front of computer screens, but our incorrect picks and pans are there to haunt us forever in black and white. When I'm reincarnated I want to come back as a financial talking head—one of those perpetually tanned generalists who is a jack of all investment trades but a master of none. They talk a good game, feel comfortable speaking from a thirty-thousand-foot view, and have a strong incentive to be quoted or interviewed to promote their firm. In fact many of these big-picture types spend the majority of their time speaking to groups or with the media and very little time doing whatever is written on their business cards—strategizing as a "strategist" or whatever.

When it comes to the little picture, they can be hilariously unprepared. You'll rarely notice this as a TV viewer, though, because the ones invited back on air time and again tend to be great ad-libbers and exude self-confidence. A forty-five-second video hit is almost never enough to show that the emperor has no clothes. Almost.

Back in 2007 when Fox Business was just getting started, the head of an investment firm, one of their regular guests, was on air when some "breaking news" was relayed into the host's earpiece. Apparently Apple had just bought a big stake in chipmaker AMD and Fox had an exclusive scoop! It certainly sounded like a head-scratcher, and I'm glad I wasn't live on the set at the time, because I would have hemmed and hawed and possibly uttered the three forbidden words of punditry: "I don't know." The guest was a pro, though, and barely missed a beat:

> Well, yeah, and AMD needs, uh—that's real smart by Apple because AMD is in trouble right now. AMD has always had two problems. Either it had a great product that was either sometimes superior to Intel but not the distribution, or it would have a terrible product that obviously they couldn't compete. And they're sort of in the middle right now. They haven't had great product offerings per se recently . . . the stock has been really just sort of muddling along, so I gotta tell you . . . I think it's a smart play by both companies to get involved with each other.

Except the host had misheard; it was the government of Abu Dhabi, not Apple. The expert barely missed a beat, and it certainly didn't hurt his broadcasting career, as he's on TV nearly every day.

Fairly recently I was on the set of another daytime financial show and the host told me and my fellow interviewee about sixty seconds before our hit what he would ask. Unlike me, my counterpart was a seasoned commentator—one of those people who appears on television so often that the makeup ladies know them by name. Also unlike me, he hadn't prepared at all and had no idea about the company he was about to analyze on national television, Amazon.com. As our host read over his notes, my fellow guest leaned over to me and asked if Amazon was profitable. That's kind of a basic thing to know for someone in his position. I told him that it had made a loss during its most recent quarter but that the company was projecting a small profit later that year.

I wanted to give him a few more details and tell him why I was wary of Amazon's upcoming quarterly results, but the studio lights went on and we put on our frozen smiles. While trying to concentrate on my own performance, I was concerned that he would flub his part of the interview. I needn't have been—he did far better than I, coming off as cool and confident in reciting what I had just whispered in his ear, along with a few generalities.

I don't know how accurate this particular guest is overall, but that encounter didn't give me a lot of confidence. Nevertheless, he's a regular while I'm only rarely asked to appear on that particular show. Around the same time, I read a paper by two economics students[8] at Washington State University, Jadrian Wooten and Ben Smith, that explained his appeal. They wrote a program that analyzed over a billion tweets about two sporting events, the World Series and the Super Bowl. They found that in terms of gaining

Twitter followers and attention, it mattered far more how emphatic one is than how accurate. For example, the gain to a professional in followers from predicting every single game of the baseball playoffs correctly was 7.3 percent. By contrast, someone who was simply extremely confident in his postings would gain 17 percent. But the most confident prognosticators actually were less accurate than those who equivocated.

"In a perfect world, you want to be accurate and confident," said Wooten. "If you had to pick, being confident will get you more followers, get you more demand."[9]

In other words, the people who are most likely to get publicity and have their "expert" views aired are those who are most self-assured and hence less likely to actually be correct. Aside from that fascinating effect, there's yet another reason to be very wary of the views of forecasters. While Robert Prechter, Charles Nenner, and other outsiders swing for the fences and occasionally homer, professional forecasters who work for a bank or asset manager rarely deviate much from the consensus. Why would they, given the asymmetric risk to their cushy jobs and sober reputations? As the great economist John Maynard Keynes said, "It is better to fail conventionally than to succeed unconventionally."

When you're presented with "consensus" forecasts, whether they're about corporate profits or the economy, most, if not all, will be from people who know this to be true. It's one reason why we're all surprised when the economy goes into recession or Enron turns out to be a gigantic fraud. Some people may see it coming, but they aren't the ones aired most prominently in the media or likely to be employed at influential brokerage or asset management firms. Negative Nellies are bad for business.

Take the *Wall Street Journal*'s monthly survey of professional

economists. In December 2007, the month that the recession officially began (it wouldn't officially be declared until several months
later), just 38 percent of economists surveyed believed that there
would be a recession *in the next year*. Asked the same question a year
earlier, only 26 percent predicted one, and the economists said, on
average, that the expansion had three and a half years left to run.

Conversely, on the other side of the recession in June 2009
(though that date wouldn't be officially recognized by the recession-
dating committee for quite some time), only 16 percent thought the
recession would end that quarter. So professional economic seers
were too optimistic before a recession had begun and then far too
pessimistic once it was ending.

The same pattern shows itself with stock market forecasters. I
already mentioned that analysts aim high, lower the bar, and then
high-five corporate management when they clear it. Strategists may
be required to use those profit forecasts but are under no obligation
to allow that to skew their view of where the market will wind up.
Like economists, though, their consensus views are tightly bunched
and generally wrong.

Each December the now-defunct *BusinessWeek* magazine (now
part of Bloomberg) used to survey its "fearless forecasters" about
what ending value they expected for the S&P 500 in the upcoming
year. Looking at those numbers through 2008 and a similar survey
done by *Barron's* since then, some interesting trends emerge. One
that I'm sure doesn't surprise you by now is that they're not very
accurate. In great years such as 1999 and 2013 they were way too
low, missing by 19 and 18 percentage points, respectively. The misses
are bigger in bad years: In 2002 and 2008 they were 32 and 44 percentage points too high.

There was a clear tendency to extrapolate the recent trend,

causing strategists to be caught off guard in years when it changed direction. By contrast, a completely robotic approach that ignores what just happened can outforecast these forecasters who earn on average a couple of million dollars annually and collectively many tens of millions. For the same period I merely plugged in the long-term appreciation of the S&P 500 each year and beat Wall Street's best and brightest 56 percent of the time with smaller average errors to boot. While I can't guarantee that you'll land a six-figure income for outsmarting professional forecasters in this way, I can say with a high degree of confidence that you're best off ignoring these annual exercises in prognostication.

One longtime Wall Streeter actually did something even better. Richard Bernstein, who was, of all things, a strategist for many years at Merrill Lynch, tried to find an effective formula to determine where stocks were headed each year. The very best measure he came up with was called the "sell-side indicator," based on the collective views of his fellow strategists. He found that it explained about 34 percent of the variability of future S&P 500 returns—far better than P/E ratios or bond yields. The twist is that one had to look at extreme optimism or pessimism in the consensus view and *do the opposite* with their money.

Can we do even better at predicting the future? Probably, though one high-profile attempt was denounced as "useless, offensive, and unbelievably stupid."[10] The idea that prompted such strong words—from a U.S. senator no less—was a pilot project within the Pentagon in the early years of the war on terror to set up a futures market for geopolitical risk. Real-money bettors would have been able to wager on the possibility of, say, Jordan's King Abdullah being assassinated by a certain date or a North Korean nuclear missile strike on U.S. soil. You can just imagine the trading pit banter:

"I'll take five hundred contracts at the close on L.A. getting smoked..."

Funding was quickly cut, but the idea—minus the unseemly aspects—lives on. So-called decision markets allow many people, including informed amateurs, to match wits with the experts and usually beat them. For example, the University of Iowa has run a nonprofit exchange to bet on U.S. presidential elections since the 1980s, with results that usually have been more accurate than pollsters and even voter surveys just before the election. The magnitude of their bets, and hence their confidence, affects market prices. By contrast, a simple poll of experts such as the *Wall Street Journal* economists survey gives equal weight to each expert, ignoring their level of conviction or past track record.

Crowdsourced predictions could soon make the earnings "surprise ratio" a thing of the past. One company that has gained traction is Estimize, which, among other things, runs a prediction survey in earnings forecasts. They claim to be more accurate than 70 percent of Wall Street consensus figures. Instead of making money from bettors, though, they sell data on the guesses to investors such as hedge funds who can make short-term profits off of "surprising" results.

Of course, there's a gigantic venue out there that already knows that analysts and other purported seers are full of it and it's called the stock market. It takes thousands of pieces of information and millions of opinions and factors them into prices instantly, for better or worse. That's the crux of the efficient market hypothesis put forward by Nobel Prize–winning economist Eugene Fama in his PhD dissertation a half century ago. The idea was popularized in the 1970s in a bestseller by Professor Burton Malkiel, *A Random Walk Down Wall Street*—a book I recommend highly to any active investor. It's no coincidence that index funds debuted around the time it was published.

The type of seer you the reader are most likely to be keeping in fine fettle is a fund manager (and, indirectly, the analysts and brokers they use). While a very small number earn their keep, it takes several years to determine which ones deserved it. The only thing that's immediately apparent, then, is their fee itself. As I'll illustrate in the next chapter, that's no small consideration. So what's the best course? Once again, I think Armstrong sums it up best in his short treatise on seers:

"Don't hire the best expert, hire the cheapest expert."

CHAPTER EIGHT

WHERE ARE THE CUSTOMERS' YACHTS?

I often ask people in my line of work if there was a book that got them interested in investing. Quite a few around my age, including me, point to Peter Lynch's *One Up on Wall Street*. Lynch retired from running the Fidelity Magellan mutual fund the year after his book topped the bestseller lists, having multiplied its net asset value twenty-seven-fold between 1977 and 1990.

That amazing track record alone would have been enough to sell hundreds of thousands of copies. What made his book both successful and memorable was its folksy but seductive premise: that you could "use what you already know to make money in the market." Few people as accomplished as Lynch would have been as modest as he was in a book written at the height of their fame. Unfortunately, lots of his readers would go on to develop an immodest sense of their own investing prowess in the booming decade that followed. Exactly ten years after he retired, the tech bubble would reach its zenith and millions of people who hadn't ever owned a stock or mutual fund a decade earlier were convinced that they themselves were investing geniuses. Many others thought they had managed to find another Lynch to invest their money. The vast majority of late 1990s superstar investment managers proved to be flashes in the pan, faltering once the bull market did.

Although it was published a half century before *One Up on Wall Street,* there was another, lesser-known book that I and many other people should have read to temper our enthusiasm. Its title, *Where Are the Customers' Yachts?: Or, A Good Hard Look at Wall Street,* relates to an anecdote that already was decades old when Fred Schwed, a former stockbroker, appropriated it. A client goes down to Manhattan's financial district and admires all of the fancy boats in the nearby marina, only to learn, after asking that naïve question, that they belong to the people who work there. Their customers can't afford such luxuries.

Aside from the title, Schwed was way ahead of his time. For example, he explained, using anecdotes, what would win another man, Eugene Fama, the Nobel Prize for a paper written thirty years later on the efficient-market hypothesis. And, thirty-five years before the first low-cost index fund was launched, he tore apart the rationale for investment trusts, a predecessor to today's high-fee, actively managed mutual funds. Throughout the book he laments, using anecdotes and even cartoons, how savers are parted from their money.

"Speculation is an effort, probably unsuccessful, to turn a little money into a lot. Investment is an effort, which should be successful, to prevent a lot of money from becoming a little."

Though plenty of authors try, it's rare to find a book like Schwed's that manages to combine real wisdom with humor, whether the subject is money or just life. Shortly before Peter Lynch's book hit the bestseller lists in 1989, Robert Fulghum's wonderful *All I Really Need to Know I Learned in Kindergarten* became a runaway success by doing just that. As I thought about how to explain in a straightforward way how and why investors waste billions of dollars a year on fund management, my thoughts drifted back not only to Schwed's book but to something I actually read in kindergarten.

In *The Sneetches and Other Stories,* Dr. Seuss tells the tale of a group of creatures who either do or don't have a green star on their bellies but are identical in every other way. Those with stars look down on those without them. Then one day a sly salesman named Sylvester McMonkey McBean shows up with a machine that will put green stars on the bellies of starless sneetches for $3 a pop—a sum they gladly cough up for that important social distinction.

Once every sneetch has a star, the ones who originally sported them, now bereft of the status symbol, are approached by McBean, who tells them that they can be special again by having the stars removed for a mere $10—still a bargain for renewed prestige. They all agree. But then the formerly starless sneetches want in on it and have their recently added stars removed, and so on and so forth, until the sneetches become penniless and can't even remember which ones did or didn't have stars in the first place.

Financial advisor Tim Courtney had a problem involving stars and wasted money too. When he would recommend mutual funds to his clients, many would check the ratings awarded by Morningstar, the leading evaluator of the investment industry's offerings, and often balk at the ones suggested. Why on earth would he put them into a three-star fund? (They're ranked, in ascending order, from one through five stars.) He became so frustrated that he commissioned a study on how worthwhile it was to invest according to the rankings. The answer over the ten-year period ending in 2009 was that they were worse than useless.

Morningstar's seal of approval matters quite a bit, though. In 2008, for example, when investors fled from mutual funds in general, yanking $111 billion from three-star funds, they poured a net $68 billion into five-star ones. In the decade through 2009, Courtney says four- and five-star funds attracted nearly three-quarters of all net inflows. As counterproductive as it is for retail investors to jump in and out of the market, this was adding yet another layer of wealth destruction to their behavior.

The first problem is that the funds that manage to earn the distinction of being rated five stars have had a hard time hanging on to it, encouraging lots of zigging and zagging by fund investors. Of the 248 five-star offerings that Courtney and his team at Burns Advisory Group counted in 1999, only 4 still were rated so highly a decade later, and 87 were no longer in business. Naturally, whatever caused a five-star fund to slip a notch or two already had occurred by the time the next Morningstar rating came out, so investors who swore by ratings would sell losers and buy new winners that might well repeat the process of becoming mediocre. Even those mutual fund investors who weren't hyperactive and stuck with the original list regretted it, though. In all but one category, the beginning stable of five-star funds from 1999 lagged the universe of all funds.

A study by Vanguard Group, the pioneer in the sort of low-cost, passive mutual funds that merely track an index, is even more damning. It calculated the probability of earning an "excess return" from active mutual funds according to how many stars they had. Five-star funds actually had the worst excess return, at negative 1.3 percent a year, and less than a four-in-ten chance of generating a positive one. The best were one-star funds, the lowest-rated ones, and their excess returns still were slightly negative.

Morningstar, which receives license fees from funds that display its ratings (nearly all funds do) and from individual investors who pay for "premium" access to its data, says it has improved its methodology and took umbrage when Courtney's study got extensive media coverage. "We never made any claims that the ratings were predictive of short-term performance, or that they can take the place of a skilled advisor," wrote managing director Don Phillips.[1]

Well, that's certainly how their subscribers interpret and use them, in much the way that someone who reads *Consumer Reports* might buy a washing machine based on its assessment of value and quality rather than consulting their skilled plumber. But let's give Morningstar the benefit of the doubt and say that under their new, improved rating system they would have picked winners, or at least not given higher ratings to poor performers. The issue for you the investor isn't only whether to trust fund raters but also the fact that all the funds did so badly on average. Every slice of the actively managed fund universe had a minus sign in front of it when it came to excess return.

The more traditional way of presenting a fund's returns is how it does relative to a benchmark. For example, large-capitalization domestic stock funds will compare their results to the S&P 500, the leading index of big American companies. According to S&P Dow Jones Indices, 82 percent of actively managed funds in that category failed to beat that index's return over the decade through 2014.[2] Now, defenders of actively managed funds—and you won't be surprised to hear that they are mostly people with a vested financial interest in investors continuing to use them—say that this isn't a fair comparison, since any alternative still wouldn't be free. What they don't point out is that even those dismal statistics are skewed in their favor for another reason.

So let's address their first claim, which is a fair one. All funds have expenses, and even a do-it-yourself investor can't just own stocks or bonds representing an index at absolutely no cost. It's only right to compare funds to funds, active versus passive, and see where the chips fall. In the ten years through 2013, Vanguard Group calculates that 31 percent of large-cap blend stock mutual funds managed to beat a low-cost index fund.

That's better than 18 percent, but it doesn't exactly inspire confidence. The fact that a fund managed by an educated person with framed degrees adorning his or her office wall usually can't beat a mindless formula is pretty damning. And it's actually worse. The odds of picking an active fund that beats passive ones need to include those funds that disappeared, since you might have picked one of those too. Once every fund is included, both living and dead, 85 percent failed to keep up with index funds.

But hey, maybe you're a glass-half-full type (or glass 15 percent full, I guess) and can point to a good performance by a specific fund manager. Maybe you've even been lucky enough to have invested your money with one. I'm very happy for you. Now tell me how likely it is that the same fund will continue to outperform the market in the future.

Today's your lucky day. Instead of paying $185 a year to Morningstar, there's a more accurate way of making that prediction that only requires a quarter (and you'll even get to keep it when you're done). While most funds don't keep up with the market, some do better than others. The odds of a good fund continuing to be good are pretty much identical to a coin flip, though.

Analysts at S&P Dow Jones Indices went through a whole lot of trouble to reach that conclusion. They looked at 2,862 actively managed domestic stock funds and chose those that in 2010 were in the top quartile (better than three-fourths of their peers). Then they repeated the exercise with only that smaller group for each of the following four years. Winnowing the group in this way, it became clear that there was no consistency whatsoever. The number of funds left was the same as a totally random process might have produced. There were two funds remaining after five years that managed to keep a streak going.

One of the two winners, Michael Cook of the SouthernSun Small Cap Fund, was commendably humble in an interview with the *New York Times* in July 2014. "One thing you don't want to do is just read about performance numbers—ours or anybody else's—and put money in an investment," he said. "Chasing past returns doesn't make sense."

Hear, hear. Unfortunately for Cook, he was a little too prescient, as one year after that interview his fund had suffered a sharp reversal of fortune and lagged its benchmark by 18 percentage points over a year. That placed it in the bottom 2 percent of its group.[3] The other winner the previous year also did poorly, so at the end of the sixth year of the study, not a single one of the 2,862 contenders managed to keep their streak going.

Another study showed something more surprising. A possible way to select an outperforming fund (well, one that outperforms other funds, at least) is to pick a past loser. Seriously. An analysis of all actively managed U.S. mutual funds showed that over two consecutive five-year periods, those funds in the lowest quintile by performance in the first period were one and a half times more likely to be in the top quintile in the next five years.

It also uncovered a less surprising fact—those funds that did poorly in the first five years were more than three times as likely to be closed or merged into another fund as the top performers. The greater likelihood of poorly performing funds losing customers and therefore being shut feeds a phenomenon called "survivorship bias" that makes overall mutual fund industry numbers look a lot better than they are. Performance data take only the average of surviving funds. While it isn't a conspiracy, studies have shown that published industry returns would be over a percentage point lower if those vanished funds were included.

I've thrown a lot of numbers and studies at you, so let's catch our breath for a moment and recap the three facts we've established. First, the vast majority of funds don't manage to keep up with whatever index they're benchmarked against. Second, they also can't keep up with actual funds run by computers that are meant to track those benchmarks—particularly when both living and dead funds are counted. Third, some funds will of course do well, beating the market, their peers, and perhaps both. But picking those winners after the fact won't help you, either. In fact, you're slightly better off choosing funds that seem bad—either because they got low ratings or just did poorly.

Now let's establish why all that is true. It isn't because mutual funds are collectively bad at picking stocks. That would actually be impossible. Professionally managed funds own so many stocks that they very nearly *are* the market. No, the reason why funds may as well be run by stock-picking monkeys and can't match the market as a group has to do with costs. Numerous studies have come to the same conclusion: You get what you don't pay for. Costs are an almost perfect predictor of performance. Don't say you weren't warned, either. A piece of boilerplate in fund brochures that people routinely skim over says, "Investors should carefully consider investment objectives, risks, charges, and expenses."

Costs are higher than people realize. The number you see when looking up a mutual fund is its expense ratio. That's a good place to start but not the whole story. William Sharpe, a Nobel Prize–winning economist and the man behind the famous Sharpe ratio used to measure portfolio risk, recently tried to calculate the all-in costs of active funds. Some aren't at all obvious. In 2013 the average expense ratio was 1.12 percent, but service charges also averaged 0.5 percent. Then there are the transaction costs within a fund—paying commissions to brokers to buy and sell stocks. That comes to another 0.5 percent. Finally, there is the fact that, unlike with an index fund, active managers usually have a little bit of cash on hand to meet redemptions or to be able to pounce on opportunities. Since the market usually is going up or at least paying dividends, having cash lying around that earns next to nothing adds another 0.15 percent.[4]

Add it all up and active funds' 2.27 percentage points of total visible and invisible expenses is 2.21 points higher than the largest stock index fund. Even if we assume that a typical fund manager can match the performance of the market exactly, that's a major drag that compounds over time and a big reason why most investors live in Lake Moneybegone.

John Bogle, the founder of Vanguard Group and the man who started the first index mutual fund back in 1976, lays out the argument in dollars and cents. His starting premise is that an active manager will neither do better nor worse than an index fund once costs are stripped out. He uses the example of a thirty-year-old making $30,000 a year who starts saving for eventual retirement at age seventy. She saves 10 percent of her salary each year and she gets a 3 percent annual raise throughout the period. If the market goes up by 7 percent a year and the fund manager can match the market return, then after forty years she would have $561,000 in a typical actively managed fund. If she chose an index fund she would have $927,000, or two-thirds more. And, of course, that's assuming she didn't jump from fund to fund, chasing five-star performers, or, even worse, pull out of the market periodically due to scary headlines. That's a gigantic difference for something that most people overlook or consider a rounding error.

The one counterargument here is that Bogle assumed the active fund only matches the market. I've already demonstrated (I hope) that it's nearly impossible to pick consistently superior managers. When I get into debates with friends and colleagues about it and the person on the other side is running out of things to say to counter the overwhelming evidence, they usually pull out a trump card: "Warren Buffett."

Yes, the Oracle of Omaha is amazing. There's just no explaining away making 163 times as much as the stock market over fifty years at the helm of Berkshire Hathaway (and a lot more if you include his stellar career running partnerships before that). Not only is he a real rarity (and not a fund manager by the way—his company owns many smaller companies outright and has influence over others), but Buffett is a devotee of value investing. It's a technique that can earn extraordinary long-run returns but also create extraordinary short-term stress for people lacking the proper mindset. (I'll discuss the opportunities and pitfalls of trying it yourself later.) But there will never be another Warren Buffett, which is why his recommendation to the person managing his estate once he's gone should be taken on board by mere investing mortals as well:

My advice to the trustee couldn't be more simple: Put 10% of the cash in short-term government bonds and 90% in a very low-cost S&P 500 index fund. (I suggest Vanguard's.) I believe the trust's long-term results from this policy will be superior to those attained by most investors—whether pension funds, institutions or individuals—who employ high-fee managers.[5]

I started this chapter by mentioning two worthwhile investing books. There's one that, to hear Buffett tell it, may be the most valuable ever written (*Security Analysis,* which I'll tell you more about in a little while). It's also—and I speak from personal experience—akin to nonprescription Ambien. A far more worthwhile and entertaining book for the layperson, and arguably even more valuable if you count money saved rather than earned, is Burton Malkiel's *A Random Walk Down Wall Street,* first published in 1973 and now in its eleventh edition. It's a powerful argument in favor of passive investing and still the best take on the academic idea that more knowledge doesn't equal better results.

It's hard to predict the future, but costs are something anyone can control. As Bogle put it, "The case for indexing isn't based on the efficient market hypothesis. It's based on the simple arithmetic of the cost matters hypothesis."

Not surprisingly, Bogle's crusade for low fees ruffled a few feathers. Edward C. Johnson III, Fidelity's chairman at the time the first index fund was launched by Vanguard, likened it to giving up. "I can't believe," he said, "that the great mass of investors are going to be satisfied with just receiving average returns. The name of the game is to be the best."[6]

And a lot of people agreed with him. A year later Peter Lynch took over Fidelity Magellan and became the poster boy for Johnson's worldview. Though Magellan was tiny in 1977, it was worth approximately fifteen times as much as Vanguard's pioneering S&P 500 tracker by the late 1980s even though there were only a handful of other index funds at the time and thousands of other active mutual funds. During his tenure Lynch trounced the market overall and beat it in most years, racking up a 29 percent annualized return. But Lynch himself pointed out a fly in the ointment. He calculated that the average investor in his fund made only around 7 percent during the same period. When he would have a setback, for example, then money would flow out of the fund through redemptions. Then when he got back on track it would flow back in, having missed the recovery.

Naturally if someone had stuck with Lynch throughout they would have done very well. But what would they have done after he left the business in 1990? The Magellan name was as good as it got in mutual funds. Unfortunately, it lagged the market in five of the next seven years and has done poorly overall, failing to keep up with the market over the ensuing quarter century. In 2010, Vanguard overtook Fidelity in total assets, and by that time Magellan was about one-fourth the size of the pioneering index fund that Fidelity's Johnson had ridiculed. So while his comment was half true—that investors would have to settle for "average returns"—it's akin to a tout on the sidewalk outside a casino telling people they have to play to win. You the reader know by now that refusing to settle for average actually lands the vast majority of investors in the decidedly below-average Lake Moneybegone.

Remember Michael Mauboussin? He makes a more sophisticated and interesting argument against passive index fund investing. He asserted in an interview that "there is a logical limit to doing this because passive managers are piggybacking on the research and trading of active managers."[7]

That seems to make sense and certainly applies to other parts of the economy. For example, if you're frugal like me then you don't order a bunch of expensive options on a new car and you wait until the end of the model year to buy when the dealer is motivated to make room for the newer ones. Between us, my wife and I have paid thousands of dollars less for our cars over the years than friends and neighbors with similar vehicles. But we're what is known as "free riders," sort of like index funds in Mauboussin's example. If all buyers did what we did, the car companies would be forced to raise base prices across the board and cheapskates like us would have ruined it for everyone.

Like the skinflint Jakab family, though, index funds are still the exception rather than the rule. There's still so much money poured into active management that Lake Moneybegone is more like an ocean. If I were a smart guy like Mauboussin and convinced that there's such a thing as investment skill, I would relish the day when those waters became a puddle and nearly everyone just stuck their money into an index fund. With so much less competition, I would assume that I could run circles around the crowd and really be "the greatest investor of our time," the way Bill Miller was described before it all unraveled.

Or would he? I explained in the introduction to this book that investing is a zero-sum game. The only way that a handful of truly great investors such as Warren Buffett can beat the market consistently is because the majority of people, each with just a fraction of his money, do so poorly. But if nearly everyone just owned corporate America in equal measure, they wouldn't live in Lake Moneybegone any longer. What's more, all those highly paid strategists, analysts, and fund managers who reap tens of billions of dollars annually from helping us invest would have to find a different line of work. I hear they're looking for car salesmen.

So since I started this chapter with a tale even a child could understand, let's end it with one written by none other than Buffett that explains what the world would look like if everyone just owned the index and also what could ruin that happy situation. In his 2005 annual report, under a section titled "How to Minimize Investment Returns," he tells the story of the Gotrocks. This extended family owns every company in America and thus all of the companies' yearly earnings. They are rich and all get richer at the same pace.

But then some family members try doing a little bit better by selling some of what they own and buying more of other things— naturally from fellow family members. People called brokers love this and encourage the activity, but after a while the family members realize that their returns are starting to lag what they used to earn.

At that point, some clever people called "Helpers" approach family members telling them that, for a fee, they can help them pick the right things to buy and sell, having expertise and credentials in this field. The Gotrocks hire them to do it. Pretty soon, though, they discover that their returns are getting even worse. Not to worry—"super-Helpers" show up, denigrating the inept Helpers, and promise better results using more sophisticated strategies that will require a slightly higher fee.

The story goes on to add yet another layer of "help" that I'll get to in the following chapter. You see where this is going, though. The Gotrocks eventually become less wealthy Hadrocks as the Helpers help themselves to fees. As a child could tell you, they subtract from their pool of wealth in the aggregate. The residents of Lake Money-begone are the Hadrocks.

"Today, in fact, the family's frictional costs of all sorts may well amount to 20 percent of the earnings of American business," wrote Buffett. "In other words, the burden of paying Helpers may cause American equity investors, overall, to earn only 80 percent or so of what they would earn if they just sat still and listened to no one."[8]

So why do investors give away a fifth of their earnings to strangers? In part it's a desire to outsmart the market and do a bit better than everyone else, but it's also a testament to how effective the giant money management industry is at marketing its services. While I really hope I can convince you to be an exception, the majority of people probably will continue to pay for them.

Sylvester McMonkey McBean would make a great mutual fund salesman. In his immortal words, "You can't teach a Sneetch."

CHAPTER NINE

HEADS I WIN,
TAILS YOU LOSE

A lan Ware had what's known as a high-class problem.

"All the Greek gods were taken."

Before he could start a hedge fund that might make him a multimillionaire, he had to come up with a snazzy name for it. His complaint to a colleague of mine was a decade ago, so things have only gotten worse for those hanging out their own shingle in the high-stakes, high-fee world of investment partnerships for the affluent.[1] Even some less likely names from mythology have been snapped up: Cerberus, the three-headed dog of hell, and Poseidon, which has unhealthy associations with being "underwater"—investing parlance for a losing position. Oedipus and Sisyphus are—and I suspect will remain—available.

Mighty trees have been claimed (Sequoia, Lone Pine, Oaktree), along with impregnable bastions (Citadel, Fortress). No wonder the trend du jour for fund names involves combining a color and a geographic feature (BlueMountain, GoldenTree, Blackstone), which, while not very original, leaves plenty of possibilities. I used a Web site called the Hedge Fund Name Generator and came up with YellowRoad Associates, SolidOcean Markets, and my favorite, Black Street Brothers.

Another name that nobody in their right mind would choose is Capital Decimation Partners, but it happens to be the moniker of a hugely successful strategy that ran from 1992 through 1999. During that period it racked up an astounding 2,560 percent return compared to 367 percent for the S&P 500. What's more, it had only six losing months out of ninety-six compared to thirty-six for the actual stock market.

The genius behind those eerily smooth 50 percent annualized gains was Andrew Lo, a professor at MIT's Sloan School of Management. But while he really is a very smart guy, the profits existed only on paper. What he did to achieve them was, by finance geek standards, pretty simple. It involved writing put options on the S&P 500 that were 7 percent "out of the money."

That essentially amounted to selling insurance policies for any willing buyers that the index wouldn't fall by at least 7 percent by the end of that period. The buyer pays a small premium that usually becomes pure profit for the seller, but he begins receiving everlarger payments when the index falls past the agreed price. As I'm writing this, for example, markets are pretty calm by historical standards, so the price I could get for selling puts is on the low side too, though not quite as cheap as in 1999 when Capital Decimation Partners called it quits.

Selling a three-month put today that was 7 percent out of the money, my profit would be wiped out if the market fell by 7.4 percent. If it dropped by 20 percent—a rare occurrence, to be sure—then I would lose three years of profits. That's happened at least eleven times since 1928. If stocks fell by at least 30 percent then five and a half years of profits would be lost. That's happened six times. In reality, though, the entire fund would likely be forced to close before that, as exchanges would demand margin exceeding the capital available—hence the name of the fictional fund.

Surely sophisticated professionals wouldn't invest in, much less construct, such a fund—right? They would if they underestimated the risk or overestimated their own abilities. In fact, some of the smartest people who ever set foot in a financial institution committed what must surely be the greatest investing miscalculation of all time. If they had been baseball players, "all-star team" wouldn't quite have cut it in describing their pedigrees. Many were the equivalent of Hall of Famers, including two Nobel Prize winners, a man mooted as a possible Federal Reserve chairman, and some of the most profitable bond traders on Wall Street. John Meriwether, among the top brass at Salomon Brothers during its heyday, described so colorfully in Michael Lewis's *Liar's Poker,* gathered this dream team in 1993. He decided to name his firm Long Term Capital Management.

Having denizens of financial Cooperstown managing your money didn't come cheap even by hedge fund standards. Investors had to part with 2 percent of assets and 25 percent of profits yearly—more than the typical "two and twenty" fee structure then typical for competitors. But customers gladly agreed, and even seemed to be getting their money's worth for the first few years. Underlying returns were 28 percent, 59 percent, and 57 percent from 1994 through 1996, respectively. Along with their record from part of 1993, that turned one dollar into around $3.50 before fees, compared to $1.60 for the S&P 500.

The fund's managers, who not only were supposed to be experts at risk but also personally had invented some of the techniques for gauging it, reckoned that these fantastic numbers involved no more potential for loss than just owning stocks passively. It was like alchemy—transforming ordinary financial risk into gold. Or at least that's what their formulas told them as they made a huge number of ostensibly boring bets. For example, they entered into the reasonable wager that a twenty-nine and a thirty-year U.S. Treasury should be very close in price even as the market offered a tiny discount for the less traded, "off the run" one of shorter maturity. Another opportunity included a seemingly irrational price discrepancy between the shares of oil company Royal Dutch Shell, listed for historic reasons in two different countries and currencies.

But then safe bets produce small returns, so the only way to turn those into heady ones that justify fat fees is to convince banks how safe they are and get them to lend you money cheaply to magnify the size of the wagers. LTCM's borrowings reached an eye-watering ratio of 28 to 1 compared to its assets.

Eventually, though, the magic seemed to wear off. The fund returned only 17 percent in 1997, or less than the stock market did in that stellar year. One issue was that LTCM's returns were no secret and many other funds piled into identical or very similar bets. The fund decided it was too big and returned $2.7 billion of "excess capital" to investors who were initially upset but would soon consider themselves very fortunate indeed.

In August 1998 something happened that financial models are useless at predicting: Russia's beleaguered leaders took the highly unusual step of defaulting on their domestic debt rather than their foreign currency borrowings. The ripple effects spread from Moscow to London, Manhattan, and, fairly quickly, to LTCM's headquarters in Greenwich, Connecticut. While LTCM hadn't bet much on the risky Russian market itself, many competitors that mimicked its strategies, such as borrowing money in Japanese yen to take advantage of that country's very low interest rates and then buying assets in other currencies, had. When their losses mounted, they were forced to sell their safe holdings and unwind those financing arrangements in a hurry. Under that selling pressure, surefire bets started exhibiting irrational prices as too many traders sprinted for the exits at once.

Irrational doesn't mean impossible—a key distinction the eggheads at LTCM failed to appreciate. As they all surely knew, the great economist (and successful investor) John Maynard Keynes famously said decades earlier that "the market can remain irrational longer than you can remain solvent." Those price moves, magnified by LTCM's gargantuan leverage, soon created gigantic losses on paper for the fund, worrying the people who had lent it well over $100 billion.

The blood in the water attracted sharks from the same firms. When those banks got a detailed look at what sorts of bets they were financing, some began making profitable trades based on the correct assumption that there was about to be a huge distressed seller—namely, LTCM. If you think that's not very nice then you're right, but it's why they say that if you work on Wall Street and want a friend you should get a dog. LTCM was so big, though, that it soon became everyone's problem and required a Federal Reserve–led rescue, wiping out the fund's investors.

LTCM's brain trust had determined that the events leading up to its collapse were a 10 standard deviation event—something that should not have occurred in the earth's entire history. But while they clearly were a wee bit off in their calculations, the PhDs knew their times tables cold. At 2 percent of assets and 25 percent of annual returns, they had made profits of about $2 billion over the preceding four years before losing $4 billion in the course of several weeks.

Remember how Legg Mason, Bill Miller's firm, profited handsomely from his fund's long run even as investors made a subpar dollar-weighted return? Hedge funds create that "heads I win, tails you lose" dichotomy on steroids. LTCM's principals happen to have reinvested their profits into the fund, becoming some of their own largest victims, but that's not usually the case. A successful run coupled with fat fees and followed by a rocky period could mean that investors in a hedge fund make a fairly pedestrian return after all is said and done while the fund's managers still walk away with huge rewards. The setup incentivizes managers to swing for the fences. And since hedge funds are secretive by nature, investors either don't know or can't understand how the returns are created. In fact, economists at Princeton University and Harvard Business School studied several successful hedge funds and determined that their risks and returns were nearly identical to the put-selling strategy used by Capital Decimation Partners.[2] It works great until it doesn't.

Naturally, meltdowns like LTCM's are rare, but the amazing thing about the hedge fund mystique is that even blow-up artists get more credit for their successes than their failures. Meriwether, for example, would go on to regain and then lose investors' trust again, opening up another firm, JWM Partners, before being forced to close it after a steep loss. There have even been threepeats.

My favorite serial offender is Victor Niederhoffer, a fascinating character on more than one level. The street-smart kid turned academic turned hedge fund star learned at the feet of the great George Soros and was one of the top-performing investors of the 1990s. In

1996 he was named the number one hedge fund manager in the world by an industry newsletter after making returns of 35 percent compounded over many years. Then he blew up in the 1997 Asian financial crisis following a disastrous bet on Thai banks.

"Blew up" is an imprecise term, but Niederhoffer's first downfall was a thermonuclear blast, wiping out the fund and rendering past performance meaningless. Ironically, Niederhoffer had just published a book I really liked (well, I still like it) called *The Education of a Speculator* that dealt, among other things, with the similarities and differences between gambling and investing. Niederhoffer became depressed after his unwise roll of the dice but eventually cheered up, formed a hugely successful new fund, won a similar award, and even wrote a new book a decade later just in time for his second collapse in 2007.

While the vast majority of hedge funds never suffer from the cataclysms that befell Meriwether and Niederhoffer, and some have had truly amazing runs, the notion that most or even many managers have unlocked a formula for reward without commensurate risk is hogwash. In relating Warren Buffett's allegory of the "Helpers" and "super-Helpers" in the preceding chapter, I said that there was one category I wouldn't mention until later. This is later, and the final stewards of the Gotrocks' fortune are the "hyper-Helpers," a not very subtle reference to high-fee investment partnerships such as hedge funds.

These friendly folk explain to the Gotrocks that their unsatisfactory results are occurring because the existing Helpers—brokers, managers, consultants—are not sufficiently motivated and are simply going through the motions. "What," the new Helpers ask, "can you expect from such a bunch of zombies?" The new arrivals offer a breathtakingly simple solution: Pay more money. Brimming with self-confidence, the hyper-Helpers assert that huge contingent payments—in addition to stiff fixed fees—are what each family member must fork over in order to really outmaneuver his relatives.

Being an allegory, Buffett's criticism is basically right but a bit too pat. It makes hedge funds sound like the Cadillac Cimarrons of investment funds. Remember the Cimarron? Named by *Time* magazine as one of the fifty worst cars of all time, it was a rebadged version of the Chevy Cavalier sold to naïve buyers for 50 percent extra.

At least hedge funds are different. They can use leverage, bet that stocks will decline, and venture into the types of investments that would be terra incognita for guys who manage mutual funds and buy their suits at JC Penney. One rarely hears about a mutual fund making a triple-digit return or, for that matter, "blowing up." Hedge fund managers have a much longer leash that occasionally turns into enough rope to hang themselves. And since the field is so hypercompetitive and deals in esoteric investments, fund managers are typically bright. Buffett acknowledges that much. "A number of smart people are involved in running hedge funds. But to a great extent their efforts are self-neutralizing, and their IQ will not overcome the costs they impose on investors," he wrote.

Aside from his own stellar track record as an investor, there are two very good reasons why Buffett is qualified to criticize the way hedge funds get paid. The first is that he ran investment partnerships himself before concentrating on Berkshire Hathaway a half century ago. But Buffett eschewed the "two and twenty" approach to getting paid, which worked out fine for him, as he never had a losing year. The arrangement paid him only if his returns were above 6 percent in a year, and if he lost money or failed to make that much then he had to get back to that watermark before earning anything else. A young hedge fund manager I know who idolizes Buffett set up his fund in an identical way, rationalizing that the commonly accepted fee structure is akin to "paying a racecar driver just to drive around the track, win or lose."

The other reason Buffett can criticize hedge funds is that he put his money where his mouth is. He had often repeated that he would make a $1 million bet that a low-cost index fund would beat a fund of hedge funds—sort of a super-duper-hyper-Helper—over a ten-year period. These charge a fee for doing research and selecting (and perhaps as important, gaining entry to) the best hedge funds available. The cumulative fees are typically 2.5 percent of assets and 25 percent of annual profits.

In 2007, Ted Seides, who ran fund of funds Protégé Partners LLC, took Buffett up on his offer. Once the winner is declared in 2017, a charity of each man's choice will receive $1 million. Buffett bet his own money, not that of Berkshire, and at the outset he estimated that his chances of winning were around 60 percent. Seides, who was allowed to divide his make-believe investment between the five best hedge funds he could find, thought his own chances were 85 percent. Clearly one of them was wrong.

Seides was confident because his fund had beaten the S&P 500 handily after fees, gaining 95 percent from 2002 through 2007 compared to 64 percent for a plain vanilla stock index fund. Like the disclaimer says, though, "Past results are not necessarily indicative of future performance." Buffett's calculation was more reasonable since he had a serious advantage. Because of the steep fees, even a fairly consistent ability to make excess returns might not be enough.

Let's say, for example, that Seides knew the funds he picked had such an edge that they could beat the S&P 500 by a steady three percentage points a year before fees. If done every year, that would be impressive, but it still depends on what the market return was. For example, let's say the market went up by 8.7 percent a year over the decade chosen—a fairly typical pace. It wouldn't change by exactly that amount each year, of course, so let's say the actual yearly change in stock prices are 5 percent, 10 percent, 15 percent, 20 percent, and negative 5 percent for the first five years, and then that repeats for the second five. Even a consistent performance of beating that by three percentage points a year wouldn't be enough to justify its fees. It would take an outperformance of 5 percent or more—a really exceptional edge. Over the last forty years, an investor able to beat the market by so much would have 240 times his starting investment.

A more apt question is whether you're getting your money's worth even when a fund does beat the market. It can only be if the results are due to some skill that can be applied consistently rather than just acceptance of market risk on steroids like Capital Decimation Partners. Researchers at Bridgewater Associates tried to answer the question. The results weren't flattering, with beta (market return) rather than alpha (investment skill) amounting to between 52 percent and 80 percent of various types of funds' returns.

Back in 2007, a boom year for hedge funds, I spoke with someone who had what practically amounted to a blank check to make a killing no matter how she made her money, but she took a radically different course. Lisa Rapuano, who learned at the knee of Bill Miller, left Legg Mason when his fund was still on top of the world to start her own hedge fund. Instead of pocketing 20 percent of annual gains, she entered into an arrangement that allowed both her and her clients to think long-term: 40 percent of three-year gains, but only what she earned above the return of Standard & Poor's 1500 stock index. Even though this was friendlier to clients, she found it to be a tough sell.[3] "Price connotes value and if you're cutting prices there must be something wrong with you," she said.

I suppose it's the reason people pay five hundred times as much for a Rolex than a Swatch that keeps better time. But then if you run in the circles in which dropping the fact that Bill Ackman or David Einhorn are managing your money impresses people, you may not need this book. Merely growing your net worth by Lake Money-begone multiples would still leave you with a roof over your head.

The fact that hedge fund strategies mostly just represent market risk should bother even people who can afford butlers for their butlers, though. I've already explained that only around 3 percent of plain vanilla mutual fund managers display sufficient skill to justify their costs. And remember, those costs are a lot more modest than hedge funds'. Is there some special knowledge that becomes available only when the word "hedge" instead of "mutual" is in front of the word "fund" that is different enough to allow them to clear that much higher a hurdle? The evidence shows that they fail to come anywhere near earning the extra fees. An index of global hedge fund performance over the ten years through 2014, the HFRX Global Hedge Fund Index, has failed to outperform the S&P 500 in nine of those years, inclusive of fees. The underperformance is an absolutely horrible negative 8.1 percent a year on average.

Ah, but hedge funds sell themselves by touting how uncorrelated they are to the market. Their "go anywhere" ability and a penchant for less liquid assets or short and long bets help them to do so. That's an advantage in that it moves a portfolio out on the "efficient frontier," meaning they don't move in lockstep with plain vanilla investments. Pension funds, and endowments in particular, care about such things and have plowed many billions of dollars into hedge funds.

But how much is it worth to you? That probably sounds like a moot point as most people reading this don't have the net worth to invest in hedge funds. The lines have been blurred, though, as hedge-fund-like products have proliferated in the world of mutual funds available to anyone and are possibly sitting in your portfolio. They go by names such as "liquid alternative," "alternative income," or "multiasset." The fees are typically around 1.9 percent on average, according to Morningstar, or far higher even than actively managed mutual funds. Their underlying costs are often higher too for a variety of reasons, such as buying illiquid assets or engaging in expensive short selling.

The first wave of hedge-fund-like mutual funds arrived on the scene in the mid-2000s with great fanfare. Known by names such as "long/short" and "130/30," they took advantage of rules that allowed their managers to bet against stocks directly for the first time with a small part of their assets, just like the masters of the universe managing hedge funds. Investment consultancy TABB Group predicted that the booming category would reach $2 trillion in assets by 2010 as investors embraced the lower volatility of the category.

In a really bad year for stocks they should have, in theory, avoided falling in lockstep with your mainstream investments. For what it's worth, they did a bit better in 2008, and the five hedge funds Seides picked for his bet with Buffett also did that, falling by only 24 percent in awful 2008 after fees compared to a loss of 37 percent for Buffett's index fund. But they didn't do well in "good" years, and investors abandoned 130/30 funds in droves. By late 2012, for example, Morningstar counted one and a half times as many shuttered 130/30 funds as those still in business, and they had less than $10 billion in assets.[4] Their mediocre performance data didn't look good, and was even overstated, as the funds that closed usually were the ones that did the worst. Similar funds have taken their place, promising uncorrelated returns under different names. "Liquid alternatives," for example, owning bank loans and other assets have grown from $72 billion in assets to $306 billion by the end of 2014.[5] Watch this space for more disappointment.

And the million-dollar bet? After what I've told you, I don't think there's much suspense remaining. Seides picked what he thought were the very best funds, and through the first seven years they eked out a total gain of 19.6 percent, while Buffett's index fund trounced it with a gain of 63.5 percent. Although the identity of the five funds he chose is a secret, Seides did break out in early 2015 how much of the yawning gap between him and Buffett was due to costs. Adding the fees back, they would have made 44 percent during that time, or not quite a third less than the index fund. They needed to do a lot better.

There still is one possible way for Seides to win the bet, but it would be the ultimate pyrrhic victory. If markets were to plunge 2008 style, his handpicked funds might beat the market by falling less. He even highlighted that fact. That shows a key difference between how investment professionals and individual investors think. No saver would celebrate losing 5 percent of his or her nest egg just because everyone else lost 20 percent. You can't feed and clothe yourself in retirement on relative return. It takes dollars and cents.

This book is, of course, about improving your relative returns, but only because my underlying assumption is that stocks and bonds will make money in the long run.

We've covered a lot of ground, and that brings us to a significant milestone: The really low-hanging fruit that makes up most of the gap between a typical Lake Moneybegone investor and the market has now been pointed out to you.

I promised that I would discuss some potential techniques for doing a little better. Before we do that, though, I want to highlight a handful of additional errors and pitfalls that don't fall neatly into the preceding chapters.

CHAPTER TEN

SEVEN HABITS OF HIGHLY INEFFECTIVE INVESTORS

I f you're old-fashioned like me then you still prefer reading books and newspapers made out of dead trees and even buying them at an actual bookstore that has shelves and a cash register. Even if you didn't pick up your copy of *Heads I Win, Tails I Win* at one, you probably still remember shopping at them before e-readers and on-line retailers won you over with their convenience and will recall that the finance and investing section is one of the larger ones. Whether it was a virtual or a physical purchase, though, I appreciate that you picked my book out of that crowded field.

Books about money are usually right near another section that's even larger—self-help and spirituality. Based on some of their titles, there's at best a blurred line between the genres. Category-straddling ones are *Think and Grow Rich, The Power of Positive Thinking, Zero Limits, Awaken the Giant Within, Unlimited Power,* and *Money: Master the Game.* Those commercially successful ones all have something in common: positive messages. They start from the premise that you're average but have greatness within you.

If that's the formula for landing on the bestseller list then I've violated it in spades by saying most investors, probably including you, should be tickled pink to earn an average return. I'm not promising to unleash an investing giant or make you *The Richest Man in Babylon* or whatever. It's when investors swing for the fences that they whiff badly.

Bolstering your bottom line and your ego just don't go hand in hand. Thus many investors are residents of Lake Moneybegone in no small part due to overconfidence and to mistakes made repeatedly in the face of overwhelming evidence. The big errors are zigging when you should zag, overestimating the value of investment expertise, paying too much for it, and failing to embrace risk at the appropriate times.

Now I'm going to get into some nitty-gritty ones, not all of which will apply to you. Coming up with a manageable list felt a bit like staring at one of those Chinese restaurant menus that leaves you spoiled for choice. I went for some of the most common items with lots of meat on them—the sweet-and-sour chickens of investing foibles. These will cost you plenty.

Telling you what not to do may violate Book Marketing 101, but I'll try to mitigate the damage by drawing inspiration from a highly successful self-help franchise. So, without further ado, here are Seven Habits of Highly Ineffective Investors:

Habit 1: Get In on That Hot New Deal

It turned out to be an offer you *could* refuse. In December 2011, red-hot video game maker Zynga, maker of *Mafia Wars, FarmVille,* and other online hits, sold its shares to the masses. In the past fifteen years, initial public offerings of technology companies had been seen as tickets to instant riches.

The first such deal to catch the public imagination was Netscape, a company that had launched a pioneering Internet browser several months earlier. Sold to investors at $28 a share, the stock price nearly touched $75 during its first trading session in August 1995 and closed at $58.25. For those who were allocated shares in the offering and sold even at the lower closing price, the 108 percent gain was the equivalent of making about a decade's worth of typical stock market returns in less than seven hours.

That was just a preview of coming attractions. Other IPOs during the heyday of the technology boom, which ran from 1998 through early 2000, did far better. Companies such as VA Linux, Foundry Networks, the Globe.com, and webMethods all rose by at least 500 percent on their debuts.

Flotations of young and exciting technology companies went ice cold for several years but resurfaced recently in a less manic echo of the dot-com boom. After some successful ones earlier in 2011, few doubted that Zynga would follow the script, perhaps posting a 40 or 50 percent first-day gain. Interest was high so that the company wound up selling shares at the top of its pricing range of $8.50 to $10. After an initial flurry of activity lasting just several minutes that saw the stock go as high as $11, though, it began to drop and, to early investors' horror, fall through the issue price.

By the end of that first trading session the $9.50 line seemed to be holding. There was a good reason for that, and also a good reason why it was a round number rather than, say, $9.53 or $9.48. The underwriters of the deal often step in to "stabilize" an issue at an agreed price, in large part to protect their reputations. They usually do so only for a matter of hours. Anyone who had immediate buyer's remorse and wanted to get out had a willing counterparty for a very short time. The share price dipped as low as $8.75 the next trading session.

Though Zynga's price briefly would rebound to above $15 a share, it wound up losing 75 percent of its value in the company's first three years on the market. This was during a good period overall for stocks when a passive investor in the S&P 500 saw gains of 72 percentage points. On an annualized basis, someone buying Zynga on the day of its IPO saw it underperform the broad market by an absolutely horrendous 35 percentage points per year.

What happened? It's hard to say precisely because the success or failure of any given offering has to do with plenty of unique factors, some of them emotional. Ultimately, of course, any stock represents ownership in a business that needs to do well, moving from promise to profits.

But people don't buy into IPOs to make a steady, boring 9 percent a year. And most unproven businesses don't sell a stake in themselves with an eye toward getting the highest price. The typical template for a hot young company is to release a number of shares that falls well short of what the public demands in order to create scarcity value. During 1999 and 2000 alone, University of Florida finance professor Jay Ritter, a leading expert on IPOs, calculates that underwriters thus left an astounding $67 billion on the table. That's the difference between the sale price and the stock's close on the first day of trading, which in 2000 reached a record high 71 percent on average.

Some naïve pundits have accused the investment banks of robbing the companies' founders. That's not the case at all, though—the owners would rather see a big pop and then hope the buzz lasts long enough for them to sell more shares later at an even more astronomical valuation. That $67 billion can be viewed as a marketing cost that was in many cases worth it for those insiders. The only people out of pocket are individual investors bedazzled by the moon-shot gains that they had little chance of realizing themselves.

Since shares in those IPOs thought likely to surge on their first day of trading are scarce, the people controlling the deal can pick and choose who gets the equivalent of that free money. In more ways than one during the technology boom it involved a quid pro quo. IPO shares often went to the personal brokerage accounts of executives of other companies with which banks such as Morgan Stanley, Goldman Sachs, or my old employer, Credit Suisse, hoped to do business. Meanwhile, hedge funds, knowing that only the very best clients would get a crack at IPO shares, sometimes would intentionally trade furiously with an underwriter to generate lots of commissions. I heard of at least one firm that was set up for the express purpose of buying and selling with no rhyme or reason in order to be a top commission payer to our firm and get allocated IPO shares in 1999 and 2000. It then flipped them for quick gains. Everyone was happy except for the poor individual investors left holding the bag.

Zynga was a rare case in which the initial buyers, unless they were very quick off the mark, expected a bonanza but were sorely disappointed. As for what happened afterward, it wasn't at all unusual. I don't have any way of predicting the few deals that fail to create instant riches, but past patterns tell me that participating in lots of IPOs and selling quickly can bring extraordinary profits on average. Even over the long run, from 1980 through 2014, Professor Ritter calculates the average first-day gain to be a very respectable 18.6 percent.

Here's the catch, though. Unless you happen to be well connected—a hedge fund manager, let's say, or a fabulously wealthy private banking client—you won't get a shot at that. Access to an IPO is like a celebrity showing up at a Michelin three-star restaurant and being quickly seated by the maître d', not standing in line at McDonald's where it's first come, first served, with your money as good as the next person's. The vast majority of people might get some tiny number of shares, but for the most part they buy the stock on the day of its debut.

Don't worry about finding shares for sale during the frenetic session after the stock becomes available to the hoi polloi in the secondary market. Of nearly five hundred IPOs that had first-day returns of at least 60 percent, almost the entire number of shares in circulation turned over. That means that, while some people hang on to their stock, others will sell it and then the buyers will sell the same shares again, repeating the process before the day is through. To put that 100 percent turnover into perspective, the average share listed on the New York Stock Exchange changes hands around three times *in a year*.

Buying on that first day and selling a few hours or perhaps a few minutes later is no better than a crapshoot. Buying and hanging on to the stock in the hopes of owning the "next Apple" is, on the other hand, more like shooting yourself in the foot—particularly when it comes to a small, unproven, and marginally profitable company.

The only unusual thing about Zynga was how quickly investors lost faith in it. Professor Ritter's calculations show that IPOs tend to lag the broad market in each of their first three years on the market. The smaller the company, the worse your odds. Companies with less than $1 billion in sales in 2014 dollars lagged the market by just over 20 percent per year on average. Those with less than $50 million in revenue do far worse.

It's only large companies with at least $1 billion in sales—often those with established businesses such as credit card issuer Visa, one of the largest IPOs of all time—that tend to do well. Not only are these easier to buy at their offer price, but they don't often skyrocket on day one. The sellers care about making top dollar, not creating buzz. I'm not endorsing their purchase but not steering you away either. As for smaller companies, you the naïve retail investor not only are the audience expected to be influenced by their buzz but one of the thousands of onlookers blowing the vuvuzela.

No doubt about it, the belief that you may have gotten in early on a company that will become a household name is intoxicating. It's like being a member of an exclusive club. If you've recently wagered on such a company, perhaps you accept Professor Ritter's numbers but insist they don't apply to your baby. Naturally, every deal is unique, and those are just averages. Consider these two commonsense warnings, though, before rationalizing in that way:

First, the vast majority of the companies touted as "the next (fill in the blank)" have no hope of realizing those ambitions. What I mean to say is that there's a tiny chance of their businesses being as successful as some established technology giant, but almost none of their stock appreciating as much. That's because people already factor in past financial bonanzas and then overestimate their odds of being part of one.

Just do the math on those that did well. An investor in Microsoft's IPO made, over many years, about a thousand times their money. By the time Google came around it was just ten times, even though that company reached a similar market value, because the widespread knowledge of what happened to Microsoft made it so much more valuable on day one. Facebook, valued at $100 billion at its IPO, actually managed to double at the time of this writing. There's virtually no chance, though, of making a thousand times your money in Facebook or seeing that business become worth $100 trillion, because that's more than the total value of every stock on every exchange in the world.

Second, even if you happened to buy a stock that rises by 10,000 percent over many years, the odds you'll still own it at that point are very small. Why? Because you're greedy and fearful like the rest of us, only probably more so if you're the type to buy such offerings. Let's say you plunked an amount of money that was significant to you into a hot new issue and it rose by 100 percent in the first month. Woo-hoo—you just doubled your money on some company your brother-in-law told you about! Do you hang on for more? Possibly. Okay, then it drops by 75 percent from there before resuming its rise to infinity and beyond. Did you hang on until losing half of your initial investment? Probably not. Because of a psychological foible called "anchoring," the original price you paid is like a mental red line. To avoid "losing" money, you'll usually sell before it gets there. Based on the same error in reverse, a person buying from you re-members how high the stock got before its 75 percent drop and fix-ates on it returning there no matter what new information has arisen.

This quirk of human nature is yet another reason why simply checking your investments less frequently decreases the odds of do-ing something silly. Professionals entrusted with your savings make the same errors and charge a fee to boot. Back in 2008, I had the idea of looking up articles about companies that had near-death ex-periences in the 2000–2002 bear market but bounced back from the brink, potentially making very brave investors hundreds of times their money. I scoured articles published at the time for the few fund managers who had something positive to say about them and admitted owning what seemed radioactive to most. I then tracked down those people to congratulate them on their prescience and ask how much they made. Without exception, they had taken a profit after the first 50 percent or perhaps 100 percent, leaving lots of money on the table.

I must sound like a curmudgeon panning these exciting technology offerings—one of those people who "don't get it." I admit that valuing a fast-growing company is more art than science and that I'm painting with a broad brush. Beyond the pitiful performance of speculative new offerings as a group, though, it seems that it's the true believers who sometimes don't get something very basic—addition and subtraction. The most famous case of an utterly nonsensical price occurred the month that the technology boom peaked, March 2000, when Palm had its initial public offering.

Remember PalmPilots? Before iPhones and even BlackBerrys, the personal digital assistants were hot stuff, and so was their maker, 3Com. The company had other businesses too, but it spun off a 5 percent stake in Palm to investors. In an upcoming tax-free deal each share of 3Com would entitle its owner to receive 1.5 shares of Palm. Palm's stock surged on its first day of trading to $95.06, but 3Com fell sharply to $81.81. Even if its other businesses were absolutely worthless, 3Com's stock should have fetched at least $145. Instead, investors, clamoring for access to the hot new thing, implied that its majority owner was worth *negative* $22 billion. The anomaly persisted for weeks, even after journalists pointed it out.

That's an extreme case, but the evidence is clear that, on average, investors overpay for hot offerings—particularly those that garner the most publicity. They are a shortcut to stock market riches that are likely to disappoint in much the same way that lottery tickets have far more chance of impoverishing you dollar by dollar than making you rich. You may know someone who claims to have made a killing on a deal, but unless he or she is a favored insider, they're the exception rather than the rule. With over five thousand listed U.S. companies in which to invest and more than forty-five thousand globally, plus numerous exchange-traded funds that slice and dice the market into characteristics to suit every taste, there really is no reason to take the risk. Today's IPO, if it isn't an outright flop, will become tomorrow's established company. Waiting a year or two to gain exposure to it is unlikely to cost you the opportunity to get in on the investment of the century because many of those took quite a while to pan out themselves.

Habit 2: Combine Your Morals and Your Money

In 2001, CalPERS, the gigantic California state employee retirement fund, decided it should throw its weight around. Still feeling flush from the dot-com boom—on paper at least, its obligations were 128 percent funded as recently as its fiscal year ended in 2000—it went on a crusade that made headlines. But its goal wasn't to, say, rein in runaway executive pay at the companies where it was a big shareholder or to force down fees charged by its outside fund managers—you know, things that could have saved retirees nationwide money, including its own, to whom it legally owes a fiduciary duty.

On the basis of labor and human rights standards, CalPERS decided to sell all of its holdings in a number of South and Southeast Asian countries. It had hired a consultant, Wilshire Associates, to grade emerging markets based on criteria that gave equal weight to social and financial factors, the former consisting of labor and human rights standards. Having a history of paying your obligations clearly wasn't one of them. Argentina made the cut based on the same scoring system.

That year the South American nation's stock market suffered horrific losses in dollar terms following the largest sovereign default in history. The Thai market, by contrast, beat the S&P 500 by about 25 percentage points. The following year, with the recommendations unchanged, Thailand, India, and Sri Lanka posted stellar returns of 136 percent, 82 percent, and 30 percent respectively, none of which were enjoyed by the current and future state retirees of California.

Today CalPERS, using very generous actuarial assumptions, is around $75 billion in the hole when assets and liabilities are compared, or just 77 percent funded. It spent $1.65 billion managing its investments in fiscal 2014, including an initiative on "sustainable investment." Barring some fantastic future investment returns, though, its current rate of contributions and expenses quite obviously isn't sustainable in the traditional sense of the word.

This is a book about how to be a better investor, not a better person. I have nothing against the latter goal but would caution you against conflating the two in the way that CalPERS has. You may not be able to afford it either. Like CalPERS, you have a duty to yourself and your family to get the best return for the lowest risk.

The funny thing is that many people put their money where their morals are without realizing it. Advocates of socially responsible investing have made big inroads in the world of pension funds and endowments. For example, part of your pension may be invested in a vehicle that shuns companies that make guns, booze, or tobacco, or those with large greenhouse gas footprints. More religiously focused ones also may ban pharmaceutical companies that sell contraceptives or hospital chains involved in abortions.

If you own individual stocks then you may avoid investing in such companies yourself, consciously or not. There even have been mutual funds that cater to specific beliefs, including Sharia-compliant ones for Muslims and a number of now-defunct ones for various Christian denominations (some had differing standards on hard liquor, gambling, or firearms but shared a devotion to high fees). Altogether there are nearly five hundred socially responsible funds with around $600 billion in assets under management.

The sad truth, though, is that not only isn't it especially profitable to be good—it's downright good to be bad. Academic studies on the subject haven't reached a firm conclusion as to why. Perhaps because they're shunned, or maybe because they happen to be in recession-proof fields, businesses like booze, gambling, smoking, and guns, the very companies that don't show up in the portfolios of do-gooders, have often been great investments. U.S. tobacco companies, for instance, had an annualized return of 14.6 percent a year from the beginning of the twentieth century through 2014, according to researchers at London Business School.[1] The overall U.S. market returned just 9.6 percent during that time. That's a huge difference over such a long period. Those investing exclusively in the sector made 165 times as much as those just owning the broad market. Smoking! Similarly, British brewers and distillers turned £1 into £243,512 over the same period for a return of 11.4 percent (there's no measure for U.S. ones since many closed down and reopened after Prohibition).

Back in 2007, I interviewed the founders of an outfit called "the Vice Fund," with a logo made up of dice, a burning stogie, a martini glass, and a target. They cited research showing that an index of "sin stocks" outperformed the market handsomely. With that evidence in hand, they expected great things, and I would have too. After all, what people are most concerned about is finding an above-average investment—right?

It wasn't a fluke either. Through early 2015 their fund continued the trend with an annualized gain over a decade of more than a percentage point higher than a leading socially responsible index fund offered by Vanguard. But as a business, the fund has been a disappointment, with less than $300 million in assets under management, a fraction of a percent of the amount invested in socially responsible funds. The fund recently changed its name to the anodyne USA Mutuals Barrier Fund to shed its bad-boy stigma.

An exchange-traded fund with the ticker symbol PUF (get it?) that invested along the same lines peaked at barely $10 million in assets and had to fold, though its underlying index—known as the SINdex—lives on. From the end of 1998 through the beginning of 2015, it had an annualized gain of 16 percent. A dollar invested would have grown nearly three times as much as the S&P 500.

Past performance is no guarantee of future returns, but that is a heck of a difference. I do understand people's reluctance to invest in companies that they personally find unsavory. When my mother-in-law retired years ago I sat down with her as she rolled her workplace 401(k) into an individual retirement account and had to choose investments. Since I knew she would trade infrequently (she's eighty and has made just a few purchases or sales since retiring), I chose a basket of bond funds and individual, dividend-paying companies for the stock portion of her portfolio rather than a low-cost index fund. One of them was Philip Morris, which has since spun off a few other companies. A former smoker, she initially balked at the choice, as I'm sure many people do. Then I asked her what effect buying those shares would have on the company's finances or on the practice of cigarette smoking. It wouldn't have any, of course—she was just buying shares from another person in the secondary market and not giving the company money. Then I suggested that if the investment did well (it has), she could donate some money to a charity such as the American Lung Association.

I would say the same thing to you. Like investment losses, charity is tax-deductible, but it sure has more impact on the world than pouring it into Lake Moneybegone.

Habit 3: Buy What's Fashionable

If your high school was anything like mine, the student body voted to decide which of their classmates was cutest, best dressed, funniest, and most likely to succeed, among other categories. The last of those was often the easiest to guess: a kid who had it all figured out and was well on his or her way to an Ivy League university followed by medical school or some other solid, lucrative path.

There isn't a vote for least likely to succeed. The point of these contests isn't to hurt people's feelings, even if they sometimes do. But if there were such a category then the recipient would be equally obvious: that good-for-nothing stoner who was late for every class and barely graduated or didn't at all.

Now imagine being able to buy a share in the future earnings of Mr. or Mrs. "Most Likely" and "Least Likely" as if they were a company. The market prices would be sky high for the former and a pittance for the latter, with good reason. Everyone else would fall somewhere in between. That's exactly how the stock market works, though the vote occurs every minute of every business day.

Whether you rely on conventional wisdom or actual surveys such as "America's Most Admired Companies," a yearly ranking put out by *Fortune* magazine, picking out the corporate crème de la crème isn't hard. But investing in them exclusively happens to be a bad idea. In fact, the least admired companies on such lists tend to outperform the best ones as measured by stock market performance.

Think back on Mr. and Mrs. Most and Least Likely, or to classmates who would have been in the top or bottom five. Some of the bad eggs probably turned things around, and while they may not be fabulously wealthy today, they're doing fine. A few of the super-achievers never really lived up to expectations. Likewise, we pay too much of a premium for respectability in the corporate world. Once a company is a blue chip, it's priced not only appropriately but at a slight premium. Translated into stock selection, going with less popular, less obvious choices is likely to be profitable. Two finance professors combed through several back issues of *Fortune*'s ranking and created a "most admired" and "least admired" portfolio. Shares of the latter outperformed the former by nearly two percentage points a year.[2]

Favoring Wall Street's redheaded stepchildren can be done systematically. One way is to buy companies that essentially are being dumped by larger corporations. Unable to sell them or unwilling to pay a big bill to Uncle Sam in the process of doing so, companies frequently spin off subsidiaries to existing shareholders in a tax-free transaction. The thing is, though, professional investors act strangely when these brand-new companies land in their portfolios. Suddenly a fund that owned, say, a large bank also has the same exact stake in a small or medium-sized insurance company. They already owned it before, of course, but it didn't have its own name and stock ticker. In a value-destroying disservice to their clients (hey, what else is new?), they decide that keeping it in their portfolio is more trouble than it's worth, so they're likely to sell their shares in the near future, putting downward pressure on its price early on.

Meanwhile, a middle-level corporate manager at the former insurance subsidiary suddenly finds himself as the chief executive of a listed company with his or her very own stock options and an even stronger incentive to do well. It may take a while, but the results are usually surprisingly good. The phenomenally successful value investor Joel Greenblatt wrote about his strategy of buying spin-offs in *You Can Be a Stock Market Genius*. Other investors have taken note. There are exchange-traded funds that buy spin-offs exclusively, and an index tracking their performance has existed since December 2006. As of this writing it has appreciated nearly 94 percent compared to just 50 percent for the broad stock market.

Another long-running, well-known, yet still successful way to profit from what's out of favor on Wall Street is to buy the "Dogs of the Dow" each January—the ten highest dividend-yielding stocks among the thirty Dow Jones Industrials. These were usually relatively poor performers in the previous year, allowing their dividend yields to rise (as price falls, yield rises as long as payouts are unchanged). Such a strategy pursued over forty-six years produced nearly three percentage points of excess return compared to the index alone. That's huge. There are many variations on the theme and mutual funds that do the work of picking the dogs for you (just don't overpay for them).

Far worse than investing in the most admired companies is having a preference for the most glamorous or exciting ones. The very first investing book I ever read, Peter Lynch's 1989 bestseller *One Up on Wall Street,* warned investors away from companies with flashy names. It specifically said that companies with an "x" in their name were to be avoided.

It seemed like a throwaway line, but it stuck in my head years later. Just for fun I decided to test it out for an investing column I was writing in 2010 for Britain's *Financial Times*. The results were surprising. I found 109 stocks in the Wilshire 5000, the broadest U.S. stock index, that began or ended with an "x," including a few that did both. Right away I could see that Lynch was on to something. Only 49 of them had been profitable in the previous year. Even after weeding out the money-losing ones, the remaining stocks were far more expensive on measures such as price-to-book or price-to-earnings than the broad market and also a lot more volatile using the measure called beta. In other words, they were both riskier and less desirable on average.

Why would there be a connection? As any Scrabble player can tell you, few words have an "x," so that letter, probably along with "z" and "q," lends itself to made-up, snazzy-sounding names. By my calculation, an "x" appears in company names seventeen times more frequently than in actual English words.

Please don't take the "x" warnings too literally, though. Lynch wrote this in an earlier era, having retired from his phenomenal run atop the Fidelity Magellan Fund before the technology bubble had even begun to inflate. A decade later, ".com" would have served the same role of attracting investors like moths to a flame. A quarter century earlier, in the Swinging Sixties, it was anything with the suffix "tronic" or the word "scientific." Hot companies included Vulcatron, Circuitronics, Astron, and the gratuitously snazzy-sounding "Powerton Ultrasonics." In his classic *A Random Walk Down Wall Street,* Burton Malkiel tells the story of a company that sold vinyl records door-to-door. Its stock price surged 600 percent when it changed its name to Space Tone.[3] The impetus for the trend in names evoking whiz-bang technology was America's reaction to Sputnik and later President Kennedy's pledge to put a man on the moon.

Fans of classic TV shows might remember an episode of *Leave It to Beaver* from 1962 (the peak of the "Kennedy bull market") that delivered a sober warning about the "-tronics." Wally is learning about stocks and bonds in class, so Ward decides that he and Beaver should get a real-life investing lesson. They each take $25 of their savings and he matches the amount to make it $100 in total. He suggests a sober utility stock and then buys it for them. Wally and Beaver dutifully check the newspaper every day to see how it's doing. It barely budges.

Meanwhile, Wally's fast-talking friend Eddie Haskell tells them about a hot electronics company and chides the Cleaver boys for being such squares. Wally and Beaver then start tracking the prices of both, and sure enough Eddie's recommendation rises consistently. They prevail upon their dad to sell the utility for Eddie's choice. Naturally, losses ensue and lessons are learned.

The fact that boring stocks are better seems to be a lesson that each generation has to learn anew. Superior bang for the buck from dowdy, out-of-favor companies was discussed as early as 1934 in *Security Analysis,* the investing classic by Benjamin Graham and David Dodd. Graham was the teacher and has served as the inspiration for the most successful investor of all time, Warren Buffett, so it's safe to say that his theories have worked pretty well in practice.

A 2012 study by the Brandes Institute, "Value vs. Glamour: A Global Phenomenon," updated and reinforced some earlier studies showing much the same thing Graham said but with a lot more algebra and statistical notation.[4] It sliced stocks into price-to-book value by decile for five-year periods ranging from 1968 through 2012. The highest-multiple stocks, a trait associated with glamour, had average annualized returns of 6.5 percent. The other end of the spectrum, the cheapest decile, had annualized returns of 14.8 percent.

Aside from price, another measure of glamour is popularity, particularly among those new to investing. When my son's high school had a stock-picking contest, I asked if I could see his classmates' portfolios. The most popular choices were highfliers such as Tesla, Facebook, and Apple. Not a boring company in sight.

A company called Openfolio that anonymously aggregates results and holdings from thousands of individual investors showed the same thing. Some 77 percent of Tesla shareholders were forty-nine or younger, while 73 percent of ExxonMobil owners were over fifty. But younger investors' love of flashy companies hurt them. During 2014 the portfolios of thirty-five- to forty-nine-year-olds lagged fifty- to sixty-four-year-olds by 2.3 percentage points. And those below twenty-five lagged the older group by a whopping 6.4 percentage points. Live and learn.

Getting burned by a glamorous stock or perhaps a fund that invested in a hot trend—dot-coms, biotechnology, 3-D printing, solar energy, whatever—can elicit the same feelings of shame as losing money in a casino. Please resist the urge to "get your money back" and thus compound the error. Consider it a one-time tuition in the school of investing.

If it makes you feel better, I had an early, expensive lesson in buying something exciting and having it blow up in my face in the most spectacular way. Back when I had just begun working for an investment bank and had put my first, modest annual bonus into a brokerage account, a Canadian fund manager by the name of Attila told me about an exciting company listed in Toronto called YBM Magnex in the business of a cutting-edge technology called "permanent magnets." It had hired a bunch of former Soviet scientists for this promising field. I didn't really know what permanent magnets were, but it sounded cool and the company appeared to be growing like gangbusters.

Excited to finally have some investment capital with which to become an investing "master of the universe," I bought some, and the stock actually went up for a while. I read everything I could lay my hands on about the technology, pored over the accounts, and felt like I was on to such a winner that I proceeded to recommend it to a good friend. Everything was great until the day the FBI raided their office and the chairman, apparently a Ukrainian mobster, vanished. The accounts and the business were fictitious. I felt awful. If I had heeded Peter Lynch's rule of thumb about "x" stocks, I would have stayed away. I immediately adopted another maxim: Never take a stock tip from a guy named Attila.

Your pet company probably isn't tainted by organized crime. Even so, paying for what's popular, and particularly what's glamorous, will boost volatility and eat into returns more often than not. I know you've heard plenty of success stories, but anecdotal evidence and typical results don't jibe for a reason. For every acquaintance you hear bragging about having made a killing, there's another embarrassed to tell you about his own YBM Magnex.

It's exciting to be a part of what you think may be the next big thing—a cure for a crippling disease or a technology set to take the world by storm. It just usually isn't very profitable. That hope, and then some, is in the price by the time you've heard of it on CNBC or the golf course. In the words of economist Max Winkler, those companies are discounting "not only the future but the hereafter."

Habit 4: Reach for Yield

"If the man wants a purple suit, sell him a purple suit."

That morsel of stockbroker wisdom was delivered to me in an exasperated tone by a grizzled older salesman when I was just months into my career as an analyst. I had asked why he had let a client of his buy into a company that I told him had poor prospects. I didn't actually cover it, but had visited its headquarters and left unimpressed (the company went bust the following year).

He explained that the fund manager was interested in buying it anyway and that we had made a bundle securing a block of stock for him. His job was to call his customers every day and generate the commissions that paid our salaries. In our business we couldn't help it if people did dumb things—we just had to make sure we were the ones who made money helping them do it.

There are millions of investors out there in search of a purple suit called income. What they want to see is a monthly or quarterly check that's as large as possible relative to their investment, and they fixate on that rather than on how exactly it's being paid. It may not be until months or years later that they look at their brokerage statement and realize that there was no such thing as a free lunch—no reward without risk. Sometimes that news hits them like a bolt from the blue. More often it's little by little, like death by a thousand cuts. Unfortunately, yield-hungry investors usually are those with a conservative bent, such as retirees who can't afford to lose a bundle, rather than gunslinging, fast-money types. But some unwittingly buy highly risky investments.

Consider the sad story of New Century Financial and the even sadder story of a family friend. An extremely bright and hardworking immigrant physician, she joined a successful medical practice and was living the American dream. Her partners practically had to twist her arm to use the fancy company car they leased for her, when she was happy driving her old clunker. The only thing she spent much money on was trips back to her native India and rescuing dozens of abandoned dogs.

She believed that the streets of America were paved with gold—particularly Wall Street. Bitten by the stock market bug, she had saved enough and made enough trading in technology stocks to retire early in the late 1990s. Then she lost a bundle and was forced to live off a smaller nest egg than she had anticipated. Less money and fixed expenses pushed her to find investments with fat yields, and New Century looked attractive. In 2005 the company showed up in the *Wall Street Journal*'s "Top Guns" list of best-performing stocks. The next year it was the second-largest originator nationally of subprime mortgage loans.

After it converted to a real estate investment trust, New Century's dividend jumped from 23 cents a quarter to $1.50 and its popularity with investors looking for income rose commensurately. By making that legal conversion it was obligated by tax rules to pay out nearly all of its income, and it also shed its tax obligations, passing them to investors. For those reasons, the jump in its payout wasn't really a reflection of greater business prospects.

Its yield at that point reached 10 percent, or around five times as much as a typical stock. It would go even higher. New Century kept on its own books many of the loans it made, increasing its profits but also its risk. By late 2006, with rumbles in the subprime market, it continued reporting profits, but its share price fell and its dividend rose to $1.90 a quarter, making for an almost irresistible 17 percent yield.

Some skeptical articles had begun to appear about the sector and the firm specifically. Short sellers were betting that its shares would fall. That was when our friend told me about her investment in this wonderful firm. She had done her homework (sort of), seeking out arguments that supported her decision while discounting the warnings. (This common mental foible is called confirmation bias.) So my warnings fell on deaf ears as she pointed out that the short sellers warning of disaster had ulterior motives.

She was right about that, of course—public prognostications about stocks are never acts of charity. But short sellers open themselves up to theoretically unlimited losses by borrowing stock and pledging to buy it back at any price, so they need to be pretty careful to last very long in that corner of the market. It's funny in such cases how people fail to take into account that management and people owning the stock and defending it have the opposite ulterior motive. As for taking comfort from the fact that some or even many analysts continue to recommend the stock, well, I hope I've put that misconception to rest.

On February 7, 2007, all hell broke loose when the company reported an unexpected fourth-quarter loss and said it would restate its financials for the previous three quarters. The stock fell by over a third. There was still time to get out, though. A Bear Stearns analyst upgraded New Century on March 1, a week before it plunged another 90 percent and trading was halted. (His own firm would need rescuing a year later, also a victim of the subprime loan crisis.) All investors, but particularly those such as people living on a fixed income who can't easily bounce back from a reduction in principal, have an irrational aversion to realizing a loss. Many held on until New Century's bitter end or close to it.

New Century is an extreme tale, of course. But plenty of income investments with very high yields have risks that aren't apparent to the unsophisticated. Another such category has been royalty trusts, financial vehicles cooked up by oilmen in the late 1970s that mostly seemed to treat their developers like royalty and ordinary investors like peasants. They made a comeback in recent years as energy prices and production surged.

A typical one is SandRidge Mississippian Trust I. Trading at over $36 a share in early 2012, it was yielding 10 percent. It has paid out a cumulative $17.82 at the time I'm writing these words, or over half of what its share price was then. That would be fantastic except for the fact that it also has lost around $34 in value as oil prices fell and its assets depleted. Unlike a normal oil company, it pays out all of its earnings and doesn't go out and drill wells.

I didn't see that caveat in a newsletter aimed at individual income investors called *Leeb Income Millionaire* selling for $399 a year. "Forget CDs that don't even keep pace with inflation. Forget about mutual funds and brokerages where the only ones getting rich are the managers, lining their pockets with your money. I can help you do much better," wrote Stephen Leeb in early 2014, touting a royalty trust. "I would conservatively estimate that investors who recognize this opportunity now could end up running $10,000 up into $50,000 or even $100,000 on one monster trade."

The message was particularly potent at the time, given the puny yields then available on conservative bonds and the recent memory of the financial crisis. Leeb pushed all the right emotional buttons, playing to readers' fear and greed.

Remember when income investors could simply buy CDs and enjoy retirement[?] And you didn't have to worry about losing your life savings on Wall Street before the closing bell? *Leeb Income Millionaire* will bring it all back. You see, my members have become accustomed to the good life, investment returns included . . . It's worth noting that the many of my members are happily retired. These folks demand safe investments that pay dividend yields of 10% a year or better.[5]

The best that I can tell from the details in Leeb's letter, the trust he was recommending (you had to pay $399 to get its name) has suffered horrendous losses as of this writing. The plunging price of oil and natural gas was one reason, but so was the amount left in the ground.

Last but not least in the world of inadvisable income investments are private or unlisted real estate investment trusts. I had the personal experience of being pitched one of these. Though I had already heard about them, I played dumb and asked the nice man sitting in my living room who had just sold me and my wife two perfectly reasonable life insurance policies what they were all about. If I hadn't known better, the sales pitch might have sounded pretty good. Great yields! No volatility! Cash out when they list on the stock exchange! My former colleague Dan McCrum, still with the *Financial Times,* was particularly eloquent in warning about these investments:

Never eat yellow snow; don't insert cutlery into power sockets; order not the Monday night fish special—clear rules to preserve health. Yet for wealth, while financial advice is plentiful, such blanket prescriptions are rare. It usually

depends on the advised's age, disposition and resources. So,
as an act of public service, here is a simple mantra to memo-
rize: do not buy an unlisted real estate investment trust.[6]

Small brokers and financial advisory firms sometimes make
half or more of their profits by selling these unlisted or private
REITs. A good rule of thumb in such cases is that the more lucrative
an investment product is for the person or organization selling it,
the worse it is for a retail investor. In April 2014 a firm that represents buyers of private REITs in securities litigation looked at the
category's return from 1990 through 2013 and found it to be well
under half of an index fund of publicly traded REITs. Yet the yield
pitched to me by the nice man in my living room was higher than
most pay. How does one explain the difference?

He wasn't exactly lying. When they're being set up and sold,
private REITs have lots of money but little or no property from
which to collect rent. They can offer those returns by paying you
back your own money for the first few years. Normally that would
come straight out of the price, but there is no price—the REIT isn't
listed or quoted. That way you can't see its value melting away. Even
worse, you're being paid out of only about 85 percent of your capital,
not 100 percent, since the outrageous commissions paid to their
sellers and originators eat up the rest. So you need to make almost
18 percent just to break even. And if you really need your money
then, in the unlikely event you can sell it to someone before the
REIT gets listed on the stock market (that can take years or may
never happen), you'll probably pay a big commission to sell it to a
"vulture" fund specializing in such situations.

Craig McCann, a former economist with the Securities and Exchange Commission and president of the firm that commissioned

the study on private REIT returns, minced no words in a 2014 interview with a colleague of mine from the *Wall Street Journal*: "Nontraded REITs are costing investors, especially elderly, retired, unsophisticated investors, billions. They're suffering illiquidity and ignorance, and earning much less than what they ought to be earning. No brokerage should be allowed to sell these things."[7]

And no investor interested in leaving Lake Moneybegone should buy them.

Habit 5: Use Exotic Products to Enhance Your Returns

Movies associated with money—*Trading Places, Wall Street,* and *Boiler Room* are three that come to mind—are typically about people who tried to make a fortune and wound up with nothing but trouble. There's only one movie I can think of in which the reverse is true: *Brewster's Millions,* the 1985 comedy starring Richard Pryor and John Candy. Monty Brewster (Pryor) receives a $300 million inheritance with the condition that he spend $30 million in a month with nothing of value to show for it. Giving it away or destroying it aren't allowed. It's a close call, marked by Brewster using much of the cash on a quixotic run for mayor of New York as "None of the Above" (he nearly wins and so almost loses the bet).

Three decades later, Brewster would have had a great way of seeing lots of money evaporate without actually setting it on fire, courtesy of Wall Street. Some investors can't get enough of products with this feature. In terms of turnover, several guaranteed-to-lose funds are among the most popular issues. Their underlying investments are diverse, from banks to the S&P 500 and even a notional measure called the VIX that's used to measure expected volatility in the stock market. What they have in common, though, is that they use borrowed money to enhance returns and reset daily. Some of the most successful ones also bet on declines in some index.

Here's the problem with that. Let's say the S&P 500 rises 1 percent and then falls 1 percent the next day. An exchange-traded note that makes three times the opposite of that will, even before any fees, have lost money, because losing 3 percent and then making 3 percent of that lower amount doesn't get you back to even—you've lost nine one-hundredths of a percent. That doesn't seem like such a high price for the excitement of making a killing. A 5 percent crash in prices, after all, would net you 15 percent, so your investment would beat the market by 20 percentage points in a single day. That logic is a lot like saying you only have to put a measly quarter at a time into the slot machine, but if it hits the jackpot you'll make thousands.

Leveraged notes will lead to ruin just as quickly and surely. The more volatile the underlying investment and the greater the leverage employed, the higher the potential for gaudy overnight profits and the faster one's investment will erode too. One fund, the Direxion Daily Small Cap Bull & Bear 3x ETF, rose 35 percent one day and has gained at least 10 percent on thirty-seven separate trading days at the time of this writing. But its small losses added up in a big way. Someone holding the fund from its debut in November 2008 would have lost 99.9 percent of their money. It took only twelve trading days for the fund to lose half of its value during one really rough (in other words, good for stocks) patch. The fund has had to undergo reverse splits in order to avoid falling below minimum stock market share price requirements by trading at mere pennies. The most volatile of these products—choppiness equals losses—are expected to lose over 90 percent of their value in a normal year.

Naturally, people own these funds for as short as days, hours, or even minutes. Where else can you make a few percent in a few hours? All you have to do is sell it at a higher price to some fool. As tempting as that sounds, the odds of you being the patsy are pretty high. Think about it. In aggregate, all the people who hold these securities for even a short while collectively own it for its whole life. You have to be pretty fortunate to be among the winners rather than the losers. It's like a hot potato that's guaranteed to singe most of the people who touch it a little bit and to give third-degree burns to some.

Other exotic products have the appearance of solidity and safety. Commodity investing is a good example. The world's running out of oil, copper, platinum, and lots of other stuff. It's a hedge against inflation too. Owning something tangible sounds a lot more reassuring than a piece of paper such as a stock, bond, or exchange-traded note. Unfortunately, people don't understand what they're buying.

Take the United States Oil Fund, which was formed in 2006 to represent an interest in crude. The average price of oil that year was $58.30 a barrel, and as I write these words, it's right around $35. Well, at least it didn't lose too much—right? Wrong. Since then an investor in the fund is down by about 90 percent. Despite the financial crisis, an investor in an S&P 500 index fund made about 180 percentage points more than someone owning the fund.

How could the return be so far out of whack with crude oil? Fees are a part of it, as usual, but the main reason is a phenomenon called contango. Investors don't own an actual barrel of oil—forty-two gallons of crude—because that would be very expensive and cumbersome to store. Instead they own a futures contract or a fraction of it. Unfortunately, when the price of crude oil available for delivery or cash settlement in a month is higher than today, then the futures price and the physical price have to converge and be identical on settlement day. If they didn't it would mean free profits for oil traders. That means a small erosion in the value of the future compared to actual oil, and that erosion is repeated each and every month that contango persists. Even if oil prices rise, it's like walking down an up escalator—you have to move pretty quickly just to stay even.

Yet another reassuring investment that's actually more risky and less promising than investors believe is a principal protected note. These sound like something for nothing and are typically marketed to retirees or conservative investors burned by a recent downturn. In a nutshell, they tell you that you can have your cake and eat it too by enjoying the gains of the stock market or perhaps the appreciation of a commodity with a guarantee of no loss. The catch is that you get only a limited amount of upside, so if the market really booms then you're out of luck.

That sounds like a fair trade-off. Unfortunately, there's nothing fair about it. What happens in practice is that a broker takes your money and invests part of it in something called a zero coupon bond that pays no interest but is guaranteed to be worth a certain amount on the date it matures. It's sold at a discount, just like those savings bonds that used to be such popular gifts for newborn babies. The rest is devoted to derivatives that give you only a fraction of the exposure to the actual index or commodity—typically call options. Those may appreciate or expire worthless, but you're guaranteed at least your initial investment back for the bond.

There are three problems with this sweet deal. First, the broker knows how to value these products and you don't, so there is a fat, invisible fee embedded in it. Even the zero coupon bond often isn't an ultra-safe Treasury but a loan given to another unit of the bank. Second, if the bank goes bust—owners of Lehman "principal protected notes" found this out the hard way—you're just another unsecured creditor and may get nothing. Third, your money is tied up in the note so you're out of luck if you need it before it matures.

The financial services industry is forever cooking up innovative products that sound great. Just remember that they are all designed as profit centers and that there's no such thing as a free lunch.

Habit 6: Trade Frequently

We all have our guilty pleasures. One of mine is watching *Fast Money,* the early evening show on CNBC featuring actual traders. One reason is to hear their smart, entertaining banter about the day's financial stories, and another is that I'm usually on a treadmill at the gym after work and it's the best thing on anyway. Beggars can't be choosers—just like when you're jet-lagged in the middle of the night in a faraway hotel room and find that an infomercial for "The Psychic Power Network" is the most entertaining show available. But only one of those programs carries the disclaimer "for entertainment purposes only." No prizes for guessing which it is.

As much as I enjoy *Fast Money,* I treat it like *Monday Night Football*—purely a spectator sport. Judging from the commercials that run during the show—ads for discount brokerages touting their active trader platforms—a significant number of viewers are there to pick up tips that they'll try to apply to their own rapid-fire trading strategies.

In the commercials for those services, a prosperous-looking man (it's always a man) in a beautiful house concentrates intently on green and red lines moving up and down on a computer monitor, and after a few mouse clicks smiles in a way that tells us he just made more money than you did all day or maybe all week. His knockout wife and perfect kids (there are pictures on the tasteful shelves in the background) are presumably off shopping or maybe even skiing in Aspen if he's really on a roll. Who wouldn't want to be that guy?

I would, but I can't, and not only because my employment agreement at the *Wall Street Journal* prohibits me from short-term trading of stocks. I can't in the same way my slight physique precludes me from getting on the field in a football stadium on Monday night. I'd get crushed. Despite the fact that I "know" a good deal about the stock market after a quarter century immersed in the subject, I also know myself well enough not to gamble my retirement savings or kids' college funds on a game stacked so clearly against me.

There are people like the traders on *Fast Money* who make a living at buying and selling stocks, bonds, and options, but they do it for a firm, their own or someone else's. Other people's money is at stake, and they still get paid even if, with all the specialized training, information, and risk management that's at their disposal, they sometimes don't do all that well. That's entirely different than putting your own savings at risk—quite aside from the fact that you don't get a nice stipend from CNBC for regaling sweaty journalists with your exploits.

I understand the appeal of trying your hand at trading. The thing I love about the financial markets—the reason reading and writing about them every day doesn't get old—is that they're the ultimate game of skill. Millions of people, plus lots of computers these days, are trying to win in what is a zero-sum game that never ends.

Even some fairly conservative investors I know, including professionals, maintain some "play money" on the side that they can afford to lose in order to get the urge out of their system. On the day I walked into my boss's office to retire from investment banking back in 2002, he asked if I would accept some other job at the firm instead. I hesitated and very nearly put my journalism plans on hold by asking him if I could be a proprietary trader, investing millions of dollars of the firm's money.

I had always had the itch to try. No longer having that option, I've been participating in a stock market game for close to a decade, doing pretty well. Of course, a bad bet in my game will never lead to an ulcer, a sleepless night, or an awkward conversation with my wife about having to cut back financially. My play money account is probably a lot like my wildly successful online fantasy poker career. The one time I tried to replicate my virtual success with real cash in Las Vegas I was tapped out faster than you can say "double belly-buster straight draw."

Typical results for individuals who trade frequently with their own money suggest the same pattern. In a study by economists Brad Barber and Terrance Odean, who examined the records of 66,465 households with accounts at a discount brokerage, there was a direct inverse correlation between trading frequency and returns even before considering commissions. They sorted investors into five groups or quintiles according to how often they traded. While average investor turnover at the time was 75 percent a year—a figure that already is too high to be healthy, in my opinion—the most active group traded at three times that average and was about a hundred times more active than those in the lowest quintile. The only group to make a positive market-adjusted return—a very slight one—was the one with the lowest turnover. The difference between the most and least frenetic traders was a massive 5.7 percentage points annually.

Those numbers, which are the difference between a healthy return and living in the slums of Lake Moneybegone, are no fluke, and they don't even include another major drag on returns: taxes. Short-term capital gains are higher than long-term ones, so frequent trading has to be more profitable than buy-and-hold investing to begin with. But another finding by the same researchers genuinely surprised me. They looked at ten thousand investors at a large discount broker and the subsequent performance of stocks investors bought versus the ones they sold. The average difference between them was negative 3.3 percent annually, and that was before counting transaction costs. Many how-to books on trading or biographies of successful speculators advise you to "sell your losers and keep your winners." Of course that only reflects those investments' performance before the day you hit that button. Based on these figures, this old chestnut is precisely backwards.

Any way you slice it, frequent trading is a loser's game. It's the equivalent of starting out a few percent in the hole and trying to climb back above the passive market return. Even before taxes, you would have to be very lucky—or maybe even psychic—to clear that hurdle consistently.

Habit 7: Use a "System"

I had intended to call this book *Rule the Freakin' Markets*. But then I remembered that Michael Parness beat me to it. Who is Parness? If you take him at his word, he went from being homeless to parlaying a few thousand dollars in savings into $7 million through a proprietary trading system he developed. He was generous enough to share this valuable knowledge with others for the low, low price of $224.75 on DVD plus shipping and handling. Guidance on what to buy and sell and when, his "Ninja Trading" service, ran an additional $429 a month. A few years ago Parness was all over the radio with his advertisements for "Trend Trading to Win."

I can neither verify nor disprove his trading claims, but Parness certainly made plenty of money from people eager for stock market riches. According to the introduction to the 2004 reprint of his book, he had by that time sold over 150,000 copies of his system on various media and was moving 5,000 of them a month. Even before the "Ninja Trading" revenue, that was $33 million. And he encouraged his ninjas to use a brokerage firm that compensated him for commissions—a source of income that may have dwarfed those others, as you'll see.

After hearing the advertisements in his thick Queens accent on the radio a few times a day back in 2007 (no offense intended, by the way—I'm a Queens boy myself), I just had to track him down for the investing column I was writing at the time. He was eager to be interviewed and talked my ear off.

It became clear pretty quickly, though, that his system had some holes in it. At the time I interviewed him, I reviewed six rapid-fire stock trades that he says he recommended during a single day. He also recommended twelve stock futures trades that day. Parness told me his average client had a portfolio of $20,000. At a typical discount brokerage commission (I don't know how much his "preferred" firm charged), six buys and sells a trading day would chew through the entire $20,000, not even including the futures trades, which might be costly for a retail investor. That means the annualized rate of return would have to be 100 percent on his recommendations just to break even. And that's before taxes.

"Yeah, but if you followed the trades you'd make a lot more than that," sputtered Parness when presented with those calculations. [8]

That's simply not credible. In that case, profits would simply be a function of a trader's bankroll. Parness, with whatever pool of money he had by then—call it $7 million or $33 million—really would rule the freakin' markets and would make far more profit with much less trouble, not to mention legal risk, trading his own account. And of course he would earn multiples of that charging a 2 percent fee and 20 percent of profits as hedge funds do for managing other people's money. Naturally, no hedge fund ever has made triple-digit returns with any consistency.

An entertaining and practical explanation of why traders with relatively little money have extremely short careers can be found in my favorite investing book of all, *Reminiscences of a Stock Operator*. Nominally a piece of fiction and a great read, it's actually a thinly disguised biography of speculator Jesse Livermore (Larry Livingston) written by Edwin Lefèvre.

In the early part of the book, Livingston gets his start in what were called bucket shops, which were eventually outlawed, before the turn of the twentieth century. Small-time speculators would show up and routinely get wiped out by making what amounted to leveraged bets on stocks. Armed with a ticker tape but not actually buying stocks for their clients (their cash went into a bucket), the bucket shops' clients easily realized gains or, more frequently, losses of 100 percent from small price moves. By the way, the real-life Livermore became fabulously wealthy but then went bust, committing suicide in the men's room of New York's Sherry-Netherland Hotel.

Another trading service that advertised heavily around the same time as Trend Trading to Win and also contacted me directly in the hope of gaining some publicity was GorillaTrades. Its mascot was a man in a gorilla suit, and its pitchman, before he died, was Monkees lead singer Davy Jones ("I'm a Believer! You'll be too!").

I know I'm being a pedant, but, technically speaking, monkeys aren't apes like gorillas. Humans, by the way, are, and a *Business-Week* investigation in 2007 described how the trading service made monkeys out of plenty of us hairless apes. They showed, for example, that GorillaTrades would have lost a subscriber money in 2006—a year when the market rose strongly. Their trades also lagged in the two other years they checked. What's more, *BusinessWeek* didn't calculate the cost of trading as I did, only the gains and losses on the recommendations themselves. Like Parness, founder Ken Berman claimed to have made a fortune trading, turning $250,000 into $5 million, according to the exposé.

"A lot of people don't know what they're doing," said Berman. "They really don't understand the concept of investing. We're trying to teach the concepts at the same time as the stock picks."

And charge them $600 for the privilege. I hope what I'm pointing out to you is crystal clear and that you'll apply the same logic when you come across any system offering you trading riches. The amounts that they charge vary widely, but the real cost is the hole they're likely to blow in your savings. Many people probably walk away after a small loss, but others hop from system to system as if searching for El Dorado always over the horizon. Some suffer far more serious repercussions.

I remember sitting at home in London one weekend with my oldest son, then a newborn, snoozing on my shoulder when some friends of my mother-in-law who were on vacation stopped by to see him. The husband casually told me that he was retiring to trade options full-time. Alarmed, but trying not to raise my voice and wake the baby, I asked him why and what he knew about derivatives.

He said he had attended seminars with a woman who had made a lot of money on Wall Street trading them, and that she had shown him how to make a very nice income using her "system."

I pointed out all the obvious flaws with this. Why wasn't she still working on Wall Street? Was he aware that traders using far more computing power than he had available often lost money on options? Did he know that writing puts or calls exposed him to theoretically unlimited losses? Speaking as the head of a research department at a major investment bank at the time, I would have thought my opinion carried some weight, but he was already mentally counting the riches he would amass and wasn't going to be dissuaded.

This was in early 1999, near the peak of an almost uninterrupted eighteen-year secular bull market. Lots of people thought they were investing savants, and I had quite a few conversations with people headed for a nasty fall. Still, here was someone who possibly stood to lose everything due to the nature of the investments. Sure enough, he did—all of his life savings are gone and, exacerbated by a serious illness, he and his wife had to declare bankruptcy.

There is no such thing as a system that turns risky strategies into consistent gains. These days there are funds that place hundreds of thousands of trades far more quickly than any human possibly could using algorithms written by some of the most sophisticated mathematicians and computer scientists on the planet with a cost per trade that is smaller than any retail investor can receive. They manage to eke out pennies or fractions thereof on most trades. It's futile and absolutely unnecessary to try beating them at this game.

As I've already demonstrated, the very practice of rapid-fire trading is hazardous to your wealth. Paying an extra fee for the privilege of being told what to buy and sell is an even worse idea.

There are very few trading geniuses out there and none of them are giving away their secrets.

What, you don't believe me? Don't take my word for it—just listen to the very pitchman that Parness had working for him in his heyday, football great Joe Theismann. Even in the sport at which he excelled, Theismann said he doubted that there really was such a thing. "A genius is someone like Norman Einstein."

CHAPTER ELEVEN

BUT WAIT, THERE'S MORE

Like clockwork—though "broken clockwork" may be a more apt description—I always seem to get the phone calls at the most inconvenient times. I don't mean those from my mother-in-law or the ones we all receive during dinner from charities or from businesses skirting the "do not call" registry. These are on my cell phone from a very nice but very persistent lady at a discount brokerage firm. I'm always in the middle of something and she always wants to "talk about my portfolio."

Since I accepted a cash bonus and some free trades when I opened the account, I feel like an ingrate telling her to stop calling, so I always explain I'm busy and ask if she can try again in a few weeks. So far she hasn't gotten the hint that I don't need or want her help. My account is in a stable of low-cost exchange-traded funds and the dividends get reinvested automatically. In other words, the whole thing runs on autopilot, never costs me a cent in commissions, and I feel no need to check it.

More to the point, I shouldn't check it, because that probably would start costing me money far exceeding the broker's modest trading fees. Using tracking software, online investment advisor SigFig studied users and found that clients who monitored their portfolios daily earned 0.2 percent a month less than average. Those who did it twice daily earned 0.4 percent less. With the minimum $100,000 deposit required for the $300 account-opening bonus at this particular broker, the latter gap would erode that cash award in just nine months. In ten years it would consume twenty-five times the windfall.

And this is compared to the typical user who checks his or her portfolio eight times a month. With apps on our phones these days, the ability to watch our net worth bounce up and down far exceeds what it was in the era when most people found out the good or bad news through a brokerage statement they received monthly in the mail. It turns out that even that is too frequent for our own good. Research by Professor Michaela Pagel of Columbia University has determined that the "model" retirement saver should look at his or her investments only once a year.

I seriously recommend taking that advice to heart. You may not be able to restrict yourself to peeking so infrequently, but I would challenge you to tell me why you need constant updates. The irony is that, between life-cycle funds, dividend reinvestment, and the services of advisors, either robotic or human, a retirement saver these days can get away with being blissfully ignorant of his or her portfolio's gyrations even though doing the opposite has never been simpler.

The obvious reason for avoiding the temptation to peek is that you're likely to do more than just look, and activity is costly. Understanding that unhealthy tendency is particularly important given what this chapter is about. While avoiding big errors and earning something closer to the market return will drag you out of Lake Moneybegone, I've hinted throughout this book that it's possible to do even better. One reason I saved it for last is that the advice I'm about to give you isn't the low-hanging fruit I've discussed so far: doing and paying as little as possible, ignoring the pundits, embracing risk at the appropriate times, and so forth.

These additional return-boosting techniques look fantastic on paper but are more demanding and may well backfire if you're the type to constantly monitor and fret over your portfolio. In fact—and I know this sounds odd—that's the reason they still work. I've urged you to be skeptical about supposed free lunches in the investing world. (Okay, maybe the $300 I got from my online broker is an exception if the nice lady doesn't give me a stroke.) What I'm going to describe, though, is the equivalent of a cheap lunch if you possess the proper temperament. If you don't, it could give you heartburn instead.

I'm going to start with what is probably the most difficult of these techniques. So, if you're ready, let's get on the long and bumpy road between Lake Moneybegone and Graham-and-Doddsville. That latter fictional town was coined by Warren Buffett, who learned how to value companies from Benjamin Graham at Columbia University (Buffett got an A-plus in his class). Graham, along with David Dodd, wrote the investing classic *Security Analysis,* considered by many to be the seminal work on the subject. I have a copy, though unfortunately not a first edition (which really would be a great investment, as they fetch $8,000 or more from collectors).

Even the fifth edition I bought for 50 cents at a garage sale, though, arguably is the most profitable book ever published. Buffett showed why in a speech given to commemorate the fiftieth anniversary of its publication in 1984 titled "The Superinvestors of Graham-and-Doddsville." He began by addressing the notion that markets are efficient. Starting with the same national coin-flipping contest example I cited earlier in the book, Buffett quipped that the same result would accrue to hundreds of millions of coin-flipping orangutans. But what, he asks, would efficient market zealots say if a disproportionate number of the orangutans lived in the Omaha, Nebraska, zoo?[1]

That cluster would warrant some investigation. Likewise, a cluster of some of the best-performing investors in the world, all of whom were disciples of Benjamin Graham, suggests not luck but a violation of market efficiency. In an article published alongside the speech, Buffett gives results of seven investors, all of whom ran partnerships that beat the market handily over various periods. Their gross returns averaged 23.5 percent compared to 7.5 percent for the Dow Jones Industrials.

All were disciples of Graham, and their shared discipline is called "value investing," a term with myriad interpretations. In theory, it means paying less for companies than their intrinsic value. In practice, it can mean something as simple as blindly selecting stocks with low price-to-earnings ratios. Calculations by money manager and author James P. O'Shaughnessy looked at what would happen if one bought only the cheapest tenth of stocks each year from 1964 through 2009 on that measure. The compound annual return was an excellent 16.3 percent, or five percentage points better than the market overall. Each dollar invested that way would be worth seven and a half times as much as one invested passively at the end of that time span and an astounding eighty-five times more than the opposite strategy of buying only the most expensive tenth of stocks.[2]

Still better results have been achieved by value managers like Buffett who look for "growth at a reasonable price." That means balancing low price with high quality. A Buffett disciple might drive a subcompact Kia Rio with manual windows and an AM radio but not a far cheaper Yugo ($3,999 new in 1985) that, while it seemed like a bargain, began falling apart almost as soon as you drove it off the lot.

Finding quality is a bit more complicated than buying what's cheapest, but it's been worth it for Buffett. Money manager Joel Greenblatt reportedly earned young-Buffett-like returns over several years in his first hedge fund, approaching 40 percent annually, owning a very concentrated and volatile portfolio of promising value stocks. More recently, he has written books on a simple, mechanical approach dubbed the "Magic Formula" that tries to select companies that are cheap and of good quality. (Yes, it is possible to quantify quality—sort of.) The simulated returns over eleven years were double that of the stock market, and he claims even better results over a longer period. Greenblatt maintains a Web site that allows retail investors to use the formula for picking their own stocks.

But here's the rub: There are long stretches when the strategy does awfully. That causes people to drop out. Someone strictly following it may look and feel like a dope for two or three years at a stretch, not just failing to beat the stock market but lagging it sharply. That, explains Greenblatt, is why it works—a concept he calls "time arbitrage."

"If value investing worked every day and every month and every year, of course, it would get arbitraged away, but it doesn't," he said in an interview. "It works over time, and it's quite irregular. But it does still work like clockwork; your clock has to be really slow."

Is your clock really, really slow? If so, then you're exceptional. A study by Jason Hsu, cofounder of a firm called Research Affiliates that I'll discuss more in a moment, calculated the tendency of investors to drop out of such strategies. In a nutshell, value mutual funds did much better than the market during the period from 1991 through 2013, but not investors in those funds. Their "dollar-weighted return"—the one that accounts for them zigging when they should have zagged and losing patience with the funds—was worse than the overall market. And the difference in the reported and underlying return was worse for value funds than other types of funds. In other words, they really try your patience, which is why your temperament is especially important if you think you want to try reaching for that extra return.

Robert Arnott, the chief executive and the other cofounder of Research Affiliates, is all too familiar with the tendency of investors to cut and run. In one of our conversations he emphasized that "markets reward discomfort." I think that's really profound. What he meant is those fantastic gains come at the price of gnawing uncertainty. Then he trotted out a famous quote from the Rothschild I mentioned earlier in the book. Many people will recognize the more-cited first half of it, but the second half is key:

"The time to buy is when there's blood in the streets, *even if the blood is your own.*"

In other words, you need to stick with it, particularly if you've personally lost money in a downturn or done worse than the market. But Arnott isn't exactly a value investor, or even an investor in the traditional sense. Instead, he and his colleagues came up with a then very controversial idea in a 2005 paper. As I write this, Arnott and his company have licensed it to firms using it to manage some $115 billion or so in investments, so the evidence has won over the skeptics.

Throughout this book I've encouraged you to pay as little as possible and do as little as possible to make sure your nest egg grows. My recommended vehicle for doing that has been low-cost index funds—the cheaper the better. For example, the largest exchange-traded fund tracking the main U.S. stock index, the SPDR S&P 500 ETF, has a commendably low expense ratio of 0.09 percent (you'll pay $9 in expenses a year for each $10,000 invested). Now I'm going to suggest paying a bit extra for a type of fund that isn't quite as passive.

You may remember Michael Mauboussin's criticism of index funds: that it makes it impossible to beat the market. He's right, of course. You'll be getting better returns than the vast majority of investors in the long run, but will very slightly lag whatever index you try to track because of expenses. Arnott's criticism of these traditional indices is different. It's that they encapsulate all the dumb things that less disciplined investors do. An index isn't just a number on a screen but a combination of hundreds or thousands of stock prices. Sometimes they get out of whack. For example, people who chased technology stocks to triple-digit valuations and then saw them crash back to earth caused those companies to become an irrationally large part of the index for a while. Even the most conservative, dyed-in-the-wool John Bogle acolytes unwittingly went along for the ride.

On a lesser scale, the same effect acts as a constant, slow grind on returns. Whatever industry was last year's hot theme, for example, got to be a bigger part of the index. But in most cases its value rose by more than its sales or earnings, reflecting investors' opinion. The inverse happened with whatever fell out of favor. But investors, as we know, are often wrong.

What Arnott and his colleagues proposed was a modified or "fundamental" index that weighted companies not on their market value, which may represent faulty human judgment, but instead on some other measure. It can be sales, earnings, employees—almost anything besides price, really. Each time the fundamental index changes its weightings, typically once a year, the same criteria are reapplied. In other words, while an index fund tracking the S&P 500 requires hardly any maintenance at all, except if companies enter and exit the index, Arnott's funds rise and fall in the same way but then rejigger themselves according to some other criteria. In that way, they avoid simply owning more of what all the people buying or selling stocks thought should be more or less valuable, respectively. The people who made them go up or down are, after all, the same silly ones who zig when they should zag and live in Lake Moneybe-gone. Buffett put it best in his Graham-and-Doddsville speech:

"When the price of a stock can be influenced by a 'herd' on Wall Street with prices set at the margin by the most emotional person, or the greediest person, or the most depressed person, it is hard to argue that the market always prices rationally. In fact, market prices are frequently nonsensical."

Fundamental indices are still indices and don't need a highly paid manager capable of cognitive errors to decide what does or doesn't belong. They rely on a formula. Naturally, though, trying to avoid the effect of the herd costs a little bit more, since such a fund has to automatically buy and sell stocks to get back to its fundamental weighting. The expense ratio for the largest ETF in the category, the PowerShares FTSE RAFI US 1000, is 0.39 percent, or 0.3 percentage points more than the leading S&P 500 ETF. But even with that headwind, it earns its keep. Since its inception in December 2005 through February 2016 it had a total return of over 98 percent, compared to barely 87 percent for the S&P 500.

Arnott's firm and others that design clever funds like this to put a twist on indices naturally get a cut for coming up with the idea. Although Arnott doesn't like being lumped in with his competitors, the broad category is called "smart beta," and it is one of the hottest trends in investing. Plenty of famous finance professors have lent their names to funds in the category. John Bogle, the father of the index fund, isn't a believer, and isn't amused, either. He has called the idea a "gimmick."

Perhaps some funds are, but the basic idea behind fundamental indexing is sound. It turns out, though, that there's an even simpler way to beat a traditional index most of the time. While most indices are "capitalization weighted"—ranked in order of size of the companies they include—just buying every stock in an index in equal measure has been shown to be superior. Doing that means you put less of your investment on those companies that happen to be large and more on those that happen to be small. For example, since Apple is as valuable and hence as represented in the S&P 500 as around a hundred of the smallest stocks combined as I write this, it has a lot of effect on an index fund. The five hundredth smallest stock, meanwhile, literally is like a rounding error—you may as well not bother owning any of it.

An equal-weighted portfolio would have the same amount of both of them. An exchange-traded fund set up to do that, the Guggenheim S&P 500 Equal Weight ETF (RSP), beat even the FTSE RAFI US 1000 fund over the period I described above, gaining over 107 percent. The only problem with this approach is that if it ever got very popular, the number of dollars chasing small companies would be unsustainable.

Of course, you could just do what Aaron Hillegass did to get a far better 350 percent return over ten years. He's not even a fund manager—he's a mathematician and an author of computer programming guides. Having read about efficient markets, he designed a program to randomly choose twenty stocks with no human input. A Web site known as Marketocracy that follows individual portfolios ranked him as one of its top virtual traders, but unlike the other winners, he had no stock tips to share. "Chance is always your master. It's just an act of accepting it," he told *Forbes* magazine in an interview.[3]

His success probably was no fluke because there's evidence that a lack of strategy can be a strategy in and of itself. In fact, as I mentioned a few chapters back, Arnott and his team conducted a similar experiment themselves. Between 1964 and 2011 they re-created one hundred portfolios with thirty stocks each picked randomly from a list of a thousand potential companies each year. These "monkey portfolios" did surprisingly well, as ninety-six out of a hundred beat the capitalization-weighted index of the same thousand stocks.

In theory, then—though I don't encourage you to actually try this—an investor could throw darts at a newspaper and pick twenty or thirty stocks at random, purchasing an equal dollar amount of each one, and do nothing else. It probably would work. Surprisingly, the complication with any such strategy comes when you express an actual opinion about the company that pops up on your screen. Joel Greenblatt has noted that investors using his Magic Formula screens will often see a company or industry about which they have a negative opinion and omit that one. Typically, though, portfolios with even a little bit of human input didn't do as well. We really are bad investors, even when we just think we're making what seems like a harmless tweak.

The final potentially market-beating strategy I'm about to mention is probably the easiest of the three when it comes to avoiding human interference. Everyone likes getting a check in the mail, making a portfolio focused on dividend-paying stocks a relatively pleasant way to eke out extra return.

From 1972 through March 2015, a $10,000 investment in a basket of only dividend-paying stocks in the S&P 500 compounded into $465,000 according to Ned Davis Research. You're probably guessing that they did better than those that don't pay them, but how big do you think the difference might be? After all, some of the fastest-growing companies eschew dividends—Apple didn't pay one for the seventeen years that include the time it rehired Steve Jobs and came up with the iPod and the iPhone. That proved to be a happy exception, but I won't keep you in suspense any longer: A basket of dividend payers was worth fifteen times as much as the nonpayers. That is a gigantic difference.

Taking the embrace of dividends too far can be dangerous, though. I've heard many people fall in love with a stock just because it had an eye-popping yield of 5 percent or higher. You really should look a dividend gift horse in the mouth when the numbers are so big. Those gaudy dividends aren't conjured out of thin air, after all. A company with such a hefty payout may be forced to cut it, and the yield may be so high only because it happens to be facing some kind of distress. In fact, a basket of all dividend payers grew to an eye-watering 215 times as much as a basket of those companies with the highest quintile of dividend yields.

What an investor should really do, then, is buy companies that pay dividends but avoid those that might not be sustainable. In the forty years from 1972 through 2012, a basket of companies that either initiated or grew their dividend earned an extra one-third as much as just a basket of dividend payers and forty-seven times as much as companies that cut or eliminated their dividends, also according to Ned Davis Research.

Rather than picking through individual stocks, investors can buy index funds that try to replicate those characteristics. The S&P 500 Dividend Aristocrats, for example, include companies that have raised their dividends for at least twenty-five years in a row. That group includes plenty of dull but reliable household names such as McDonald's, Coca-Cola, Procter & Gamble, and Chevron. Over the ten years ending August 2015 they had an annualized return three percentage points better than the broad stock market. That pace would have left an investor with a third more money. Extrapolating it over forty years would leave an investor with nearly three times as much.

There are a lot of variations on the dividend theme. I counted nearly forty exchange-traded funds with varying approaches. I'm not endorsing any specific product but will divulge that I personally own (and buy more of regularly through automatic reinvestment) shares of the SPDR S&P Dividend exchange-traded fund (ticker symbol SDY) that has a formula similar to the "Aristocrats." In the process of doing my research, though, I found that the cheapest fund in the category in terms of expense ratio was the Schwab U.S. Dividend Equity ETF (ticker symbol SCHD), and I'm considering reinvesting my future dividends into that fund instead.

Unlike fundamental indices and value, dividend investing should be ulcer-free—right? Not always. In looking back at the one-decade history of the fund I own personally and comparing it to an ETF that passively owned the entire S&P 500, for example, I noticed that it did better overall but that its one-month trailing performance was worse nearly half of the time. There were 134 days when I could have logged into my brokerage account and found it trailing the plain index fund by a whopping five percentage points over a month. Even with something as dull as this, then, checking how your dividend fund is doing too often could short-circuit those superior gains.

If you weren't aware of that temporarily poor performance, though, then it would be like a tree falling in the woods. I'm reminded of the old joke about the newlyweds who travel to Las Vegas on their honeymoon. Unable to sleep, the husband tells his wife he's going down to the casino for a while. He stops at the roulette table and puts $5 on red. Having guessed correctly, he doubles his money. Then he keeps playing, putting the $10 on red, winning again, and so forth. By the tenth spin of the wheel a large crowd has gathered to cheer him on and, as he again guesses correctly, his bankroll swells to $5,000. By the fifteenth round he has nearly $165,000 in chips on the table and the nervous casino manager has come out to observe the spectacle. This is already enough for the man to pay off his mortgage, but, being on such a roll, he decides to give Lady Luck one more chance. Unfortunately, he loses. When he returns to his wife in the hotel room, she asks how he did.

"Not bad—I lost five bucks."

In real life, people show a lot less equanimity about losses, even with house money. The formula for success in unlocking extra gains from volatile strategies such as value, fundamental indexing, and dividend investing would seem to be remaining oblivious to the market's ups and downs.

Unfortunately, never seeing a negative number on your brokerage statement is unrealistic. There have been periods exceeding ten years when, even with dividends, U.S. stocks showed paper losses. A moderately higher pain threshold will reduce the odds but not eliminate them.

It's hard not to peek for years on end at your portfolio. Your odds of losing willpower are highest when your local paper has the headline "Stocks Plunge," and that's the very worst time to look. And, practically speaking, most people will check their portfolio at least annually in order to file income taxes.

Many people who walk into a casino promise themselves that they'll stop if they lose more than a certain amount. Whether they actually follow through is another matter, but it makes sense since you're almost guaranteed to lose if you stay there long enough. Doing the same for investing is a recipe for disaster, though. Almost no matter what number you make your line in the sand, there's a good chance of crossing it one day. History shows that it will be precisely the wrong time to do that.

James O'Shaughnessy looked at the fifty worst months in stock market history going back to 1871 in terms of trailing ten-year stock market return. The average annual loss over those periods was 4.6 percent, which is truly awful, turning an initial $100,000 into a little over $62,000 including dividends. The times when these losses are fresh have been the best ones to be fully invested, though. Over the next three, five, and ten years there were zero instances of a negative total return. The average annual gain was about 15 percent annually.[4]

That's pretty compelling, but keeping your cool is hard even after being presented with those numbers. It takes a fairly rare mental makeup to extract the extra returns that have enriched people like the superinvestors of Graham-and-Doddsville. What's more, the ability to be greedy when others are fearful isn't an attribute like, say, having blue eyes or not. Instead, it's more of a continuum like height. Not only aren't most people tall enough to play center in the NBA, but some (like me) aren't even able to reach the shelf above their refrigerator without standing on a chair.

What's an investor to do? While you can't get taller past a certain age, you can get wiser. The next chapter will try to deliver what is, literally and figuratively, some age-old wisdom.

CHAPTER TWELVE

FAR FROM THE
MADDENING CROWD

You get some funny calls when you write for a newspaper. Most are from perfectly nice, friendly people with a question, but there are some angry or even deranged ones too, so my guard is always slightly raised when the phone rings and I don't recognize the number. Every once in a while, if you're lucky, the person on the other end of the line is really special.

That was the case eleven years ago on the Monday morning after a column I had written appeared in *Barron's* magazine, the investing weekly. The faint, raspy voice of the man who wanted some more details threw me right away. It sounded like I was talking to Methuselah, and it turns out I wasn't that far off. When we finished chatting he asked if I could send him some of my source material.

"Sure—what's your e-mail?"

There was a long pause. He asked if I could fax it to him instead. Even in 2005, though, I had no idea where to find the machine tucked away in our newsroom, not to mention the time to print out documents and feed them into the tray. I insisted on using e-mail and he slowly—very slowly—recited his address to me.

"I-R-V-I-N-G ... then there's a period ... K-A-H-N ... then there's a thing that looks like an 'a' with a circle around it ..."

I finally got the whole thing but wondered who this guy was. Googling his name, I found out that I had been speaking to a living Wall Street legend. Then age ninety-eight, he not only was the oldest money manager still in business but had gotten his start working for Benjamin Graham, the father of value investing and a second father to Warren Buffett. He was Graham's first research assistant and helped him write the 1934 classic *Security Analysis*.

Before that, though, back in the summer of 1929, he made his first big stock trade while still a clerk, selling short (betting on a falling price with borrowed shares) Magma Copper, the Tesla of its era. The market peaked just weeks later and crashed that October, doubling his money.

I was recounting this tale to a colleague a few years later while working at the *Financial Times* and she asked why I didn't give him a call and ask him what he thought about the world. After all, we were smack in the middle of the worst financial crisis since he had made that lucky trade at the start of his career. It turned out he was still at it and pleased to share his wisdom. He was telling his clients at the time to ignore the headlines and buy beaten-down, high-quality stocks. With the benefit of hindsight, that turned out to be great advice, though at the time unemployment was ticking higher and economists thought the U.S. economy remained in a deep recession.

What I also found interesting was his take on his masterful 1929 trade. He dismissed it as a dumb move on his part. Rather than basing it on analysis—he didn't really know anything yet, just having started in the business—Kahn relied on his perceptions. Young stock traders were zipping in and out of the market. "They were all borrowing money and having a good time and being right for a few months and, after that, you know what happened," he said in an NPR interview.[1]

I also sought out Roy Neuberger, then 106 years old (he retired at the tender age of 99). The fund manager had shorted Radio Corporation of America, the Apple of its day, in the Great Crash of 1929. Too frail to speak, his protégé Marvin Schwartz, a sixty-eight-year-old whippersnapper, told me the secret to his success. "In almost each and every instance, he advised us to buy in what would be a passing negative period," he said.[2]

Neuberger wrote in his memoirs that memories of 1929 helped his firm, Neuberger Berman, trounce competitors after the 1987 stock market crash.

I was too late to speak with yet another long-lived investing legend, Sir John Templeton, who had passed away just a year earlier at the age of ninety-five. Back in September 1939 when Nazi tanks were rolling into Poland, he borrowed $10,000 to buy a hundred shares in every issue on the New York Stock Exchange trading for less than a dollar. He made a killing. In early 2000, when only old fogies who "didn't get it" weren't in the market, Templeton sold all of his technology stocks just ahead of that bubble's bursting. His motto was "to buy when others are despondently selling and to sell when others are greedily buying." The right time to make the plunge was "at the point of maximum pessimism."[3]

Being profitably contrarian isn't unique to the twentieth century. N. M. Rothschild of the fabulously wealthy family—yeah, the one from the card game—increased that hoard during the Napoleonic

Wars. He famously said, "Buy on the sound of cannons, sell on the sound of trumpets." Going back even further than that—to the time of the world's very first stock market in seventeenth-century Amsterdam—a keen observer named Joseph de la Vega described herd behavior, bubbles, and crashes in his book *Confusión de Confusiones* that seem entirely familiar today. Of emotional investors he wrote, "They will sell without knowing the motive; and they will buy without reason. They will find what is right and they will err for fault of their own."

He also spoke of the excessive regret that Meir Statman told us is a trait of poor investors. "Unexpected news arrives, and shareholders panic. Shares are sold, but shareholders soon feel a sense of despair; they feel mistaken, and after some time they discover that they were wrong in their dealings."

He saw irrational exuberance three hundred years before Alan Greenspan uttered those words:

"They are not afraid of the fires, nor do they fear the earthquake."

And blind panic as well:

"They exaggerate the risks so much that the onlookers think they are witnessing death, even to the point to preferring death and disaster to anything else."[4]

Having the gumption to resist the pull of the crowd has been a rare and, as I hope I've convinced you, extremely profitable trait throughout history. If it seems it's even rarer than it once was, there's a good reason for that. When we read about the exploits of an "investor" today in the newspaper—someone who not only pits himself against the market but has enough cash to warrant media coverage—we now usually mean someone tasked with managing other people's money. However gutsy and contrarian he or she may be, the people who entrusted them with their savings usually aren't and often will yank the money away when their emotions get the better of them.

That's one of the reasons why some hedge funds are able to amass more impressive track records than mutual funds. The barriers to getting in and getting out are significantly more complicated and time-consuming than a few keyboard clicks, and so they're able to pursue strategies that take a while to work out. Even they get undercut, though. The case of Dr. Michael Burry described in Michael Lewis's *The Big Short* stands out. He was absolutely correct about how the subprime mortgage crisis would play out and was the first to bet against the dodgy loans—the sort of trades that would make John Paulson a multibillionaire and Wall Street legend. But his investors lost patience before the bets paid off.

It's no coincidence, then, that the most successful investor today and, measured in total wealth, of all time is eighty-five-year-old Warren Buffett. His investment vehicle represents permanent capital. It never pays dividends or faces redemptions. On the not infrequent occasions when investors have fretted that he was losing his touch they could simply sell the shares on the stock exchange to someone who felt otherwise. Buffett isn't bothered or affected by the ensuing fluctuations in Berkshire Hathaway's stock price or, for that matter, about the gyrations of the broader stock market overall. He has cited an allegory that his mentor Benjamin Graham put in his classic *The Intelligent Investor* as the advice that is "most conducive to investment success."

Graham said one should imagine market prices as coming not from millions of people but a single, emotionally unstable business partner, Mr. Market. Sometimes he's euphoric and other times despondent. Sometimes he will want to sell you his interest at a low price, and other times he will want to buy yours at a ridiculously high one. Luckily, he won't be offended if you ignore him.

But, like Cinderella at the ball, you must heed one warning or everything will turn into pumpkins and mice: Mr. Market is there to serve you, not to guide you. It is his pocketbook, not his wisdom, that you will find useful. If he shows up some day in a particularly foolish mood, you are free to ignore him or to take advantage of him, but it will be disastrous if you fall under his influence.[5]

Ignoring the market's siren song is easier said than done, of course, and people mostly succumb to it at great cost. Having read this far, you've seen overwhelming evidence to back up that statement. Now you're hearing about some of the people who are most skilled in reaping the reward from the behavior of millions of overly skittish investors. They wouldn't have gotten where they were without a pretty strong tide to swim against. At the same time, millions of less disciplined investors were going with the flow and being carried straight onto the shoals of Lake Moneybegone.

If even a small amount of these investors' age-old wisdom rubs off on you, it could be a real boon to your investment results. I don't mean taking the plunge with borrowed money or selling everything in anticipation of a crash, by the way. "Professional driver, closed course, do not attempt," as they say in the car ads to avoid being sued. Just avoiding the temptation to panic or speculate blindly will leave you well ahead of your peers. I can't tell you whether there will be another 1929, 1987, 2000, or 2008 in your investing lifetime.

The odds are pretty good, though. The lessons to be learned from how these wealthy contrarians navigated the really high peaks and low valleys of the market apply to plenty of situations that come in between too, not just calamities or bubbles. Even less extreme swings of fear and greed cause investors to zig when they should zag.

How will you recognize one of these perilous junctures? There certainly are anecdotal ways to take the market's temperature. Depending on how long you've been investing your own money, you probably remember people flipping houses or obsessing about real estate circa 2006, falling in love with profitless dot-coms in 1999, or selling everything and vowing never to buy another stock again in 2009.

Popular culture yields plenty of clues too. You've heard, for example, of the *Sports Illustrated* cover curse. A team or athlete hot enough to appear in that coveted space often stumbles badly soon after, failing to win a championship. The reason has nothing to do with being on the cover, of course. It's called reversion to the mean—putting in a performance that is a bit more ordinary than the unusually excellent one that got them there in the first place.

The same principle holds for nonsports magazine covers when the subject happens to be stocks or the economy. Two of my favorite examples occurred within weeks of the end of the crushing 1973–74 bear market that was then the worst since the Great Depression. In September 1974, a *Newsweek* piece titled "Is There No Bottom?" stated, "The plain fact is that there is simply not enough good economic news to sustain a real economic comeback." Less than a month later, *Fortune* had a story titled "A Case for Gloom About Stocks." The same publication had, less than two years earlier, written, "The flush of robust prosperity is suffusing the economy."[6] Probably the most famous contrarian cover story was *BusinessWeek*'s "The Death of Equities" in 1979, thirteen years into a secular bear market.

At the other extreme was *Time*'s "Home $weet Home" cover in the summer of 2005 asking, "Will your home make you rich?" just months before the peak in real estate prices. Most egregious was a sensational article in *Ladies' Home Journal* on the eve of the 1929 stock market crash by speculator John J. Raskob. "Everybody Ought to Be Rich" actually suggested buying stocks on margin—a strategy that financially wiped out anyone who tried it.

Bestselling books mirror the same crazy swings. For example, the peak in technology stocks in 2000 was preceded by titles including *Dow 36,000: The New Strategy for Profiting from the Coming Rise in the Stock Market*; *Dow 40,000: Strategies for Profiting from the Greatest Bull Market in History*; and, hey, why not, *Dow 100,000: Fact or Fiction*. In just a few years, with those titles in the leftover bin out back, new business books included *Conquer the Crash* and *Financial Reckoning Day*. By 2006 the good times were rolling again (stocks would peak the next year) and *The Next Great Bubble Boom* was published. Showing some really impressive emotional flexibility, the very same author followed this up with *The Great Depression Ahead* in 2009 when a lot of people were inclined to let bygones be bygones and believe him again.

Back when I was an analyst, I got to experience the same cycle of euphoria and despair in an even more compressed period. Like dog years, time in emerging markets is sped up. Clients who told me in 1997, for example, that the epic rally in the Russian market would make us all rich and then in 1998 after losing 90 percent of their funds' investments there that they would never, ever invest a dime in that awful country again were back at it in 2003.

Here in the developed world the ups and downs are a little less extreme and the peaks and valleys farther apart. The market is also established enough for there to be some long-running measures we can use to quantify investor anxiety. My favorite gauge, dating from 1987, is a weekly survey conducted by the American Association of Individual Investors. (In case you're not familiar with it, AAII is a good, unbiased, nonprofit information resource.)

For the survey, AAII polls its membership to determine whether they're bullish, bearish, or neutral on the stock market. The numbers can swing a lot from week to week, but I've found that the extremes are telling and can be a great contrarian indicator. Between 1987 and 2014, for example, I sorted over fourteen hundred surveys on the gap between bullish and bearish responses.

In the year following the ten most pessimistic weeks the S&P 500 rose by a whopping 22.1 percent on average. In fact, there was only one instance when the market failed to go up—a nasty reading in January 2008 when the financial crisis was just getting warmed up. Not surprisingly, the lows came around times of crisis such as the anxious run-up to the first Gulf War. The best yearly rise was 58 percent that coincided with the 2009 trough in the stock market following the financial crisis. It really is darkest before the dawn.

By comparison, the times when investors were most exuberant proved to be pretty lousy. The average one-year gain following the frothiest ten weeks was barely positive for the S&P 500. The market fell four times out of ten in the following year and the biggest gain was just 10.4 percent.

Clearly, then, sentiment can tell you a lot. As they say, though, talk is cheap. Wouldn't it be nice if there were a single number based on people who put their money where their mouths are? There is— sort of. The most famous of these is what journalists call the stock market's "fear gauge." It's a misnomer, but the CBOE Volatility

Index, or VIX, is an interesting and useful indicator of how much traders are willing to pay to sleep better at night.

The VIX as we know it today was developed by a Vanderbilt University professor in 1992 and is based on a Nobel Prize–winning 1973 option pricing formula by Fischer Black and Myron Scholes that, through some complicated math, tells us how much stock volatility is expected over the next thirty days. The higher it is, the more nervous traders are.

The VIX isn't always right, though. In fact, it's frequently wrong because actual volatility in the market rarely resembles what traders assume. Rather than being a reason to ignore the VIX, it's why people who don't trade options should consider paying attention to it. Like sentiment measures, the VIX's pendulum will swing too far on its arc in the direction of complacency and then back toward despair.

All too often, I read stories about a spike in the VIX that suggest some sort of ominous warning signal has gone off. Naturally, the VIX doesn't rise sharply out of the blue—it follows some scary headline or selloff in stocks. Reacting to it is like shutting the barn door after the horse has bolted. If anything, it's a buying signal or, ideally, a "stay put and don't do anything dumb" signal.

The VIX only has been around since 1993 and the CBOE went back and calculated it only as long ago as 1990, but newsletter writer Bill Luby, a contributor to *Barron's*, estimated what the VIX might have been for some major turning points of the twentieth century. The average of the official closing VIX values, just for reference, has been a bit under 20.

Not surprisingly, Luby estimates that the two highest VIX readings ever would have been immediately after 1987's Black Monday, and Black Tuesday in 1929 when he calculates it reached about

112 and 111, respectively. The third, and also the highest spike since the VIX's invention, was a reading just below 90 after the collapse of Lehman Brothers in 2008. Other high points include the 9/11 terrorist attacks, Germany's invasion of Poland (when Templeton was backing up the truck and buying stocks), and the collapse of hedge fund Long Term Capital Management in 1998.

As you might have guessed from my reference to Templeton, buying when the fear index is highest can be very profitable. On the other hand, unusually low readings—there have been some eerily calm stretches when the VIX was below 10—are less auspicious. A lot less. Just during the period when a daily VIX has been calculated, the average one-year gain in the S&P 500 was a blistering 26.4 percent following the highest 1 percent of all readings. At the other end of the spectrum, the average return was a barely positive 0.3 percent in the year following the lowest 1 percent of VIX readings when traders saw nary a cloud on the horizon.

By no stretch of the imagination am I endorsing any type of trading strategy based on investor surveys or the fear gauge. Sentiment indicators can be a useful sanity check at market extremes to help you stay the course, though, and I'm using the word "sanity" on purpose. Charles Mackay, a nineteenth-century journalist and author, penned my favorite quote on how we lose our grip in bubbles or panics in his classic *Extraordinary Popular Delusions and the Madness of Crowds:*

"Men, it has been well said, think in herds; it will be seen that they go mad in herds, while they only recover their senses slowly, one by one."

This book is about presenting you with the odds so you can stack them in your favor. By definition, panics and bubbles make it very hard for you to do that. They wouldn't occur if a significant part of the population made up of otherwise rational individuals didn't succumb to a sort of temporary madness. You may even reconstruct facts in your head.

For example, when asked by fund manager Franklin Templeton in 2010 what the stock market's performance had been in 2009, two-thirds of investors surveyed recalled that it had dropped. In fact the S&P 500 had risen by a very good 27 percent. Asked the following year about the year 2010, nearly half gave the same answer despite the fact that the market had risen a still respectable 15 percent. Naturally, most savers don't follow the market down to the last percentage point, but at least people should know if it rose or fell. The effect faded as the awful 2008 and early 2009 bear market receded in people's memories.

The effect when stocks are surging and have been for some time—in other words, in the later stages of a bubble—is just as dangerous. A survey done at the height of the dot-com boom published in the *Journal of Psychology and Financial Markets* found that the average investor expected annualized returns over the following decade far in excess of the historical norm. Nearly a third thought they would get over 20 percent a year, and nearly nine in ten believed they would earn at least 10 percent. Not a single respondent expected a negative return, but, even with dividends, they would lose a tenth of their money in the S&P 500 over the next decade.[7]

Hysteria, bubbles, and panics are part of investing, and I suspect they always will be. If someone could devise a perfect indicator to tell them when a bubble was near bursting or a crash near bottoming, he or she would be the greatest speculator of all time. There is no foolproof warning signal that will allow you to sell profitably to a greater fool or swoop in to pick up stocks at half price. But, as I hope I've shown, there are plenty of clues that the market has reached an emotional extreme. You need to remind yourself at such times that these are the forks in the road for investors. One direction leads to a happy place and the other to Lake Moneybegone.

One reason so many take the wrong road is that both giddy times and awful ones seem to last just a little bit longer than our patience. That, in turn, leads to a conclusion that Sir John Templeton called the four most dangerous words in investing: "This time is different." When it comes to extremes of sentiment, it never really is but sure seems that way. As Irving Kahn, who passed away at age 109 the month I began writing this book, said to me eight decades after he had kept his nerve and made a killing in the Great Crash and was about to do so again, "History mostly repeats itself, but it's never exact."

CHAPTER THIRTEEN

THE HUNGARIAN GRANDMA INDICATOR (OR WHY YOU MAY NEED AN ADVISOR)

There's a great scene in the 1983 comedy film *The Man with Two Brains* in which famous neurosurgeon Michael Hfuhruhurr (Steve Martin) asks a portrait of his dead wife for a sign that she objects to his feelings for Dolores (Kathleen Turner), a beautiful gold digger. The lights start to flicker, gusts knock over all the furniture, the painting spins on the wall, and a disembodied voice screams, "No . . . no . . . noooo!" As the howling stops and the wind dies down, he keeps staring. "Just any kind of sign—I'll keep on the lookout for it."

When it comes to investing, we hear what we want to hear. And while the signals may not be as glaringly obvious or the response quite as clueless as Dr. Hfuhruhurr's, it's close. My goal in writing this book was to help you look at investing in terms of probabilities so that you can tilt them in your favor. It really is the best advice I can give. Unfortunately, I worry that many of you won't take it, and not because your reading comprehension is poor or you think I'm full of it. It's because learning about money is different from most anything else. Knowing what to do and even making a conscious decision to approach a certain situation such as a bear market differently the next time doesn't mean you actually will.

Some exceptionally bright people who understand investing foibles far better than I do still are prone to money mistakes, particularly near market extremes when most of the damage is done to our portfolios. Take Daniel Kahneman, the psychologist who won the Nobel Prize in Economics for his pioneering work in behavioral economics whom I've mentioned throughout this book. I was amused to read a recent interview with him about his own financial decisions. He said that even though he knows all about cognitive errors—heck, he discovered many of them—he continues to make those mistakes again and again with his own portfolio.

I've focused a lot on selloffs and bear markets, but the tendency to make mistakes exists during boom times as well. As Charles P. Kindleberger, who was a preeminent scholar of speculation, observed in his classic *Manias, Panics, and Crashes,* "There is nothing so disturbing to one's well-being and judgment as to see a friend get rich."[1]

My favorite "smart people doing dumb stuff with their money" quote comes from Harrison Hong, who not only holds a PhD in finance from the Massachusetts Institute of Technology but is an expert in, of all things, financial bubbles. He held off on buying technology stocks in the late 1990s but finally took the plunge just before the market peak, meaning he not only lost a bundle but didn't even enjoy some of the upside like most people did.

"My sister's getting rich. My friends are getting rich . . . I think this is all crazy, but I feel so horrible about missing out, about being left out of the party," he said to a colleague of mine at the *Wall Street Journal.*[2]

The ideal solution would be for some sort of flashing light to go off and tell us we're about to do something dangerous—sort of like those "lane departure warning" systems they put in luxury cars these days. A vague feeling of unease based on knowledge, whether from reading things like this book or even from years of theoretical study as in the cases of Kahneman and Hong, often won't cut it. Those little voices in their heads were drowned out by the cacophony of a crowd that convinced them of a risk or opportunity too significant to ignore.

Humans have put on clothing and read books for 1 percent of our existence and lived a poor, solitary, nasty, brutish, and short existence for the other 99 percent. It's hardly surprising, then, that fear and greed trump theory and logic. Running in the opposite direction from the crowd would have cost our primeval ancestors a meal or put them in mortal danger, eventually removing such contrarian thinkers from the gene pool. So here's one last investing insight that may be the most important one in this book, if only because the other ones may be useless to some of you without it. It stems from personal experience.

It was the autumn of 1999 and I was making a visit to my mom's house in Queens. I don't know how it is in your social circle, but my parents' generation takes an unusual amount of vicarious pride in their offspring. They all arrived from Hungary as adults, mostly as penniless refugees, and put all of their energy into making a living and turning their kids into successful Americans. Since they had started from zero, a disproportionate marker of "success" was financial.

Although my smarter and more erudite little sister was finishing her PhD in literature at the time, I was the one who was hot stuff since I had succeeded in the lucrative field of investment banking. Though there's really no connection, to them I was at my most influential about anything having to do with money.

I was also a new father and was there with my oldest son, then an infant and now a teenager. I know that everyone thinks their child is the most adorable in the world, and I'm no exception. Suffice it to say, though, that putting any baby, much less a cherub like him, in front of a pack of late-middle-aged Hungarian American women was like throwing raw meat to starving lions. They were all over him, much in the way that they probably had been with me thirty years earlier.

But then a funny thing happened. They quickly lost interest in pinching his cheeks and instead began asking me questions about the stock market. All of them had taken to watching CNBC for hours on end, and here was a real live stock analyst who was on TV and everything standing in the living room in front of them with no commercial interruptions.

I proceeded to hem and haw and suggest that they reduce their risk as things looked awfully frothy. Rather than listen to what I had to say, though, they then tuned me out and began one-upping one another with tales of stock market killings: "I made 30 percent last month in Lucent" or "I bought [Internet incubator] CMGI at $60."

I should stop now and tell you that these are some of the most frugal, cautious people you will ever meet. Being reduced to a net worth of zero in a strange country where you don't speak the language and having to scrimp and save for decades will do that to you. Now that most of them were in or on the cusp of retirement, I was horrified that they might be setting themselves up to lose a chunk of their hard-won nest eggs on some overhyped Internet stocks.

But then they were infected with the same bug that had spread nationwide—tech stock fever. I didn't want to be too strident with the Hungarian Grandmas, because, after all, these women not only were twice my age but probably had wiped my bottom at one point. All they wanted from me was affirmation of how clever they were rather than a word of caution. If I had told them to sell Internet Stock A and put the money into Internet Stock B, which was a can't-lose double-bagger, they probably would have rushed to the phone to call their brokers that second. But telling them to give up on the prospect of free money forever was getting me nowhere.

At least something positive came out of the episode, aside from the inspiration to write this book. After her friends left, I asked to see my mother's retirement portfolio. The good news was that it had swelled in value. The bad news was that it was 94 percent in stocks—mostly technology companies she had heard of by watching CNBC for hours on end. Newly retired, this is a woman who, except for the evening news, had never watched TV in her life. Now she welcomed David Faber, Joe Kernen, and Maria Bartiromo into her living room and trusted them and their guests with her savings. And who's to blame her—she had made a small fortune (on paper) by taking their advice.

The other Hungarian Grandmas were too tough of a nut to crack, but my mom was another matter. In my family our finances are an open book—there was never "my money" and "your money"—and I insisted that she sell a big chunk of her most speculative stocks, pay the capital gains, and put the remaining proceeds in boring Treasury bonds. We went through her portfolio that very afternoon and I told her what to dump. It was a painful process—a lot like forcing someone to throw out or give away belongings with sentimental value when they need to downsize—but we sold most of the stocks she needed to sell.

I'm happy to tell you that my mom is comfortably retired today. She spends much of the year traveling and is able to maintain an apartment back "home" in Hungary as well as one near my house in New Jersey. Though she's still retained a lot of her frugal habits, she doesn't need to. If she had gone with her emotions rather than my advice, the situation might be a lot different.

I'm not telling you this to portray myself as some sort of hero or genius. I'm doing it to make a point. Because she trusted me, because her finances and risk tolerance were completely transparent to me, and because I was able to look at her situation rationally rather than emotionally, my mom's finances potentially were saved from a ruinous outcome. A lot of the stocks she owned lost 90 percent, and in some cases 100 percent, of their value in the next two years.

Your chicken paprikash may not be as good, but you're not so different from the Hungarian Grandmas. Like them, when it comes to crunch time, fear and greed are likely to overpower common sense. Depending on your emotional makeup, everything you read in this book and every other piece of sensible advice you've heard may have about as much impact on you as Dr. Hfuhruhurr's wife did from beyond the grave at those junctures.

I've noted some ways to inoculate yourself from market stress. One is to simply check less often on your investments, but that becomes more difficult when stocks become front-page news—precisely the times when people make the biggest dents in their portfolios by zigging when they should zag. Another is to automate the decisions in some way—through regular, formulaic rebalancing or a life-cycle fund—but those processes still can be short-circuited through a few anxious mouse clicks.

You probably don't have a close relative with financial expertise who can and will ask to see your portfolio, and even if you do, he or she may not be able to look at it in an emotionally detached way or prevail upon you to stop doing something stupid. But there are people and companies out there who get paid to do that: financial advisors.

My advice to you is to pay for only the services you need and no more but also no less. Several chapters ago I went through the services that a so-called robo-advisor can provide. Aside from constructing a portfolio for you as good as anything a human can concoct, many are keenly aware of the emotional side of investing. From the way they present results to the frequency with which they contact you, they try to avoid causing you to do something counterproductive.

In terms of costs alone, humans can't really compete. A fee-only advisor typically charges at least four times as much. Assuming he or she invests in low-cost funds and designs a similarly efficient portfolio, a "robo" portfolio might be worth 15 percent more than one managed by a human over two decades. Or it might not. If you're prone to panic or exuberance at market extremes, then a human may save you that much in the course of a single bear market.

And then there are in-between steps. For example, an outfit called LearnVest will, for a $299 setup fee and $19 a month, pair you with a certified financial planner. They won't manage your assets, but they come up, based on a questionnaire and a conversation, with a plan for your assets and provide ongoing advice. Compared to a traditional planner assisting a person with $150,000 in assets, that comes to about a third of the cost in year one and an eighth of the cost going forward. But then you have to do your own legwork and will have contact with a representative only by phone or e-mail—perhaps not the ideal setup for those panicking after a five-hundred-point drop in the Dow Jones Industrials. And, of course, you're on your own when it comes to buying and selling stocks or funds.

While I've urged you throughout this book to pinch pennies, human advice may be your best bet sometimes. Financial advisors these days mostly are different from old-fashioned brokers who pitched investments and were out to churn your portfolio in a way that maximized their compensation, often at your expense. The most suitable advisor is one who only charges a fee, usually a percentage of your assets, so that he or she is as interested as you are in seeing your nest egg grow. Someone who tries to sell you a complicated annuity, nonterm life insurance policy, or unsuitable investments such as an unlisted real estate investment trust or pooled commodity account should throw up red flags.

Reputable ones are members of organizations such as the Financial Planning Association and National Association of Personal Financial Advisors. They have credentials such as "Certified Financial Planner," "Certified Investment Management Analyst," "Chartered Asset Manager," or "Personal Finance Specialist." But I found nearly one hundred different credentials in my research, and some, while they sound similar or impressive, have minimal requirements and no complaint procedures. You can and should check to see if an advisor has had disciplinary action taken against him or her through the Financial Industry Regulatory Authority (FINRA).

A big caveat here is that you need to have some substantial assets already to be worth the time of many financial advisors. Some will take on what the industry calls "Henrys"—people who are high earning not rich yet—but your salary and net worth may require fees that are higher than 1 percent to get much face time. Furthermore, some of the additional services that only a human can provide—estate planning and moves to minimize your taxes— may not really be of use to someone of more modest means. Finally, a financial advisor typically will offer little guidance for a workplace retirement account. Doing it yourself may be your best bet in that case.

And even if you are in the right tax bracket to avail yourself of an advisor, there's no guarantee that having a human being a phone call away will put you on the financial straight and narrow. The decision about whether to engage a human advisor really depends on your unique circumstances. Everyone has some complication: a choppy income, an unemployed spouse, infirm parents, a special needs child, divorce, a family business, and so on. Robots are clever but aren't designed to deal with wrinkles like those.

But the biggest reason you may want a person to hold your hand is the wrinkly organ inside your skull. All the facts, figures, and investing books in the world may not be enough to avoid expensive errors. Reading this book or others like it and resolving to do better next time may or may not happen in the breach. It's almost like we have two brains sometimes.

CHAPTER FOURTEEN

LEAVING LAKE MONEYBEGONE

It seems like almost every time I buy something online or have to deal with customer service these days, a survey arrives in my e-mail in-box within minutes from the company in question. Although they say they send them out "so we can serve you better," I know it's just a cheap way of doing market research. Delete.

Now that you've finished reading *Heads I Win, Tails I Win,* I'm going to give you a two-question survey that's entirely for your benefit, not mine. Here we go:

Do you think you're an above-average investor?

I bet your answer is a lot more nuanced than it was a couple of hundred pages ago. As with driving or looks, more of you would have said yes than no.

Now you know enough to divide your answer into two parts. Even if you're better than most, the odds are you're still a resident of Lake Moneybegone in terms of your actual returns. The good news is that you're now far better equipped to narrow that gap.

The wildly successful hedge fund manager Michael Steinhardt once was asked what the average investor could learn from him. His answer: "I'm their competition." So here's my second survey question: How does that make you feel?

Before you cracked this book open, hearing that and reading about Steinhardt's record might have produced one of two unhelpful reactions. For most people it would be despair, reinforcing their view that the odds are stacked against the "little guy" succeeding as an investor. Others would want to learn everything they could about the secrets of such pros to emulate their success, almost certainly with awful results.

Those attitudes weren't going to lead you out of Lake Moneybegone, but now you know that a clear path does exist and that people like Michael Steinhardt aren't the ones blocking it—you are.

Yes, Steinhardt is your competition, but there can be lots of winners in this gigantic zero-sum game called investing. A billionaire investor like him can trounce the overall market only because lots of people with far smaller pots of money do worse. And tens of thousands of lesser lights in the financial world can afford their metaphorical yachts only if lots of people send them their money for nothing much of value. Today is the day you stop subsidizing them. Don't worry, they'll be just fine without you.

I promised you in the introduction that the advice I put down in these pages would be the best I could give. I also said that I had condensed all of this into a two-minute speech that I've repeated innumerable times to strangers and acquaintances. The reason you just read more than seventy-five thousand words isn't only because my publisher would have taken back its advance if I had delivered a manuscript consisting of seven bullet points. It's that the short version isn't all that persuasive on its own.

I often think of something my wise colleague Jason Zweig, the author of some great books and several hundred columns about investing, said when asked at a journalism conference what his job was:

> My job is to write the exact same thing between fifty and a hundred times a year in such a way that neither my editors nor my readers will ever think I am repeating myself. That's because good advice rarely changes, while markets change constantly. The temptation to pander is almost irresistible. And while people need good advice, what they want is advice that sounds good. The advice that sounds the best in the short run is always the most dangerous in the long run. Everyone wants the secret, the key, the road map to the primrose path that leads to El Dorado: the magical low-risk, high-return investment that can double your money in no time.

The advice in *Heads I Win, Tails I Win,* replete with statistics and anecdotes, was meant to be both convincing and memorable. It needs to be because it's got some very tough competition. Lined up against me is not only an industry with a huge marketing budget and tens of billions of dollars in profits at stake but readers mentally hardwired to ignore my advice. So, for the sake of clarity and persuasiveness, I'm going to take a page out of Jason's playbook and repeat myself one last time. Here are the key takeaways from this book that you should feel free to fold up and put in your wallet or recite to friends, neighbors, and airplane seatmates until their eyes glaze over:

Know yourself: Most people earn abysmal returns without knowing it, and very few people have an accurate idea of how well or poorly they've done. Although it seems illogical and a bit like the flip side of the children in Garrison Keillor's Lake Wobegon, the typical investor is way below average. The first steps to improving are understanding that performance gap and how your personality might be contributing to it.

Stop zigging when you should zag: The largest portion of that incredible gap between the typical investor and the market is entirely self-inflicted. Our need to be in control and ultimately our fear and greed cause us to make decisions that are, in the aggregate, disastrous for our returns. The way to stop this isn't to try becoming an investing genius. The answer is to decide to leave ourselves with as few decisions to make as possible and to remove the need or temptation to do so in the future.

Learn to be cheap and lazy: Investing must be the only pursuit in which your results are inversely proportional to your effort and in which you get what you don't pay for. Low-cost, passive funds that require as little input from you as possible are your best bet.

Don't confuse luck and skill: Still convinced there are investing superstars out there who can deliver superior results? It might seem that way, and, with the benefit of lots of hindsight, there may even be some people who were worth it. Your odds of identifying one of those stars are very poor, though, and your chances will be even worse if you go with someone else's recommendation. Save your money and avoid disappointment.

Turn lemons into lemonade: Bad times are inevitable, and they're especially bad for typical investors. Not only are markets dropping, but at such times the gap between your returns and those returns tends to be widest and mistakes the most costly. Instead, embrace risk by refusing to panic and rebalancing your portfolio on schedule. You'll be capturing extra returns on autopilot.

History doesn't repeat, but it does rhyme: Treating the market like a predictable money machine is an almost certain path to disappointment. There's a lot of uncertainty, and savers need to understand what levers they can control: time, savings, and portfolio construction. On the other hand, certain patterns do repeat themselves. When stocks are historically cheap or expensive, the odds of their returns being good or bad, respectively, increase. Likewise, when measures of fear or complacency reach extremes, the near-term performance of the market tends to be the opposite of what the crowd expects.

Don't be afraid to ask for help, but only as much as you need: For many people, choosing and rebalancing a stable of shares or funds may be daunting. There is help out there, and some of it is cheap and robotic these days. Even for those who aren't overwhelmed by the complexities of setting up a passive portfolio, the ups and downs of markets may be too much to handle. A human advisor is more expensive than a robot but may save you money in the long run by acting as a sanity check.

Well, that's all, folks. If I gave you a shock at the start of this book by pointing out how bad we retail investors are as a group, or if you looked back through your old brokerage statements and realized how much worse you're doing than you thought, cheer up. We may let hope triumph over experience, but harnessing the experience of others provides plenty of reason to be hopeful about the future. Now do it. The road out of Lake Moneybegone is in front of you and the first step is the hardest.

ACKNOWLEDGMENTS

It's a bit ironic to wrap up a book about money by reminding you that money isn't all-important. If I didn't really believe that, though, then *Heads I Win, Tails I Win* wouldn't be sitting in your hands.

I'm actually more concerned with financial security than most people. Nevertheless, I mde a decision fourteen years ago to leave a very lucrative field that bored me for one in which I write about people who make multiples of what I do. I haven't regretted it for a minute.

Being an investment analyst glued to financial spreadsheets all day made my decision possible in two ways. Practically speaking, the job allowed me to build up a financial cushion that made me comfortable enough to go out on a limb in a new field, journalism. It also gave me the confidence to forecast that, even with some events I didn't anticipate at the time—a global financial crisis and a third child, for example—I could still afford to retire one day.

ACKNOWLEDGMENTS

Obviously I could have a nicer car, a bigger house, and go on more lavish vacations doing my old job, but health, happiness, family, friendships, and fulfillment are so much more important. Without financial security, though, all of those can suffer strains. So, yes, I suppose money actually is pretty important, if only as a means to an end. I really hope reading this contributed in at least a small way to your family's financial well-being and happiness.

That sentiment is a nice way to begin the part of the book where I thank people, because my family is at the top of the list. My wonderful wife, Nicole, and my three sons, Jonah, Elliott, and Daniel, have been my biggest boosters. As they can tell you, though, a book doesn't write itself. Writing this while working full time meant a lot of evenings, weekends, and holidays without Dad or being very, very quiet while I worked. You can turn up the volume on the PlayStation now, guys.

My mother, Veronica, the best Hungarian Grandma ever, and sister, Judy, were wonderful too. Both read early versions of the manuscript. I'm the one in the family who writes for a living but they're the ones who live to read and this book benefited from their input.

I'd also like to thank a member of my family who never got to read this book but nonetheless played a huge role. My dad, John, passed away thirty years almost to the day before I sent in the final draft. He came to this country as a refugee from a communist country and fell in love with capitalism. My dad always had a well-thumbed issue of *Barron's* magazine with him and tried to teach me about the stock market at a young age. I'm afraid I disappointed him by being a bit slow on the uptake and not especially interested at the time. I wish I could sit down with him today and talk about our shared obsession.

While the apple didn't fall very far from the tree, my dad was "exhibit A" for this book. I can't reconstruct his returns, but I know that the final figure was a pale reflection of the time and savings he devoted to making what he hoped would be a fortune as an investor. He was a very smart man but, as the subtitle says, smart investors often fail.

His yellowed brokerage statements from Merrill Lynch show that he was both very active and way ahead of the crowd on a couple of big trends. But he was swimming against an awfully strong tide along with millions of other residents of Lake Moneybegone.

Aside from a supportive family, *Heads I Win, Tails I Win* is sitting in your hands or on your screen thanks to a whole bunch of people not named "Jakab." Their names don't appear on the cover but they deserve a great deal of the credit. Since he was literally involved in this project from a blank page to the last word, my profound thanks go to Eric Nelson, my thoughtful and patient editor at Penguin Random House. His talented colleagues Adrian Zackheim, Vivian Roberson, Tara Gilbride, Will Weisser, and Tori Miller all made this book better too.

My coworkers at *The Wall Street Journal* get a huge shout-out as well—particularly my editor and friend David Reilly, who supported this project and was fairly patient with me as I juggled writing it along with my day job. I really love working at the *Journal* and particularly with the crew at "Heard on the Street." Here's to Steve, Miriam, Justin, John, Aaron, Charley, Alex, Abheek, Jacky, Stephen, Helen, Paul, and Richard. You are the sharpest, most insightful, not to mention funniest, financial journalists around.

I also need to mention a longtime *Wall Street Journal* colleague who recently left the industry but is responsible for my being in it: Gabby Stern. Had she not asked me on that flight to London fourteen years ago if I was interested in financial journalism I might still be glued to spreadsheets somewhere.

My friends were a fabulous source of support but also occasional anxiety. I always felt guilty for sneaking away from my desk stacked high with notes and having them ask, "How's the book going?" The finished product seemed impossibly far away at times. Special thanks go out to Gregg Lambert, Shane Leonard, and István Máté-Tóth, who also read early chapters and gave me useful advice.

The latter two people I befriended while working at Credit Suisse. I know I poked a lot of fun at my former employer and profession in this book, but I really do consider myself very fortunate to have worked there. I learned how to think and to push myself to the limit and I had my eyes opened up to the world. There were and still are a lot of good people there. I wouldn't hesitate for a second if one of my sons wanted to work at my old firm or for one of my former bosses there.

And finally, I want to thank you for reading my book.

NOTES

Chapter One: Lake Moneybegone

1. Markus Glaser and Martin Weber, "Why Inexperienced Investors Do Not Learn: They Do Not Know Their Past Portfolio Performance," *Finance Research Letters* 4, no. 4 (2007), available at SSRN:http://ssrn.com/abstract=1002092.
2. Jennifer Erickson and David Madland, "Fixing the Drain on Retirement Savings: How Retirement Fees Are Straining the Middle Class and What We Can Do About Them," Center for American Progress, April 11, 2014, https://www.americanprogress.org/wp-content/uploads/2014/04/401kFees-brief3.pdf.
3. Meir Statman, "Investor, Know Yourself," *Wall Street Journal,* April 21, 2013.
4. Martin Conrad, "The Money Paradox; It's Easier to Talk Contrarian Than Be Contrarian," *Barron's,* December 31, 2011.
5. Brad M. Barber and Terrance Odean, "The Behavior of Individual Investors," September 7, 2011, available at http://ssrn.com/abstract=1872211 or http://dx.doi.org/10.2139/ssrn.1872211.

6. "3 Lessons from Our Teachers: Why Teachers Are Better Investors Than Pretty Much Anyone Else," Openfolio, https://openfolio.com/teachers/mar-2015/.

Chapter Two: Timing Isn't Everything

1. *Annual SIA Investor Survey: Attitudes Toward the Securities Industry,* SIA, November 4, 2004, https://www.sifma.org/uploadedfiles/research/surveys/2004investorsurvey.pdf.
2. Kathy Yuan, Lu Zheng, and Qiaoqiao Zhu, "Are Investors Moonstruck? Lunar Phases and Stock Returns," September 2002, http://deepblue.lib.umich.edu/bitstream/handle/2027.42/36301/b2092645.0001.001.pdf.
3. Stephen Miller, "Granville Was Market Timer with Flair," *Wall Street Journal,* September 10, 2013.
4. Barry Ritholtz, "Worlds Greatest (and Worst) Market Timer," *The Big Picture,* August 30, 2014, http://www.ritholtz.com/blog/2014/08/worlds-greatest-market-timer/.

Chapter Four: Who Wants to Be a Billionaire?

1. James K. Glassman and Kevin A. Hassett, *Dow 36,000: The New Strategy for Profiting from the Coming Rise in the Stock Market* (New York: Times Books, 1999).
2. James Grant, "Real Estate 36,000," *Grant's Interest Rate Observer,* September 10, 1999.
3. Jennifer Lawler, "Target Date Fund Pros and Cons," Bankrate.com, http://www.bankrate.com/finance/retirement/target-date-fund-pros-and-cons-1.aspx.

Chapter Five: Actually, Timing *Is* Everything

1. Spencer Jakab, "The Long View: When Analysts' Consensus Spells Danger," *Financial Times,* August 1, 2010.

Chapter Six: The Celebrity Cephalopod

1. Michael J. Mauboussin, *More Than You Know: Finding Financial Wisdom in Unconventional Places* (New York: Columbia Business School Publishing, 2007), 50.

2. Andy Serwer, "The Greatest Money Manager of Our Time," *Fortune,* November 15, 2006.

3. Ian McDonald, "Bill Miller Dishes on His Streak and His Strategy," *Wall Street Journal,* January 6, 2005.

4. Bing Liang, "The 'Dartboard' Column: The Pros, the Darts, and the Market," November 1996, available at http://ssrn.com/abstract=1068.

5. Tom Lauricella, "The Stock Picker's Defeat," *Wall Street Journal,* December 10, 2008.

6. Eleanor Laise, "Best Stock Fund of the Decade: CGM Focus," *Wall Street Journal,* December 31, 2009.

7. Steve Johnson, "Active Fund Managers Really Can Pick Stocks," *Financial Times,* May 17, 2015.

8. Mark Hebner, "Survivorship Bias—Things Are Not as Good as They Look," Index Fund Advisors, May 11, 2013, https://www.ifa.com/articles/survivorship_bias_things_are_not_as_good_as_they_look/.

9. Karen D'Amato, "When It Comes to Fund Performance, History Is Often Written by the Winners," *Wall Street Journal,* August 6, 2012.

Chapter Seven: Seers and Seer Suckers

1. Tom Harford, "How to See into the Future," *Financial Times,* September 5, 2014, http://www.ft.com/intl/cms/s/2/3950604a-33bc-11e4-ba62-00144feabdc0.html.

2. Burton Malkiel, *A Random Walk Down Wall Street: The Time-Tested Strategy for Successful Investing,* 11th ed. (New York: W. W. Norton, 2015), 157.

3. Ibid., 97.

4. Anne Tergesen, "What the Pros Are Saying," *BusinessWeek,* December 19, 2007.

5. William A. Sherden, *The Fortune Sellers: The Big Business of Buying and Selling Predictions* (New York: John Wiley & Sons, 1998), 97.

6. Philip Mattera, "Rigged Research: Wall Street Stock Analysts Under Fire," Corporate Research Project, Corporate Research E-Letter No. 23, April 2002, http://www.corp-research.org/e-letter/rigged-research.

7. Roni Michaely and Kent L. Womack, "Conflict of Interest and the Credibility of Underwriter Analyst Recommendations," February 1999, http://turtletrader.com/pdfs/boost1.pdf.

8. B. O. Smith and J. J. Wooten, "Estimating Consumer Demand for Information Attributes Using Twitter Data," Under Review at Economics E-Journal (2013).

9. "Confidence Trumps Accuracy in Pundit Popularity," May 28, 2013, https://news.wsu.edu/2013/05/28/confidence-trumps-accuracy-in-pundit-popularity/.

10. Francie Grace, "Betting on Terror," CBS News, July 29, 2003, http://www.cbsnews.com/news/betting-on-terror/.

Chapter Eight: Where Are the Customers' Yachts?

1. Don Phillips, "What Really Shines Through in the Morningstar Ratings for Funds," Morningstar, June 1, 2010, http://news.morningstar.com/articlenet/article.aspx?id=339449.

2. Matt Egan, "Investing Guide: 86% of Investment Managers Stunk in 2014," CNNMoney, March 12, 2015, http://money.cnn.com/2015/03/12/investing/investing-active-versus-passive-funds/.

3. Jeff Sommer, "Who Routinely Trounces the Stock Market? Try 2 Out of 2,862 Funds," July 19, 2014, http://www.nytimes.com/2014/07/20/your-money/who-routinely-trounces-the-stock-market-try-2-out-of-2862-funds.html?_r=0.

4. John Bogle, "The Arithmetic of All-In Investment Expenses," *Financial Analysts Journal* 70, no. 1 (January–February 2015).

5. Mitch Tuchman, "Warren Buffett to Heirs: Put My Estate in Index Funds," *MarketWatch,* March 13, 2014, http://www.marketwatch.com/story/warren-buffett-to-heirs-put-my-estate-in-index-funds-2014-03-13.

6. "Convergence! The Great Paradox: Just as Active Fund Management Becomes More and More Like Passive Indexing, So Passive Indexing Becomes More and More Like Active Fund Management," remarks by John Bogle, founder and former chairman, the Vanguard Group, before "The Art of Indexing" conference, September 30, 2004, Washington, DC, http://www.vanguard.com/bogle_site/sp20040930.htm.

7. N. Mahalakshmi and Rajesh Padmashali, "'In Investing, There Are Many Ways to Fail but There Are Many Ways to Succeed Too,' Michael Mauboussin, Head of Global Financial Strategies at Credit Suisse," *Outlook India,* February 2, 2013, http://www.outlookbusiness

.com/special-edition/masterspeak/in-investing-there-are-many
-ways-to-fail-but-there-are-many-ways-to-succeed-too-1324.

8. Berkshire Hathaway Annual Report, 2005.

Chapter Nine: Heads I Win, Tails You Lose

1. Ianthe Jean Dugan, "Why Hedge Funds Hunt for Animals, Search the Stars," *Wall Street Journal,* July 25, 2005.

2. Brendan Conway, "Is Your Hedge Fund Secretly a Pricey Put-Selling Strategy?," *Barron's,* May 27, 2014.

3. Spencer Jakab, "Street Savvy: Fear of Falling for Hedge Fund Fees," *Dow Jones Newswires,* May 2, 2007.

4. Steven Johnson, "The Decline, Fall and Afterlife of 130/30," *Financial Times,* May 12, 2013.

5. Rob Copeland, "Can Hot New Bond Funds Burn You?," *Wall Street Journal,* April 26, 2015.

Chapter Ten: Seven Habits of Highly Ineffective Investors

1. James Mackintosh and John Authers, "Sin Stocks Pay as Alcohol and Cigarettes Beat Sober Rivals," *Financial Times,* February 10, 2015.

2. Deniz Anginer and Meir Statman, "Stocks of Admired and Spurned Companies," *Journal of Portfolio Management* 36, no. 3 (Spring 2010).

3. Burton G. Malkiel, *A Random Walk Down Wall Street: The Time-Tested Strategy for Successful Investing,* 11th ed. (New York: W. W. Norton: New York, 2015), 58.

4. "Value vs. Glamour: A Global Phenomenon," Brandes Institute, November 2012, http://www.brandes.com/docs/default-source/brandes-institute/value-vs-glamour-a-global-phenomenon.pdf.

5. "Go Ahead. Add Another Zero to Your Account Balance," http://www.leebincomemillionaire.com/content/lim01141?spMailingID=LMP2.

6. Dan McCrum, "Do Not Trust Hawkers of Unlisted Reits," *Financial Times,* March 25, 2015.

7. Robbie Whelan, "Nontraded REITs Are Hot, but Have Plenty of Critics," *Wall Street Journal,* June 15, 2014.

8. Spencer Jakab, "The Trend May Not Be Your Friend," *Dow Jones Newswires,* March 22, 2007.

Chapter Eleven: But Wait, There's More

1. Warren E. Buffett, "The Superinvestors of Graham-and-Doddsville," *Hermes* magazine, Columbia Business School, 1984.
2. James P. O'Shaughnessy, *What Works on Wall Street: The Classic Guide to the Best-Performing Investment Strategies of All Time,* 4th ed. (New York: McGraw-Hill, 2012), 84–85.
3. Maggie McGrath, "Leaving Your Portfolio's Fate to an Algorithm's Whims," *Forbes,* December 10, 2014.
4. Presentation by James O'Shaughnessy, Big Picture Conference, October 17, 2012.

Chapter Twelve: Far from the Maddening Crowd

1. Sam Roberts, "Irving Kahn, Oldest Active Wall Street Investor, Dies at 109," *New York Times,* February 28, 2015.
2. Spencer Jakab, "Veterans of 1929 In It for the Long Run," *Financial Times,* October 3, 2009.
3. Obituary, "John Templeton," *Economist,* July 17, 2008.
4. Teresa Corzo, Margarita Prat, and Esther Vaquero, "Behavioral Finance in Joseph de la Vega's *Confusion de Confusiones,*" *Journal of Behavioral Finance* 15, no. 4 (2014).
5. Berkshire Hathaway, letter to shareholders, 1987, available at http://www.berkshirehathaway.com/letters/1987.html.
6. Robert Frick, "Bear Market Diary," *Kiplinger's Personal Finance,* October 1997.
7. David Dreman, Stephen Johnson, Donald MacGregor, and Paul Slovic, "A Report on the March 2001 Investor Sentiment Survey," *Journal of Psychology and Financial Markets* 2, no. 3 (2001): 126–34.

Chapter Thirteen: The Hungarian Grandma Indicator (or Why You May Need an Advisor)

1. Charles P. Kindleberger, *Manias, Panics, and Crashes: A History of Financial Crises* (New York: John Wiley & Sons, 2000), 13.
2. Justin Lahart, "Bernanke's Bubble Laboratory: Princeton Protégés of Fed Chief Study the Economics of Manias," *Wall Street Journal,* May 16, 2008.

INDEX

You Can Be a Stock Market Genius
(Greenblatt), 192
Brandes Institute, 194–95
Bridgewater Associates, 172
brokerage accounts/firms, 2, 19, 23,
32, 56, 83, 143, 196–97, 207,
209–11, 216–17, 228, 257
Brown Brothers Harriman, 90
Buckingham, John, 128–29
Buffett, Warren, 3, 30, 160
advice of, 34, 157–58, 161–62,
235–36
and bet with Seides, 171, 174–75
criticizes hedge funds, 169–71
and Graham-and-Doddsville,
218–19, 223
inspired by Graham, 194, 218–19, 232
and value investing, 113, 157–58, 220
bull market, 32, 38, 42–43, 46, 51–52,
55–61, 70, 75, 88, 90–92, 117, 124,
149, 214
Bureau of Economic Analysis, 57
Burns Advisory Group, 151
BusinessWeek, 126, 144, 213, 238

CalPERS, 186–87
Capital Decimation Partners, 164,
168, 172
Carlson, Ben, 30–31, 44, 61
CGM Focus Fund, 111
Charles Schwab, 83
Chicago Board Options Exchange
(CBOE), 239–40
Clipper Fund, 105
Cohen, Abby Joseph, 128
Columbia University, 108, 217–18
commissions, 18, 135, 156, 181, 197,
202, 209, 211, 217
commodity investing, 73, 81,
205–6, 251
compound
annual return, 19, 52–54, 64, 67, 95,
111, 219

average return, 75–76, 110
interest, 2, 4, 14, 30–31, 44, 91
contango phenomenon, 205–6
Cook, Michael, 154
Countrywide Financial, 109
Courtney, Tim, 150–52
Cramer, Jim, 118, 128
crashes, 76, 234, 242
of 1929, 39, 51, 54, 92–93, 123–24,
232–33, 236, 238, 240–41, 243
of 1973–74, 75, 237
of 1987, 33, 39–40, 51, 125–26, 233,
236, 240–41
of 1998, 33, 166–67, 238
of 2008, 33, 40, 47, 50, 61, 84, 126,
174–75, 236, 239, 241–42
Credit Suisse, 181
CXO Advisory Group, 128–29
cyclically adjusted P/E (CAPE), 92–95

Dalbar, 13–14, 16, 32–33, 37, 74
decision markets, 146
DiMaggio, Joe, 98, 102, 104
Direxion Daily Small Cap Bull & Bear
3x ETF, 204
dividend investing, 54, 216–17, 226–29
Dodd, David, 194, 218–19
dot-com boom, 132, 179, 186, 193, 195,
237, 242
Dow Jones Industrials, 42, 251
beating it, 219
dividend-yielding stocks of, 192
drops in, 33, 45, 52, 125–26
increases in, 46, 88
and mutual funds, 152
predictions of, 121, 123–26
Dreman, David, 128–29
Drudge Report, The, 46–47

Eastman Kodak, 101, 109
economic
contractions, 50, 52–54
growth, 49, 52, 57, 71

INDEX